Data Communications

An Introduction to Concepts and Design

APPLICATIONS OF MODERN TECHNOLOGY IN BUSINESS

Series Editor: **Howard L. Morgan**
University of Pennsylvania

COMPUTERS AND BANKING: Electronic Funds Transfer Systems and Public Policy
Edited by Kent W. Colton and Kenneth L. Kraemer

DATA COMMUNICATIONS: An Introduction to Concepts and Design
Robert Techo

Data Communications

An Introduction to Concepts and Design

Robert Techo

Georgia State University
Atlanta, Georgia

PLENUM PRESS · NEW YORK AND LONDON

ISBN 0-306-40398-6

A Division of Plenum Publishing Corporation
227 West 17th Street, New York, N.Y. 10011

Printed in the United States of America

Preface

This book has evolved primarily from lecture notes for data communications courses taught at Georgia State University since 1969. Additional material was derived from seminar presentations that were made during this period as well as from consulting work. Teaching data communications in the College of Business Administration influenced the point of view of this material, giving it a semitechnical orientation. This point of view has been extended to the preparation of this book. Only those technical details were included which, it was felt, would lead the student to a better understanding of the subject. References are provided for those who desire further information in particular areas.

The reader for whom this book is intended is the nontechnical person who has some knowledge of computer technology and who wishes to extend that knowledge to the field of data communications. The two key points stressed in this book are terminology and concepts. The objectives of this book are to enable the student:

1. To read articles in the field of data communications with an understanding of their content.
2. To be able to engage in knowledgeable discussions with communications engineers on the subject of data communications.
3. To design and implement the hardware aspects of applications using data communications. The software that would be involved is beyond the scope of this book except where protocols are considered.

4. To effectively evaluate proposals for the implementation of data communications systems.

The pedagogical approach used in this book is briefly summarized as follows:

First, there is the introduction of data communications into the computer system. This is developed in a brief historical summary in Chapter 1.

Second, an overview of the data communications system with all of the terminology is presented in Chapter 2 to illustrate where and how all of the component pieces fit together. This is an exposure chapter with the expected level of comprehension being low. The teaching philosophy is that subsequent exposures, while repetitious, offer the student a "feeling of familiarity" with the subject matter.

Third, certain concepts mentioned earlier are covered in more detail. Chapters 3 and 4 lead toward an understanding of the concept of channel capacity in terms of signal speed. Chapters 5 and 6 extend this understanding to bits per second capacities. Different types of channels are described in Chapter 6. Next, the use of the telephone system (because it was there) for data transmission and the inherent difficulties of using such channels are taken up in Chapters 7 and 8. This covers the major concepts.

Fourth, the design of a data communications system in terms of its hardware and service components is presented. Chapter 9 describes the services available from the common carriers. The characteristics of modern equipment are discussed in Chapter 10. Terminals are described in Chapter 11. Chapter 12 discusses how all of the ingredients are put together in a systematic manner.

Fifth, discussions are presented in Chapter 13 on communications codes and error control, and in Chapter 14 on communication protocols. These last two topics round out the essential functions found in all communications-control equipment. The final chapter discusses future areas where developments in data communications can be expected.

Along the way, material that may be omitted because of great detail is indicated in sections marked with asterisks (**).

I am indebted to many people for their advice and assistance in the preparation of this manuscript. Foremost are the many helpful comments of the Georgia State University graduate students who took the course on which this text is based. I would like to thank Susan Webb and William McMullan of the Georgia State University Computer Center for their comments and suggestions on different portions of the manuscript. Finally, I would like to thank Anne Herron for her patient typing and retyping of the manuscript.

Atlanta, Georgia Robert Techo

Contents

Chapter 1

The Technology of Data Communications

The computer-oriented individual historically has viewed the field of data communications with some disdain and, more recently, with some trepidation. The field has grown too quickly and it has grown too complex. The prevailing attitude of systems programmers, analysts, and application programmers has been: if data communications can be ignored, then maybe it will go away because there are more important problems to be considered. But, it has not gone away!

Instead, the field of data communications has experienced a growth that can only be described as phenomenal. New hardware that was but a dream a short decade ago has appeared to support computer applications that had been deemed impossible. Terminal devices, routinely using light pen and sensors [e.g., point-of-sale (POS) terminals], now input data to computer systems located a considerable distance away. The technology that put man on the moon had a large role in this growth through the creation of spin-off processes, such as the proliferation of minicomputers and then the development of microprocessors for data communications applications.

These innovations resulted in the development of new computer system concepts, such as distributed processing, distributed data bases, packet switching, etc. New programming considerations, such as concurrent operations, synchronization of processes, and emphasis on real-time, have become important in applications programming of computers. All of these developments threatened the computer professional with technological obsolescence. At the same time the increased complexities compounded the problem for the neophyte to the field of computing. The purpose of this book is to present the concepts of data communications technology for understanding and utilization by the computer-oriented individual and by the managers of teleprocessing applications.

1.1. DATA COMMUNICATIONS AND TELECOMMUNICATIONS

Data communications is a subset of the field of telecommunications, which encompasses all forms of point-to-point communications by means of electrical, light, or radio signals. Radio signals are sent through space while electrical signals are sent over wires or some conducting medium. Currently, light waves are being sent over optical (glass) fibers. Telecommunications includes voice transmission by telephony, telegraphy, and short-wave and long-wave radio, video (or television), commercial, educational, and amateur radio broadcasting, methods of radiolocation, radio navigation, and telemetry, to name but a few of the more familiar applications. Table 1.1 illustrates several common telecommunications systems and describes their seven functional components. These same components are required in typical data communications systems that will be discussed in succeeding chapters. Historically, telecommunications developed as a branch of electronics that was the domain of the electrical engineer, and all of its technicalities and its circuit orientation presented a formidable barrier to study by the layman. But in recent years, engineers have gained a clearer understanding of the general principles of telecommunications and can now describe them in terms the layman can grasp.

1.2. THE PROBLEM OF TERMINOLOGY

Data communications is the transmission of digital (computer or machine-generated) data by means of electrical or radio signals. Early computer applications using data communications were joint efforts by professionals from several different disciplines, each of whom saw the implementation in a different way. The communications (or electrical) engineer considered data communications to be the transmission of information as electronic signals that are subject to noise and distortion.

The computer programmer, or analyst,* viewed data communications as the use of a transmission medium, other than the standard computer input–output

*The term ''analyst'' is used as the generic for the person or persons responsible for the design, development, and implementation of the computer system.

Table 1.1. Examples of Common Telecommunications Systems Described in Terms of Their Functional Components

Data source	Translator (transducer)	Transmitter	Transmission channel	Receiver	Translator (transducer)	Data sink
A scene being televised	Video camera	Transmitter station	Airwaves networks	Television set	Picture tube	Viewing audience
A radio announcer	Microphone	Transmitting station	Airwaves (radio signals)	Radio receiver	Radio speakers	Listening audience
Person fills out form for telegram	Clerk types message on paper tape	Teleprinter device	Wire cables	Teleprinter device	Message on paper tape	Delivered telegram
	Clerk keys message on telegraph	Telegraph sender unit	Wire pairs on poles	Telegraph receiving unit	Message written down by clerk	Delivered telegram
Person calling another person	Telephone handset converts acoustic sound to electrical pulses	Telephone handset connects to exchange offices	Telephone network	Telephone handset receives signal from exchange offices	Telephone handset converts electrical pulses to acoustic sound	Person being called

(I/O) channels, for the purpose of transferring data between remote peripheral devices under control of some software discipline. Thus, emphasis was on the computer programs and program development. This viewpoint has evolved to what is known as "communications protocol." Its development closely parallels the development of the computer I/O channel (see question 6 at the end of this chapter).

The computer-systems manager or project leader looked at data communications as the mechanism for the transmission of information from remote points in a timely and optimum manner. The need for timely information in the computer application provides the justification for the existence of data communications as a component of the system. The term "optimum" is a catch-all phrase that typically means "most economical" or "most reliable," i.e., with fewest errors.

Each of these individuals described the implementation using the terminology of his discipline, and much effort was devoted to gaining a common understanding of what was desired. The focus of attention fell upon the dialogue between the computer people and the communications specialists as they tried to bridge the semantic differences of these disciplines. It is essential to realize that at that time (early 1960s) communications specialists had to tailor-design each system using specially designed hardware components wherever data communications was required. More often than not, the case was that these communications specialists did not understand or appreciate what the computer specialists desired, and vice versa. This was exactly the problem that had existed between the computer designers and the computer programmers in the 1950s. The computer designers were primarily concerned with the construction of faster-and-faster arithmetic calculators that happened to be called computers. The computer programmers, on the other hand, desired machines to facilitate problem solving, i.e., machines whose instruction set would include array or vector processing statements, iterative while- or until-type statements, etc.

Recent developments have made available more standardized (off-the-shelf) hardware components, diminishing the requirement for specially designed electronic circuits and tailored data communications systems. This in turn had the effect of changing the role of the communications specialist in the design of the computer applications to a less technical one—a role which can be understood by the computer specialist.

The terminology, however, remains as the largest single barrier to the layman in understanding the functions of the products and the services available from the communications industry. In data communications nomenclature, one finds several generations of telephone terminology, samplings of amateur ("ham") radio operator terminology, and what may be considered as "recent" communications terminology. All of this adds to the confusion, because many of these terms are used interchangeably in the periodical literature. A glossary is given at the end of this text to provide a convenient reference for terms encountered in the reading material.

Computer-industry terminology is used to describe computer products and services, and in the same sense, communications-industry terminology is used to describe communication products and services. In order to effectively evaluate, design, develop, and implement a total computer application using data communications, the computer-system designers must understand what the communications specialists are talking about when equipment or services are being described. It is imperative that technical management understand the elements of data communications whenever they propose or authorize the expenditure of funds for such equipment or services. This text hopes to clarify this terminology and the concepts they represent.

1.3. EVOLUTION TO DATA COMMUNICATIONS

Data communications evolved through the adaptation of telecommunication techniques to the computer system. We shall briefly examine how this evolutionary process occurred in order to gain some understanding of where the data communications subsystem fits into the computer system organization. More detailed narratives of the historical developments of computer technology may be found elsewhere.[1-4]

1.3.1. Batch Processing Systems

The computer systems of the mid-1950s consisted of what is now referred to as "batch processing systems." This mode of operation required the creation of punched, or tabulating equipment, cards from source documents for program and data preparation. This transformation of information from a human-readable form to machine-readable form has been, and still is, a major problem in effective computer utilization in the computer industry.

The punched cards were input to the computer mainframe [i.e., the primary memory storage and the central processing unit (CPU)] as the job stream (or sequences of programs and data) via a card reader peripheral device. The results of each job were output to a line printer. This operation of batch processing jobs serially is shown schematically in Figure 1.1. As computer technology (of the late 1950s) advanced, it became apparent that the computer processor resource was being wasted by idleness, because the internal speeds of the computer, measured in microseconds and then nanoseconds, were outstripping the speeds of the electromechanical peripheral devices such as card readers and line printers, whose operations were measured in millisecond units. The batch processing

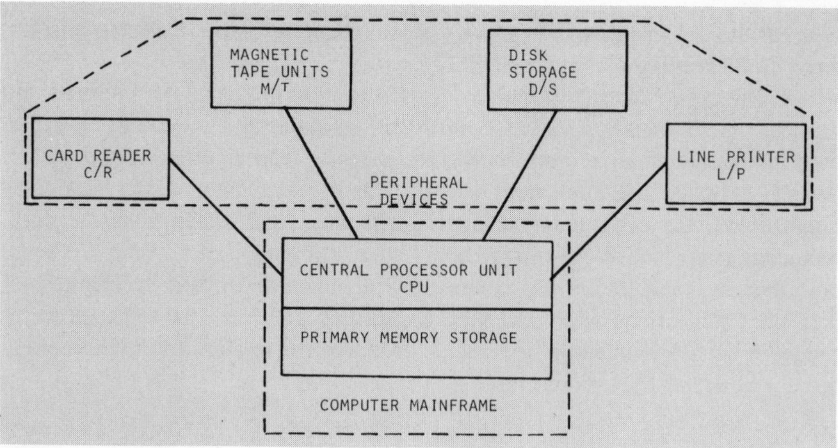

Figure 1.1. A schematic of a batch-processing computer system. All of the computer resources are dedicated to the particular program (or job) during its execution.

computers were being forced to wait on the peripheral devices during the I/O operations.

1.3.2. Multiple Satellite Computers

The concept of satellite computer systems as depicted in Figure 1.2 was introduced as one way to alleviate the CPU delay problem. This multicomputer system was designed using the smaller satellite computers strictly for I/O operations. The data, prepared on punched cards, were read in by a satellite computer whose sole function was to read cards and output the information on reels of magnetic tape (M/T). The main computer, being a larger-scale machine than the satellite computers, would input the job stream from magnetic tape, perform the required calculations, and then output the results to magnetic tape. The output tapes would then be read by (other) satellite computers whose sole function was to print the information on line printers. The major effect of these computer systems was to increase the speeds of the I/O operations to the main computer by using magnetic tape data transfer rates rather than direct card equipment data transfer rates. Table 1.2 illustrates some typical data transfer rates of various peripheral devices. Cost considerations as well as further technological advances diminished the use of these types of satellite computer systems.

1.3.3. Multiprogramming

In the early 1960s many hardware innovations were incorporated: the programmable interrupt, the I/O channel, concurrent I/O, privileged instructions,

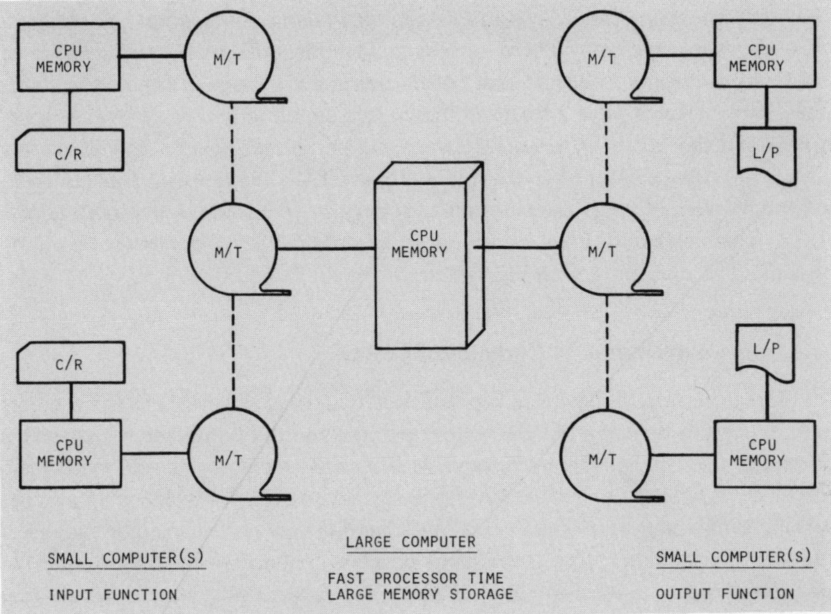

Figure 1.2. A schematic of a satellite batch-processing system. This approach was used to increase the rates of information flow to and from a large processor using magnetic tape transfer rates which are much higher than either card-reader or line-printer transfer rates.

Table 1.2. Data Transfer Rates for Various Devices (bits/s)

Card readers	3000-27,000
Card punch	1000-8000
Paper tape reader	75-10,000
Paper tape punch	75-2400
Line printer	600-64,000
Typewriter	45-150
Teletypewriter	45-300
CRT	8000-550,000
Magnetic tape unit	50,000-3,200,000
Disk	1,000,000-3,000,000
Drum	1,000,000-8,000,000
CPU	2,000,000-20,000,000

memory protection, etc. These innovations led to the development of sophisticated operating systems. These operating systems utilized multiprogramming and multiprocessing concepts that set the trend for current computer systems. Many such systems have a feature, known as "spooling," that allows the input of data and the output of results between the peripheral devices and secondary storage to proceed without interfering with the CPU's operations. This ability to have concurrent I/O operations through processor cycle stealing (memory access by I/O channels) definitely enhanced the development of computer-operating systems. The multiprogramming system is shown in Figure 1.3.

1.3.4. Communications in Computer Systems

A requirement of the more sophisticated operating systems was the need for communication between the computer operator and the computer system. This led to the use of the operator's console which was initially a typewriter or a teleprinter device, but now is a cathode-ray tube (CRT) or video display tube (VDT). At this stage one could conjecture that if the computer operator had direct access to the computer, then it should be possible to allow a user (programmer) to have direct access to the computer. Initially, the systems programmer would find it advantageous to modify the operating system by direct interaction through a keyboard device. Proceeding with this conjecture, if there was one user, then why not have many keyboard devices concurrently providing access to the computer? And why couldn't these devices be located at a distance from the processor, in other words, outside of the computer room? This connection of a teleprinter directly to the computer allowed the programmer to interact more efficiently during program development because the card preparation and batch

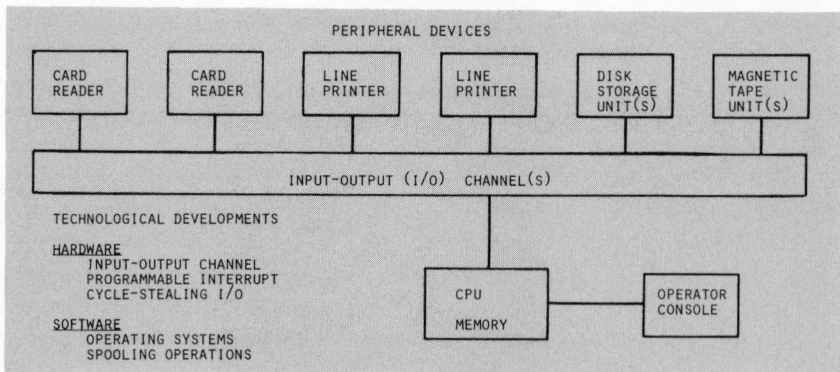

Figure 1.3. A schematic of a multiprogramming computer system. This system allows the time-interleaved execution of more than one computer program over an interval of time. It was made possible by some of the indicated technological developments.

processing steps were eliminated. Multiprogramming, which allowed access to the computer by several programmers, added to the efficient use of manpower.

In the early 1960s several universities were engaged in projects using computers in an interactive manner. One such experiment known as Project MAC was undertaken to demonstrate that a relatively large number of terminals could be connected to a single computer system.[(5)] The work of Kemeny and others resulted in the development of a time-sharing system using a simple but powerful compiler, BASIC.[(6)] This further enhanced the idea of many programmer's "conversing" with the computer system during program development and debugging operations, each unaware of the others' presence. This subsystem evolved into what is known as the communication link.

As long as the distances of the cables connecting the various devices were short, data communications facilities were not required and these devices were considered to be peripherals to the computer system. Now, as the number of devices increased and the distances between devices increased, the use of data communications became a necessity. First, with increasing numbers of terminal devices being involved, concepts had to be developed for handling the message traffic among them without involving the CPU. Secondly, when the distances increased, a point was reached at which the signals could not be received intelligibly without some form of signal enhancement being used. Another step in the evolution of data communications in computer systems was the adaptation of the telephone system, which is primarily a voice transmission network, for use in transmitting digital data signals.

The effort involved in handling the traffic of a large number of terminal devices and in the problem of signal enhancement over larger distances led to data communications being considered as a separate and required subsystem known as the communication link.

Concurrent developments in telemetering of data as used by process-control computer* systems also contributed to the emergence of a body of data communications concepts. These systems also required a communications link for the retrieval and dissemination of monitoring and control data. Data communications not only allowed the efficient use of manpower, it also increased the efficiency of the data input procedure.

From these modest beginnings, the capabilities of the communication link were refined and expanded to allow higher transmission speeds with lower error rates. As the idea of remote access to the computer gained acceptance, computer systems were designed to permit the attachment of any of the peripheral devices at distant sites (see Figure 1.4). Today, it is commonplace to have remote

*A process control computer is a computer that is adapted for concurrent input and output by many analog and contact closure devices in addition to the usual peripherals. These computers are suitable for monitoring and controlling industrial processes (or factory equipment).

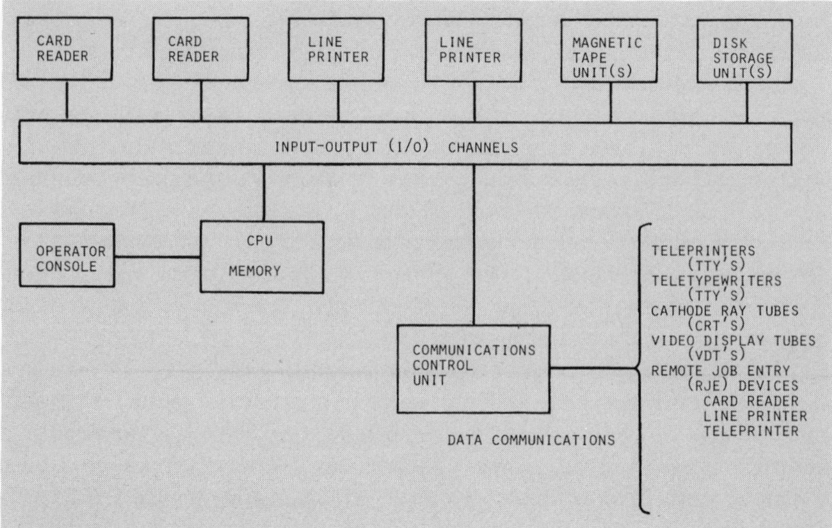

Figure 1.4. A remote processing system incorporates a special peripheral device to control the data flow and to increase the distance between the central processor and various input-output devices collectively referred to as terminals.

terminal stations consisting of line printers, card readers, and keyboard devices access computers using data communications.

Within a short time, the nature of computing has undergone a dramatic change. It is now possible for many users to have the impression of executing their jobs, or programs, on large-scale computers independently of each other. The real-time processing system, as shown in Figure 1.5, emerged in data processing applications. In these systems the data and the results of the calculations interact with the environment to form a feedback loop with the computer.

The concepts of remote batch entry (RBE, also known as remote job entry, RJE), interactive programming, and conversational progammming have enhanced the popularity of computing for many individuals who would not be interested in using the computer if batch processing were the only means of access. This growth of interest has brought about the development of new terminals and a reduction in the costs (lease/purchase) of various common terminal devices, which, in turn, has provided a stimulus to further growth in teleprocessing.

The method of providing data input has changed drastically from the punched card to direct interactive input using terminal devices. This evolutionary process is depicted in Figure 1.6. Where once there would be a roomful of key punch operators, now there is a roomful of terminal operators interacting directly with the computer system. Scenes such as shown in Figure 1.7 have become

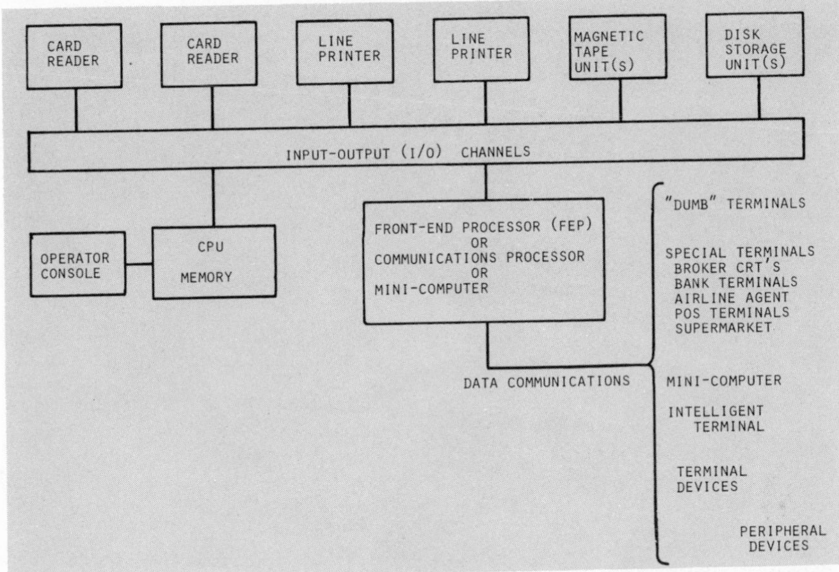

Figure 1.5. Increased sophistication in the communications processor as well as the terminal peripheral devices led to the development of real-time applications where the data are input as they are generated, and the processed results influence the subsequent production of new data.

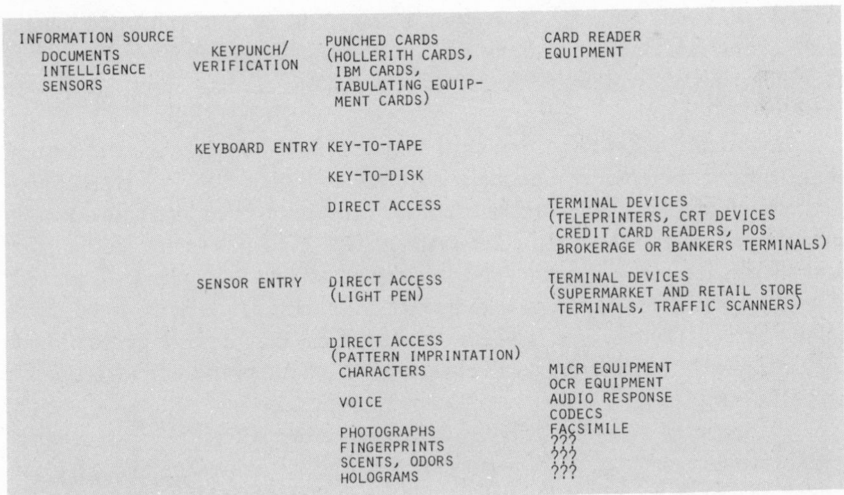

Figure 1.6. The changing nature of computer data input is depicted as the evolutionary process from punched cards to direct computer access.

Figure 1.7. Instead of keypunch operators, these terminal operators interact directly with the computer to input transaction data and obtain up-to-date query responses. (Courtesy of Eastern Airlines.)

commonplace with today's technology. The major theme in this changing pattern is that both data communications *and* some form of computer processing are becoming more involved with the transformation of data from human- to machine-usable form.

And finally, at today's frontiers of computer technology there is the concept of distributed computer processing as depicted in Figure 1.8. This type of configuration represents the incorporation of the data communications network as an integral part of the total computer system. This kind of system may contain several general purpose computers, referred to as host computers, to provide shareable processor support to a wide variety of terminal devices. In addition, minicomputers, known as message processors, located at network nodes provide the capability of transferring data between host computers and terminals quickly and efficiently.

The essential idea of distributed processing is that a computer job (or application) would consist of tasks performed by different processors located at different geographical sites. For example, transaction data might be input and partially processed in a data base update at the local site, and the results transmitted to a distant host for update of a centralized data base. Supermarket terminals could input data to computers at each store while also performing cash register check-out functions. These store computers could transmit data to a regional center computer. Several regional centers could send their data to the organization headquarters. Market analyses, buying trends, and pricing information might be sent back to the individual stores. Distributed processing entails that each site processes the data it acquires and transmits the results on to the next site.

The ultimate goal of distributed processing systems is to have host–host interaction. An application might be initiated from a terminal to a host computer, say host A. Host A then causes a search of data bases located at the sites of host B and host C computers and the appropriate data transferred back to host A. Host A then allows host D to process some of the data because it has more processor capability. The results are generated and, when collected by host A, transmitted back to the initiating terminal. All of the host-to-host interaction is not observed by the terminal user; in the 1980s such capabilities will be available. The key point is that the technology already exists to attain these goals.

1.4. THE EXPLOSIVE GROWTH OF DATA COMMUNICATIONS

In the preceding section we briefly described the evolution of computer systems from batch processing to those of today using data communications. One

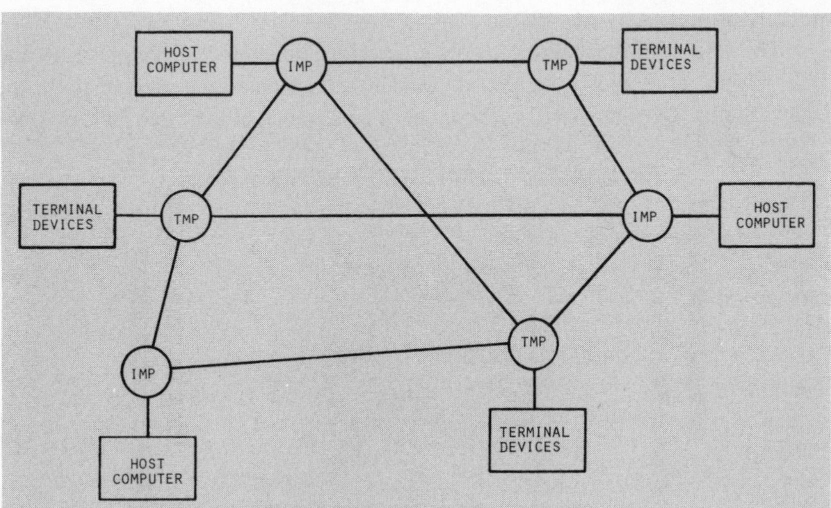

Figure 1.8. A distributed processing system where separated, shared processors are interconnected by a computer message-switching network. (IMP = interface message processor, TMP = terminal message processor.)

might reasonably ask, How could this have taken place in such a short period of time? In retrospect, this writer is of the opinion that there were three factors that influenced this technological growth.

First, as computers were evolving, people would foresee applications where it was economically feasible to use computers. In other words, a market was being created for the use of computers in a wide variety of applications that required teleprocessing. Airline ticket reservations, stock exchange transactions, and banking transactions were examples of such applications.

The second factor was the United States' space program, which put a man on the moon in the late 1960s. The technological spin-offs of this program provided a wealth of new devices, such as integrated circuitry, circuit miniaturization, microprocessors, etc. Figure 1.9 shows a processor and its size relative to ordinary staples. The technology was there to use in computer teleprocessing applications.

The third factor was the abrupt turnabout in governmental regulatory policies for the communications industries in the United States. Historically, the common carrier telephone companies, which provide virtually all of the data communications facilities and services, were considered protected, regulated monopolies. All of this was changed by three far-reaching decisions by the Federal Communication Commission (FCC) that had the effect of encouraging competition in the data communication field. These developments are discussed in detail in Chapter 9. The result of these decisions was the birth in the late 1960s of a new industry, the interconnection industry, whose sales grew to hundreds of millions of dollars by the 1970s.

The effects of these three factors are vividly illustrated in Figures 1.10 and 1.11. Figure 1.10 shows the growth statistics for remote data terminals in the United States. Consider 1970 as the point of confluence of the three factors; since

Figure 1.9. A MAC-8 microprocessor (framed by two ordinary staples) containing over 7000 transistors and capable of executing over 400 different instructions at microsecond speeds is used in many teleprocessing applications. (Courtesy of Bell Labs.)

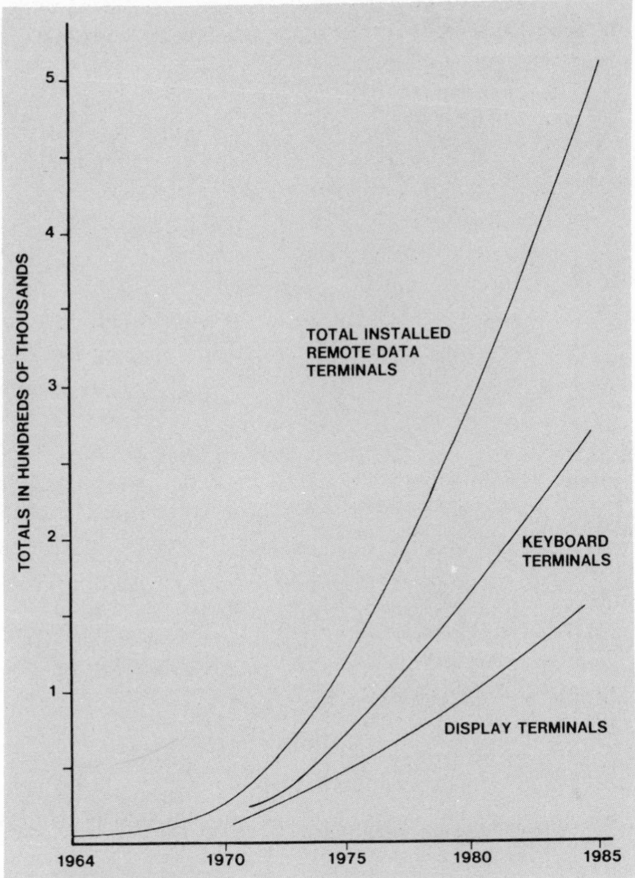

Figure 1.10. Growth statistics for remote data terminals illustrate the phenomenal rise since 1970.

then, the growth is truly remarkable. Figure 1.11 illustrates the growth potential in terms of investments in data communications equipment and services. The data are from a report by Frost and Sullivan.[7]

In summary, we have a classic situation where the technology for data communications existed, but a monopolistic marketing position slowed its development. Once this barrier was lowered, the market forces were strong enough to cause a rush of technological development in response to the waiting applications. The immediate beneficiaries were consumers who were provided with a wider variety of services and equipments at lower prices because of competitive forces. This atmosphere of competition improved existing equipment and services and fostered new innovations in equipment and service. Teleprocessing

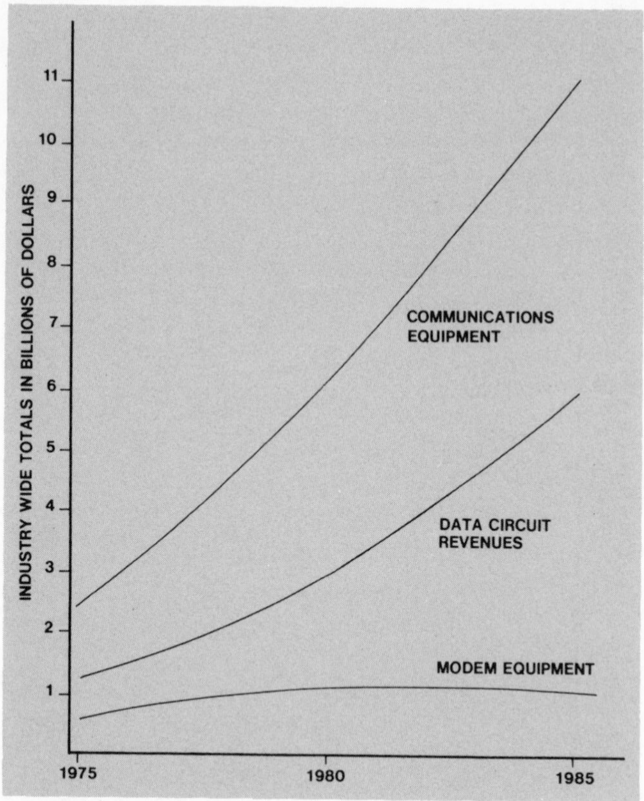

Figure 1.11. Data communications equipment growth is forecast to be strong into the 1980s.

applications that were but dreams in the sixties have become realities in the seventies.

PROBLEMS

1. In this chapter numerous terms were used without a detailed exposition of their meanings. Define the following terms and cite a reference source. (If considered adequate, personal knowledge may be considered as a reference source.)

batch processing	on-line, off-line, real-time
machine-readable form	time sharing, time slicing
multiprogramming	remote job entry
multiprocessing	interactive programming
cycle-stealing	conversational programming

2. What would you consider the most important single computer hardware feature that makes multiprogramming a possibility?

3. Characterize and give examples of what is meant by large-scale computers, medium-scale computers, small-scale computers, and minicomputers.

4. Go to the current periodical literature and obtain the specifications for one specialized type of terminal that is linked to a computer processor in an on-line manner. Advertisements or new product announcements should be referenced.

5. From your personal experience, develop an additional example to those cited in Table 1.1, and describe it in terms of its functional components.

6. The I/O channel of the modern computer system is a processor with a limited instruction set. Describe the evolutionary steps in the development of the I/O channel. At what points were the programmable interrupt and the cycle-stealing concepts introduced?

Chapter 2

An Overview of Data Communications

Data communications components are usually described as supplements to the conventional (mainframe/primary storage/secondary storage/peripheral devices) computer systems. As a result, computer specialists concerned with data communications tend to emphasize transmission channels and terminal devices even though similar channels (viz., selector channels, multiplexor channels, etc.) and device controllers have existed in conventional systems. The purpose of this chapter is to present data communications as a complete integral subsystem. This overview will describe all of the essential components of a data communications system and their relationships to one another in a concise form. Many new terms will be introduced and briefly explained. References to succeeding chapters of this text will be given where more detailed explanations may be found.

2.1. THE DATA COMMUNICATIONS SUBSYSTEM

The functional components of a data communications subsystem are shown in Figure 2.1. The computer programmer might refer to this subsystem as the "data link," which is established for the purpose of "carrying" information from a data source to a data sink. The terms "data source" and "data sink" refer to the originators and receivers of data and could be any of the input or output devices listed in Table 2.1.

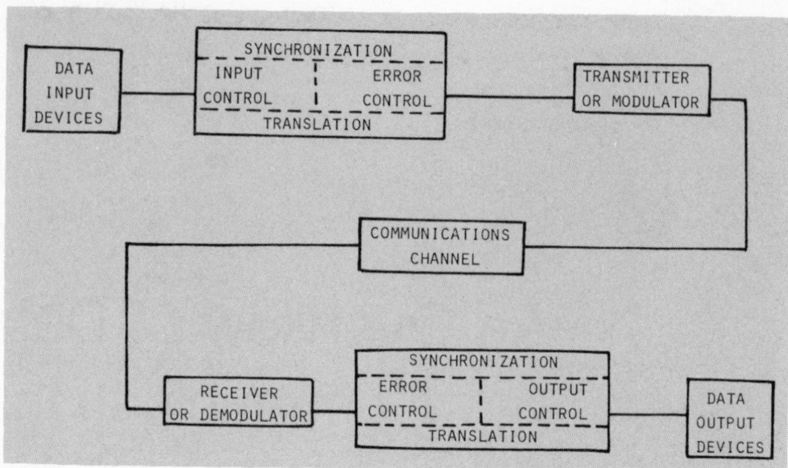

Figure 2.1. The data communications subsystem, often called the data link, consists of the indicated functional components which are required in every data communications system.

2.2. THE COMMUNICATIONS CONTROL UNIT

In the data communications subsystem, the communications control unit has been given various names by different manufacturers. For example, it may be called a communications controller multiplexor, communications processor, front-end processor, etc. This device should not be confused with the computer I/O channel inasmuch as the functions differ. The communications control unit is required in addition to the I/O channel.

The communications control unit performs several important functions on the data communications subsystem. The various functional components of this unit may be freestanding pieces of equipment or combinations of components [of integrated circuit (IC) or large-scale integration (LSI) modules] in one or more equipment units. The components, however, must exist in one form or another in the data communications subsystem. The functions performed by these components as shown in Tables 2.2 and 2.5 are:

1. Input and output line control, or line protocol
2. Code translation
3. Error control
4. Synchronization
5. Transmission and reception of the signals

These functions may be performed entirely by hardware devices (such as concentrators, multiplexors) in a hardwired manner, or they may be performed entirely by software (such as programs in minicomputer systems), or they may be per-

Table 2.1. System Components of a Data Communications Subsystem

Data input or output devices	Communication control units
Keyboard	Memory or buffer storage
P/T reader (paper tape)	Magnetic core
C/R (card reader)	Magnetic drum
M/T unit (magnetic tape)	Shift registers
Facsimile	Delay lines
Badge reader	
Microfilm reader	
CRT/VDT (cathode-ray tube/visual display tube)	
MICR (magnetic ink character recognition)	
OCR (optical character reader)	
Transducers	
Senors	
A/D equipment (analog to digital)	
Computer processors	

Transmitters or receivers	Communication links	Data output devices
Modulators/demodulators	Telegraph lines	P/T punch
Modems	Telephone plant	Card punch
Datasets	Radio	Line printer
Acoustic couplers	Microwave	Teleprinter
Dataphone®	Coaxial cable	Teletypewriter
Line adaptors	Wire pairs	M/T unit
		CRT/VDT
		Plotter
		Recorder
		Dials and gauges
		Computer processors
		COM (Computer output microfilm)

formed by combinations of hardware–software devices. For the purpose of providing an overview of the data communications system, we shall briefly describe each of these functions. The essential point is to introduce new terminology and concepts with the idea of showing where these pieces fit together in the overall picture. Detailed discussion of the functions is deferred to later chapters.

2.2.1. Line Control or Line Protocol

Line protocol is the mechanism by which the data-communications subsystem controls or regulates the flow of data into and out of the system as messages.

Table 2.2. The Functions of the Communications-Control Unit and Some Examples

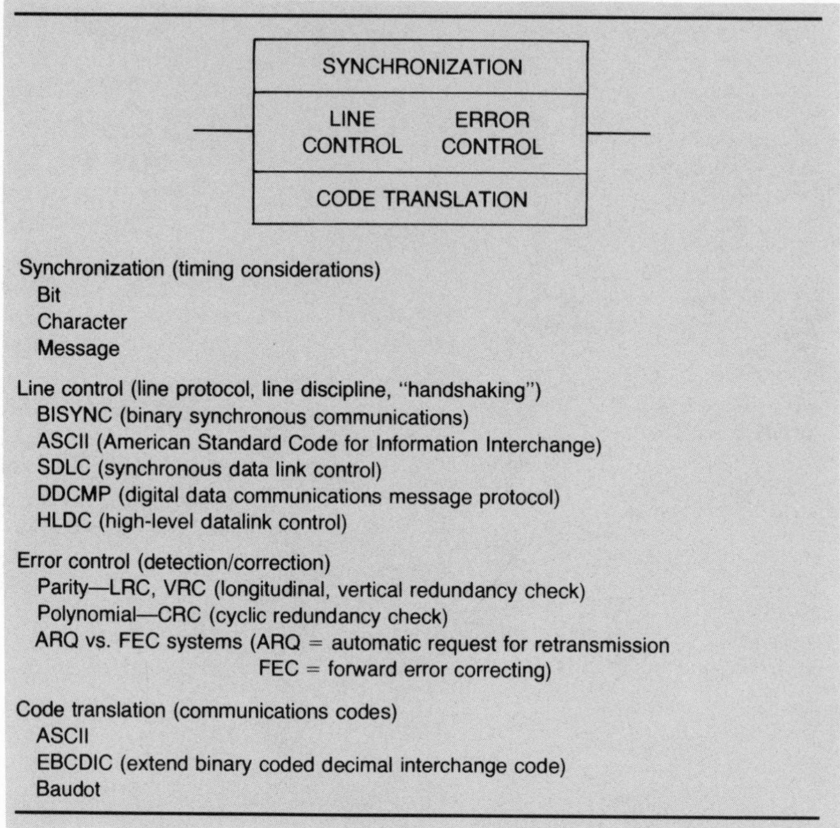

SYNCHRONIZATION

LINE CONTROL | ERROR CONTROL

CODE TRANSLATION

Synchronization (timing considerations)
- Bit
- Character
- Message

Line control (line protocol, line discipline, "handshaking")
- BISYNC (binary synchronous communications)
- ASCII (American Standard Code for Information Interchange)
- SDLC (synchronous data link control)
- DDCMP (digital data communications message protocol)
- HLDC (high-level datalink control)

Error control (detection/correction)
- Parity—LRC, VRC (longitudinal, vertical redundancy check)
- Polynomial—CRC (cyclic redundancy check)
- ARQ vs. FEC systems (ARQ = automatic request for retransmission
  FEC = forward error correcting)

Code translation (communications codes)
- ASCII
- EBCDIC (extend binary coded decimal interchange code)
- Baudot

An important distinction to be made here is that the computer system sees messages as information to be transmitted between the sender and the receiver, while the data communications subsystem looks at these transmissions as data upon which certain operations are to be performed. The control of these operations is currently known as *line protocol* and it is becoming more and more important as the sophistication of the subsystem increases.

Line protocol used to be called "handshaking," but this term has now been relegated to specify the process by which the channel connection is established. For example, in the use of the dial telephone, handshaking refers to the lifting of a telephone handset off the hook, listening for the dial tone, the dialing process, hearing the ringing signals, and the receiver being lifted. Line protocol includes the control of all of the above actions and, in addition, the message etiquette concerned with right party calls (or wrong numbers), the conversation itself, and the termination of the call.

Line protocols are currently being formalized, and they are beginning to be known by specific acronyms. Some of the better known protocols are BISYNC (IBM's Binary Synchronous Communications), ASCII (American Standard Code for Information Interchange), and SDLC (IBM's Synchronous Data Link Control). The topic of line protocols is covered in greater detail in Chapter 14.

2.2.2. Code Translation

Code translation is required because communication codes differ from the internal codes of many hardware devices such as computer systems. Computer codes are the bit representations of "graphic" display characters such as the digits, the alphabet, special characters, etc., for communication purposes. However, there is the added requirement that the codes provide for a representation of control information. This is necessary because communications systems generally must transfer both data and control information serially over one circuit path. Some of the more common communication codes are EBCDIC (Extended Binary Coded Decimal Interchange Code), an 8-bit code developed by IBM; ASCII (American Standard Code for Information Interchange), a 7-bit code developed by the American National Standards Institute (also known as ANSI); and the Baudot code, a 5-bit code used in the earlier teleprinter systems. The topic of codes is covered in more detail in Chapter 13.

2.2.3. Error Control

The mechanism by which errors occurring during the transmission process are detected and corrected at the receiver is known as *error control*. Traditionally, voice and teleprinter communications between humans have a great tolerance for errors (manifested as static or garbled transmission, etc.) because of the large amount of redundancy which exists in a natural language (such as English, German, French, etc.). Data communications, however, is concerned with serial transmissions of characters that are usually in a symbolic language form, which inherently has a minimum amount of redundancy. Therefore the problem of error control is to determine how much redundancy must be added to the transmissions, how to detect the erroneous messages with a high degree of accuracy, and how to correct the detected errors.

At present there are two major ways of achieving error correction. The first is known as the *ARQ method,* which means automatic request for retransmission (a term derived from amateur radio). In this method, a receiver sends a positive acknowledgement (ACK) message back to the transmitter for every message correctly received, and a negative acknowledgement (NAK) message for those messages in which an error has been detected. The NAK message requests the transmitter to resend that particular message. The ARQ method may also be referred to as the ACK/NAK system.

The other method, the forward error correcting (FEC) scheme, provides enough redundancy in the transmission for the receiver to correct any errors detected in the message.

Because of the increased logical capability requirements in the receivers, the FEC method is more expensive than the ARQ method of error control. Currently, the costs of the FEC system can be justified only where the time-value of the messages is high, such as in military, missile, or rocketry applications. However, if the present trends of circuit miniaturization and cost reduction continue, then FEC methods will be economically justifiable for routine data communications applications.

There are two major methods of error detection. The first method is to use simple parity bits for added redundancy. A parity bit may be added to each character of the message, in which case they are known as vertical redundancy check (VRC) bits. In addition, parity bits may be added to all the particular bits of all the characters in a message block, in the form of a single longitudinal redundancy check (LRC) character. The second error-detection method is known as cyclical redundancy check (CRC) and involves using polynomial operations upon the bits of the messages to create characters which are appended to the end of a message block. The CRC methods are more powerful for error detection than VRC/LRC methods and can be extended in complexity for error correction. Error-control methods are discussed in more detail in Chapter 13.

2.2.4. Synchronization

Determination of the correct timing for transmitting and receiving the signals is known as synchronization. It is perhaps the most important function in the data-communications subsystem, and yet it is the least emphasized, because (1) it is a highly technical subject and (2) synchronization of a communications system by its very nature either works or it does not work.

For purposes of this discussion, it is important to realize that data transmissions are serial in nature (i.e., one bit behind the other) and contain both control information and the message data in the same signal stream. This differs from computer transmissions (e.g., memory-to-peripheral device, memory-to-CPU, etc.) which occur in parallel with control information being sent on channels (e.g., interrupt lines) separate from data channels (e.g., multiplexor or selector channels). Hence, the data-communications synchronization problem reduces to how to correctly determine (1) when a bit is transmitted; (2) when a character is transmitted (i.e., which is the first bit of a character); and (3) when is a message transmitted (i.e., when is a character the first character of a message).

From the preceding, it becomes obvious that different levels of synchronization between the transmitter and the receiver are required. Typically, it is assumed that the timings are known for the transmitter and that the signal suffers distortion during transmission over the communications channel. Thus the major problem lies with the receiver's correct detection of the original signal. Bit synchronization determines when the receiver must sample the incoming signals to correctly identify a bit (or a signal pulse) without incurring interference from adjacent bits (pulses). We use the term pulses because, as we will see later (cf. Chapter 5), more than one bit may be transmitted in each pulse. The design and trouble-shooting of equipment for bit synchronization is properly the domain of the electrical engineer, and in this regard, the equipment either works or it does not work.

Character synchronization requires the receiver to sample the incoming stream of bits to determine which bits correctly define each character. This is made possible in the specification of communication codes, and, in turn, is one of the reasons for having communication codes. Parituclar characters, called synchronization, or SYN, characters, contain a unique pattern of bits such that whenever a pair of SYN characters is received, all of the possible left or right shifts of bits yield improbable or undefined characters.

For example, the ASCII character SYN is represented by the bit pattern 0110001. As shown in Table 2.3, the SYN character is a unique pattern which does not replicate itself under left or right translations.[1] While a pair of SYNs is

Table 2.3. An Illustration of the Use of the SYN Character

Left-shifted bits	1 = 110001*x* ≠ SYN	Cannot yield any valid characters which can be used to start a message
	2 = 10001*xx* ≠ SYN	
	3 = 0001*xxx* ≠ SYN	
	4 = 001*xxxx* ≠ SYN	
	5 = 01*xxxx* ≠ SYN	Except when next character begins with 10001*yy* which could be M, X, h, x, none of which can be used to start a message
Right-shifted bits	1 = *x*011000 ≠ SYN	Cannot yield any valid character which can be used to start a message
	2 = *xx*01100 ≠ SYN	
	3 = *xxx*0110 ≠ SYN	
	4 = *xxxx*011 ≠ SYN	
	5 = *xxxxx*01 ≠ SYN	Except when preceding character is *yy*01100 which could be A, E, I, M, none of which can be used to start a message

sufficient, many systems use four SYNs in the transmission to check the receiver's synchronization.

Message synchronization is the objective of line protocol, which is discussed in Chapter 14. The reason for its inclusion as a synchronization function becomes evident when communications networks are considered.

2.3. TRANSMITTER AND RECEIVER IN THE COMMUNICATION LINK

In the data communications subsystem, the transmission of the data signals over the communications channel is performed by a transmitter device, and the reception of the data signals from the communications channel is performed by a receiver device. The signals of data communications transmissions may be either *analog* or *digital* in nature. An analog signal consists of a continuously varying (e.g., sinusoidal) waveform of electrical energy. Another way of saying this is that the amplitude (or strength) of the signal varies continuously with time. A digital signal, on the other hand, consists of discrete pulses of electrical energy usually representing the bits zero or one. Such digital signals may also be referred to by the terms space (zero) or mark (one).

When data transmissions over the communications channel are analog in nature, the transmitter–receiver device is commonly known by the name *modem,* which is a contraction of modulator–demodulator. Since analog transmissions were used in the early data communications systems, where the process of modulation was important, the name modem became universally established. Stand-alone modems are typically uninteresting-looking boxes.

A modem may also be referred to as a *dataset* (which should not be confused with the computer term for the storage of data on disk devices), or *Dataphone*®, which specifically refers to AT&T modems (manufactured by the Western Electric Corporation) and is a registered trademark of AT&T (see Figure 2.2). Table 2.4 summarizes modem terminology and functions.

An *acoustic coupler* is a portable modem which transmits and receives tones when placed (coupled or cradled) in the ear-and-mouth (E&M) piece of a dial telephone handset. An acoustic coupler is typically a slow-speed device (under 600 bits per second), but its prime advantage is mobility and ready access to almost any dial phone in the country. Because it is mobile, an acoustic coupler may be categorized as a soft-wired device.

All other modems are categorized as hard-wired devices, in the sense of being permanently connected to a communications line. From 1969 to 1977 it was a requirement by telephone company tariffs that foreign, meaning non-Western Electric manufactured modems, have a data-access-arrangement (DAA) device in the line for protection of the dial telephone network. This part of the

Table 2.4. Modem Functions and Terminology

TRANSMITTER	RECEIVER
MODULATOR	DEMODULATOR

Terminology	Modulation method
Transmitter/receiver	Analog
Modulator/demodulator	Amplitude modulation (AM)
Modem	Frequency modulation (FM)
Dataset	Phase modulation (ϕM)
Dataphone	Digital
Acoustic coupler	Pulse (PAM, PDM, PFM, PPM)
Line adapter—erroneous usage	Pulse code modulation (PCM)

Figure 2.2. In the foreground is an AT&T Dataphone® modem which can be used to send digital data over the telephone network. The CRT terminal is the Dataspeed 40 with a keyboard and printer. In the background are several teletypewriter terminals. (Courtesy of AT&T Corp.)

tariff has been the subject of much controversy and has been replaced by a licensing or certification arrangement. This aspect is discussed in Chapter 4.

The modem may be erroneously referred to by the term *line adapter*. Since a device known as a line adapter really exists in many data communications systems, confusion naturally arises in nomenclature. A synonomous term for line adapter is *line driver*. The function of the conventional line adapter or line driver is to modify (or act as an interface for) the various electrical voltage and current levels which may exist between the communications channel and the different hardware communications devices. On the other hand, the function of the modem is to modulate a carrier signal for transmission and to demodulate the received signal.

A modem is not required when the data transmissions are digital in nature, but a line adapter device is always required. In digital transmission the line adapter devices are used at the communications control unit of the computer. Elsewhere, line adapter or line driver functions are performed by devices called channel service units, terminal service units, etc.

2.3.1. Modulation

Signals emanating from terminal or computer devices are said to be at their originating frequencies or in *baseband* form. The process of modifying the analog characteristics of a higher frequency carrier signal by the baseband signal is known as *modulation*. Those analog characteristics that can be modified are the signal amplitude, as in amplitude modulation (AM); the signal frequency, as in frequency modulation (FM); and the signal phase angle, as in phase modulation (ϕM) transmission. These are illustrated in Figure 2.3. Commercial AM, FM, and television broadcasting are examples of modulation systems.

The baseband signals may also be modulated digitally. *Digital modulation* exists in two forms: (1) Pulse modulation, of which there are many variants such as pulse position (PPM), pulse duration (PDM), pulse amplitude (PAM), pulse frequency (PFM), etc.; and (2) pulse-code modulation (PCM).

The primary purpose of modulation is to increase the transmission capacity of a communications channel by utilizing higher frequencies. A more detailed discussion of modulation methods is given in Chapter 5.

2.4. COMMUNICATIONS CHANNEL

In the data communications system, the communications channel is the path over which the electronic signals travel from the transmitter to the receiver (i.e., modem to modem). Of principal concern is the amount of distortion that the signals are subject to when traveling over the communications channel. This distortion influences the capacity of the channel for the data transmission (i.e. the

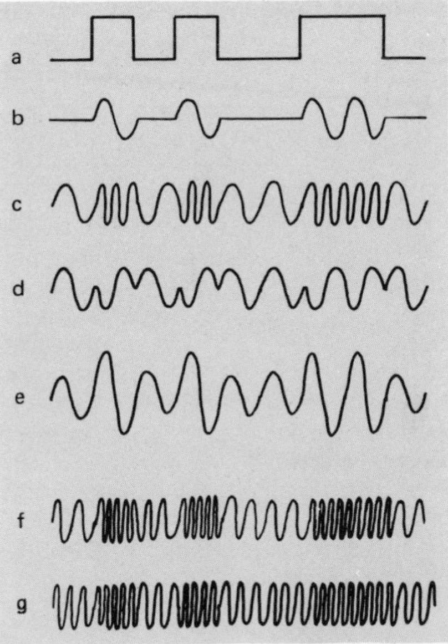

Figure 2.3. Types of analog modulation. (a) Input binary pulses; (b) on-off AM or ASK; (c) frequency-shift keying (FSK); (d) phase-shift keying (ϕSK); (e) carrier AM; (f) carrier FM; (g) carrier ϕM. When the digital baseband signal directly alters the carrier, this is known as shift-keying; otherwise, it is referred to as carrier modulation. Note that carrier frequency modulation and carrier phase modulation have similar waveforms.

maximum rate at which data can be sent). The various distortion manifestations and their countermeasures are discussed in Chapter 8.

Whenever specific media or equipment such as wire pairs, coaxial cables, microwave radio, etc., are described, the term *communication link* is used. The communication channel, on the other hand, may be comprised of many different kinds of communication links combined in a system as a service. This is generally referred to by the term *communication facilities*.

The communication channel may also be characterized in a number of different ways. Some of these are

1. Channel transmission modes
2. Transmission speeds
3. Transmission methods
4. Facilities type
5. Facilities organization type
6. Channel type

These characterizations serve to describe the capabilities of the communications channel in the system and are summarized in Table 2.5.

Table 2.5. Communications Channel Characterizations

COMMUNICATIONS CHANNEL

Channel modes	Facilities organization type
Simplex	Point-to-point
Half-duplex (HDX)	Multidrop
Full-duplex (FDX)	Switched
Transmission speeds	Network
Bits per second (bps)	Channel type
Characters per second (char/s)	Baseband
Words per minute (wpm) (note: one word contains six characters)	Narrowband
Baud (note: Baud is the plural)	Voiceband
Transmission method	Wideband
Serial-by-bit } Asynchronous or	Multiplexed (FDM/TDM)
Parallel-by-bit } synchronous	Carrier service
Facilities types	Transmission link
Wholly owned private system	
Private leased (PL)	
Public system (DDD)	

2.4.1. Channel Transmission Modes

A communications channel may operate in a simplex, a half-duplex, or a full-duplex mode. In *simplex* mode, transmissions are in the same direction at all times. Computer-driven video displays of airline arrivals and departures at airports would be an example of a simplex mode of transmission. *Half-duplex* (HDX) describes a transmission that may be in either direction, but only in one direction at a given moment of time. Half-duplex systems are sometimes referred to as two-wire transmission. Many computer terminal systems are half-duplex in operation. The computer sends (transmits) a message to the terminal, and then awaits a reply (in the receive state) message from the terminal. When transmissions can occur simultaneously in both directions, the mode of operation is known as *full-duplex* (FDX). This is sometimes referred to as four-wire transmission. Historically, the communications link had to be four physical wires for full duplex capability on a physical pair of wires. Table 2.6 shows these different modes.

While the communications channel may have full-duplex capability, it is the capability of the modem equipment, or the terminal equipment, that determines whether full-duplex transmission actually can be used. Currently many systems are operating in half-duplex mode because of the lack of hardware or software capability to support a full-duplex operation and not because of communications channel limitations!

2.4.2. Channel Transmission Speeds

Communications channel transmission speeds may be described using several different units. Computer specialists are interested in the channel throughput in *bits per second* (bps or b/s). Since control information and data are transmitted serially, the units of bps may be further refined to a net "information bits per second," which have been referred to in communications literature as TRIB (transfer rate of information bits) or NDT (net data throughput).[2,3]

Transmission speeds of keyboard equipment are usually given as *characters per second* (char/s). Conversion to bits per second requires a knowledge of the number of bits per character, which in turn depends upon the communications code being used. *Words per minute* (wpm) is another unit for describing transmission speeds; it is a holdover from the early days of teleprinter transmission systems. In this instance, a word is defined to contain six characters, so that, as one might suspect, words per minute divided by ten yields characters per second.

Finally, we have the *baud* (named in honor of J. M. E. Baudot, an early developer of telegraph systems) as a unit of transmission speed. The baud rate of a communications channel is the maximum rate at which the signal pulses are transmitted, or the modulation rate of the channel. In binary transmission systems the baud and bit per second are synonymous, because each signal pulse carries one and only one information bit. In multilevel or *M*-ary (the *M* here replaces the *bin* in binary to indicate a code with *M* elements) systems, the baud rate indicates the number of signal pulses that are transmitted per second, with each pulse carrying more than one information bit.

Just as computer specialists are interested in the bit rate, communications

Table 2.6. Data Communications Link Directionality Terminology

Symbols	ANSI	U.S. telecommunications industry	CCITT[a]	Historical reference to physical link requirements
→	One-way only	Simplex		2-wire
⇄	Two-way alternate	Half-duplex (HDX)	Simplex	2-wire
↔	Two-way simultaneous	Full-duplex (FDX)	Duplex	4-wire

[a]Consultative Committee on International Telegraphy and Telephony.

specialists are interested in the baud rate of a communications channel. Unfortunately, the terminology is getting mixed up in the current literature, with computer people talking about data chennel line speeds of "9600 baud" when they really mean "9600 bits per second." Baud and bits per second are being used synonymously even though they may be entirely different values. This usage is another example of a holdover from telegraphy. The differences between baud and bits per second will be discussed in Chapter 5 on modulation.

The term baud as a unit of signaling speed contains reciprocal time units in its definition. Hence, it is redundant to say "baud per second." Furthermore, the term baud is plural, so that it is also incorrect to say "bauds." Unfortunately, both of these usages are heard frequently.

2.4.3. Channel Transmission Methods

The transmission method used on the data communications channel is some combination of *asynchronous* or *synchronous* with *serial-by-bit* (one bit follows the other) or *parallel-by-bit* (or serial-by-character: one character follows the other). There are relatively few parallel-by-bit transmission systems, the majority being *serial-by-bit*. The majority of the lower-speed (under 600 bps) systems use asynchronous transmission while the higher-speed systems use synchronous transmission methods. Figures 2.4 and 2.5 illustrate these methods.

Asynchronous transmission, sometimes known as start–stop transmission, consists of inserting a prefix bit to the information bits of the character to indicate

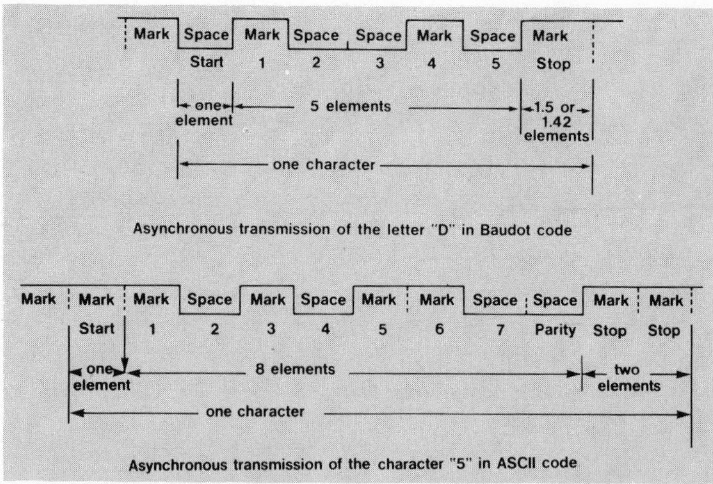

Figure 2.4. Start-stop, or asynchronous, transmission requires the addition of a start bit and one or two stop elements. Characters from two different communication codes are shown as they would be transmitted asynchronously.

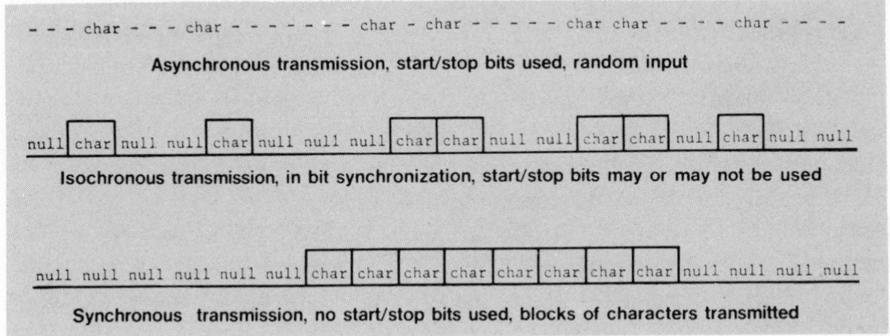

Figure 2.5. Synchronous transmission of blocks of characters (without any start-stop elements) are compared to asynchronous transmissions where the input is random. A recent innovation is isochronous transmission with characters input in a random manner and the transmitter-receiver maintains character position synchronization by either clock timing or sending null characters.

the start of the character and inserting one or more bits as a suffix to the information bits to indicate the end of the character, or character-stop (Figure 2.4). When transmissions ae not taking place, the asynchronous communications channel holds either a steady mark or space. Asynchronous transmission occurs character-by-character, as in a typewriter or teleprinter system, with each character providing the start-bit as a "flag" to activate the receiver to receive and properly decode the character, and one or more stop bits to deactivate the receiver. Thus, in asynchronous transmission systems the characters may be transmitted at varying or irregular time intervals corresponding to the operation of a keyboard device.

On the other hand, synchronous transmission systems require that characters be transmitted over the communications channel at all times, even when there are not any information characters being transmitted (Figure 2.5). For this purpose communications codes have defined idle (IDLE) or synchronization (SYN) characters. The start and stop bits used in the asynchronous method are not required in the synchronous method. Groups of characters making up message *blocks* are transmitted in synchronous systems.

Asynchronous systems are cheaper to build and easier to maintain, but because they operate at lower speeds, they are wasteful of line capacity. For high transmission rate requirements, synchronous systems are employed. These concepts are discussed in the chapter on modem equipment.

2.4.4. Facilities Types

The communications channel is categorized by facilities type according to its economic organization. The communications system may be *wholly owned private, private leased,* or it may be a *public* system. Wholly owned private systems are communications systems built for the private use of corporations or organizations within private land areas (such as factory sites, etc.), or on acquired right-of-way land. They are granted permission to operate by the Federal Communications Commission (FCC) with the understanding that such services may not be leased or sold to outside parties. Electric utilities and railroads are examples of companies that have private communications systems.

Companies that operate communications systems under FCC regulation and sell or lease such services are called *common carriers*. The prime examples are the familiar telephone companies which include American Telephone and Telegraph (AT&T), General Telephone and Electronics (GTE), the Bell Companies, the U.S. Independent Telephone Companies (USITA), and Western Union. The common carriers lease communications systems for exclusive use by customers (referred to as subscribers), subject to a published *tariff*. In a tariff, the nature of the service provided is described, the obligations of both the carrier and the customer are detailed, and the charges for such services are given. Such systems are called *private leased* or *tie-line* systems.

Under different tariff specifications, common carriers also sell communications services that are available to the public on an "as used" basis. The prime examples are the *public switched network,* or the *direct distance dialing* (DDD) system, offered by AT&T, and the telegram or mailgram service offered by Western Union. The distinction between the private leased system and the public system is that in the former, the communications channel between points exists for all time; while in the public system, the channel exists only for the duration of the message transfer (call connection). These concepts are discussed in more detail in Chapter 9.

2.4.5. Facilities Organization Arrangements

There are several distinct ways in which a communications facility (or data-communications system) may be arranged according to topological and utilization considerations. Topologically an organization may be either point-to-point, multipoint, or a network. In terms of utilization a system may be either switched, nonswitched, or a message-switched network. Each of these is discussed in the following paragraphs and illustrated in Figure 2.6.

The simplest arrangement is *point-to-point,* which defines the existence of a channel between two stations. Remember that a channel may be made up of one or more segments with each segment consisting of different communication links. For example, one segment may consist of wire-pair cables, a second segment may be part of a microwave relay system, etc. Point-to-point service, then, is indicative only of the kind of connection between two stations, and not what kinds of links make up that connection. In the United States the costs of communications services offered by the common carriers are based strictly on

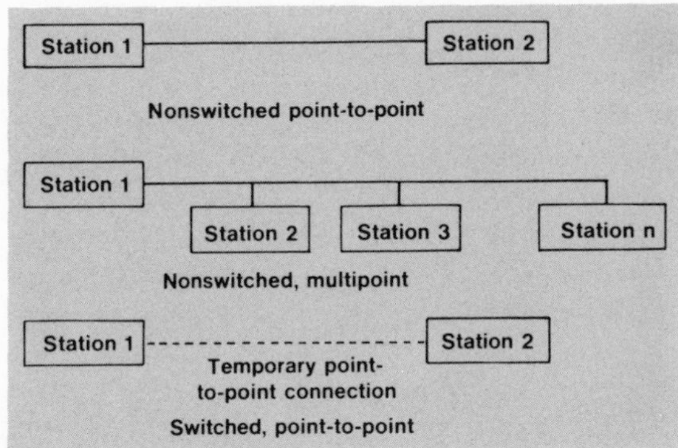

Figure 2.6. Channels may be described as point-to-point or multipoint (or multidrop) and switched or nonswitched as they connect to different stations.

airline mileage between the stations and not on actual channel path mileage. Point-to-point service is comparable to telephone private-line service.

Another type of arrangement is known as *multipoint* or *multidrop* and is comparable to a telephone party line service. In a multidrop system, any station can communicate with all other stations. Therefore, each station must have the capability of recognizing its own address so that it can respond to messages addressed to it and ignore all other messages.

The third type of arrangement is the *network* where many point-to-point connections exist among three or more stations. In a network arrangement, each station usually has the capability of relaying messages on to other stations, in addition to transmitting and receiving its own message traffic. These kinds of networks are called *message-switching networks* (or systems). Examples of message-switching systems are Western Union's Telegram service or the U.S. Postal Mail Service.

Networks may topologically be categorized as centralized (or star) networks, decentralized (or distributed) networks, and loop networks (Figure 2.7). Typically, where an installation consists of one large computer system with connections to a number of data terminals, we see the *centralized network* as the organization type. Systems containing several large computers with a large number of terminals may be arranged as *decentralized networks*. The term *distributed computing* describes an organization consisting of a (mini-) computer-driven message-switching network connected to several large computers (called host computers). Many data terminals provide the capacity for concurrent execution of jobs on more than one host computer. The type of arrangment known as a *packet-switched network* is an implementation of a computer message-switched system and is discussed in more detail in Chapter 9.

The data communications system may be either *switched* or *nonswitched* in

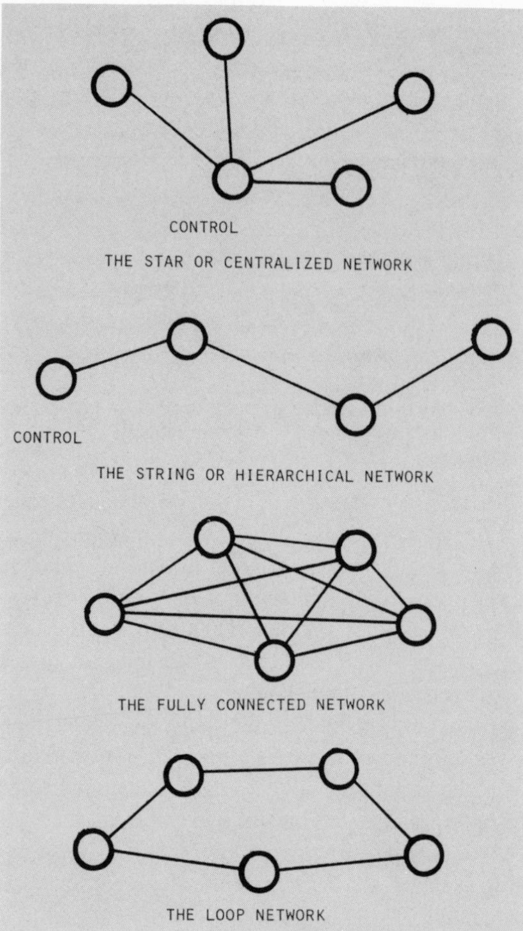

Figure 2.7. Several different kinds of networks may be used to connect the different stations (or nodes) depending upon the purpose of application.

its utilization. Switched means that station calling capability exists (usually by dialing). A switched system implies that the communications channel exists only for the duration of the call, or message transfer, and does not exist at other times. This differs from systems described as point-to-point or multidrop nonswitched where the communications channel exists even though there is not any message transfer taking place. This distinction is important when considering communications channel costs and utilization factors compared to message traffic. This is discussed in more detail in Chapter 9.

2.4.6. Channel Capacity Types

Communications channels may be categorized according to the capacity for carrying data, or type of speed range used for transmissions. Sensors, terminals, and computers, generate a data stream at originating frequencies which is called the *baseband signal*. These signals can be transmitted over particular communication links, such as wire pairs, for up to 2000 feet without requiring modulation. Systems using this type of transmission are called *baseband systems*. To transmit baseband signals over long distances in the presence of channel distortions, modulation to higher frequencies is required.

When the transmission is at low speeds, i.e., up to 300 bps, the channel is referred to as being a *narrowband* channel. The channel is known as a *voice channel* or *voice-band channel* when it has the capacity for transmission rates of 600 to 10,800 bps. For transmission rates at 19,200 bps and higher, the term *wideband* channel is used. Typical speeds for wideband channels, are 19.2, 40.8, 50, 56, 230.4, and 250 kilobits per second (kbps).

A transmission channel can carry the combined signals of several lower-speed channels through a process known as *multiplexing*. For example, a voice channel can carry several narrowband channels; a wideband channel can carry several voiceband channels, and so forth, according to different multiplexing

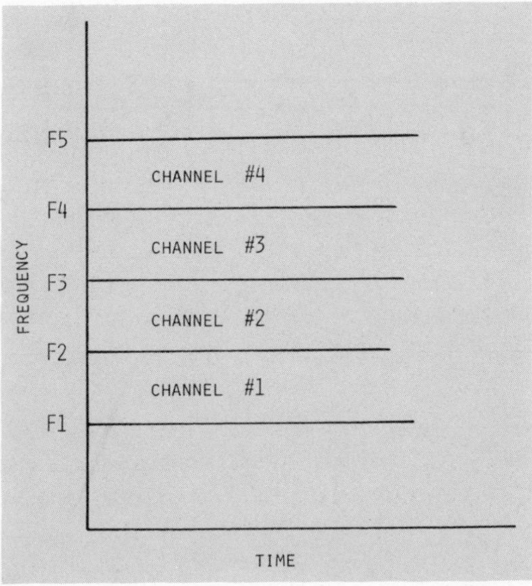

Figure 2.8. In frequency-division multiplexing (FDM), a channel carries the signals of several lower-speed subchannels. Each of the subchannels is allocated a specific frequency range.

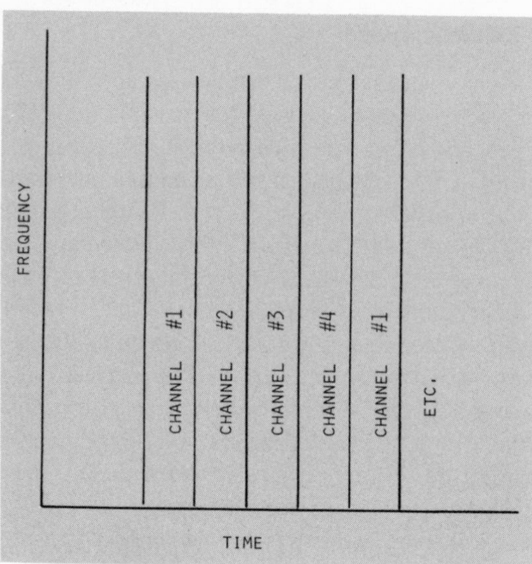

Figure 2.9. Time-division multiplexing (TDM) is a technique where each subchannel is allocated a portion of the transmission time.

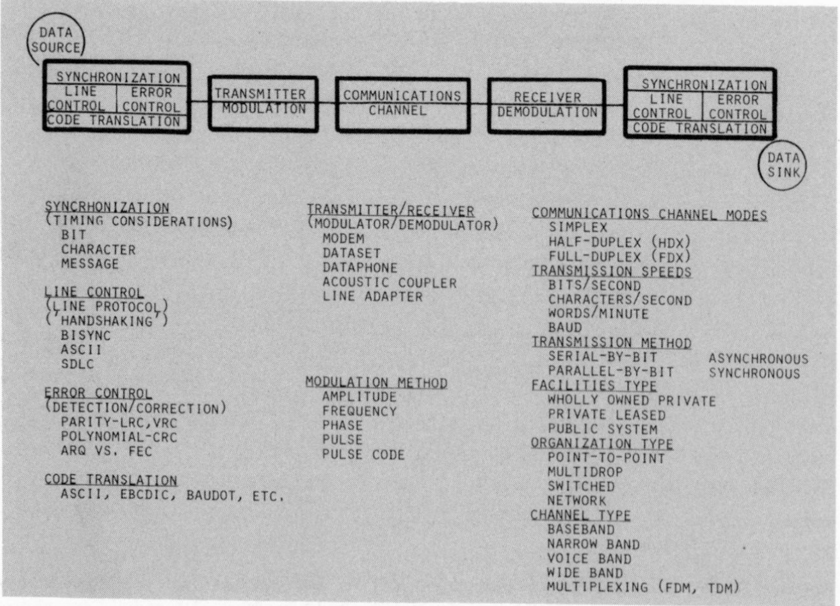

Figure 2.10. The data communications subsystem with its components as discussed in this chapter.

schemes. Two principal multiplexing schemes used in data communications systems are illustrated in Figures 2.8 and 2.9. They are *frequency-division multiplexing* (FDM), and *time-division multiplexing* (TDM). In the former method, the channels are stacked adjacent to one another in frequency space, while in the latter method, the channels are interleaved with one another in time. Multiplexing is discussed further in Chapter 6.

2.5. SUMMARY

An overview of the data communications system is shown in a summary form in Figure 2.10. This should give the reader a perspective on how everything fits together, even though most will not fully understand what it is that is fitting together. This chapter serves only as an introduction to the terms and the concepts behind those terms. No attempt has been made to give complete or detailed explanations. The remaining chapters will cover these concepts in the detail required for successfully putting together a data communications system.

PROBLEMS

1. Describe the differences between the I/O channel and the communications channel.
2. Identify and briefly describe the five basic functional components of any data communications subsystem.
3. Why is code translation required in data communications?
4. What are the two primary methods for correcting detected errors in a data communications system?
5. Discuss the concept of redundancy with respect to its role in the error control process of a data communications system, and of a natural language conversation over a telephone channel.
6. What is meant by line protocol?
7. How does an analog signal differ from a digital signal?
8. When should an asynchronous transmission system be used instead of a synchronous system? Describe each method.
9. What is the purpose of the modem in the data communications system?
10. Are modems used in digital transmission systems?
11. What are the advantages/disadvantages of an acoustic coupler?

Chapter 3

Originating Signals

3.1. PRELIMINARY REMARKS

Before getting into the actual data communications concepts, a few remarks of an introductory and elementary nature are in order. Fundamental to this discussion is the nature of the flow of electricity. We can think of it as the movement of electrons in a conductor such as copper wire.

When wires from a light bulb are connected to the terminal posts of a battery, as in Figure 3.1a, electric current flows from the positive terminal to the negative terminal under the force of a voltage (pressure difference) between the two terminals. This is an example of a direct current (dc) system. The light bulb glows because its filament (a wire) resists the flow of electricity and becomes hot. Figure 3.1b shows the same circuit as Figure 3.1a in a schematic form.

Another type of electricity, or flow of electrons, is alternating current (ac). In Figure 3.1a, imagine instead of a battery a device in which the polarity of the terminals reverses itself a number of times each second [i.e., the positive (+) terminal becomes negative (−) while at the same time the (−) terminal becomes (+)]; because current always flows from (+) to (−), the direction of flow alternates—hence the name alternating current. Such a device is called a generator.

The number of times that these reversals occur every second is referred to as the *frequency* of the alternating current. Frequency is expressed in cycles per

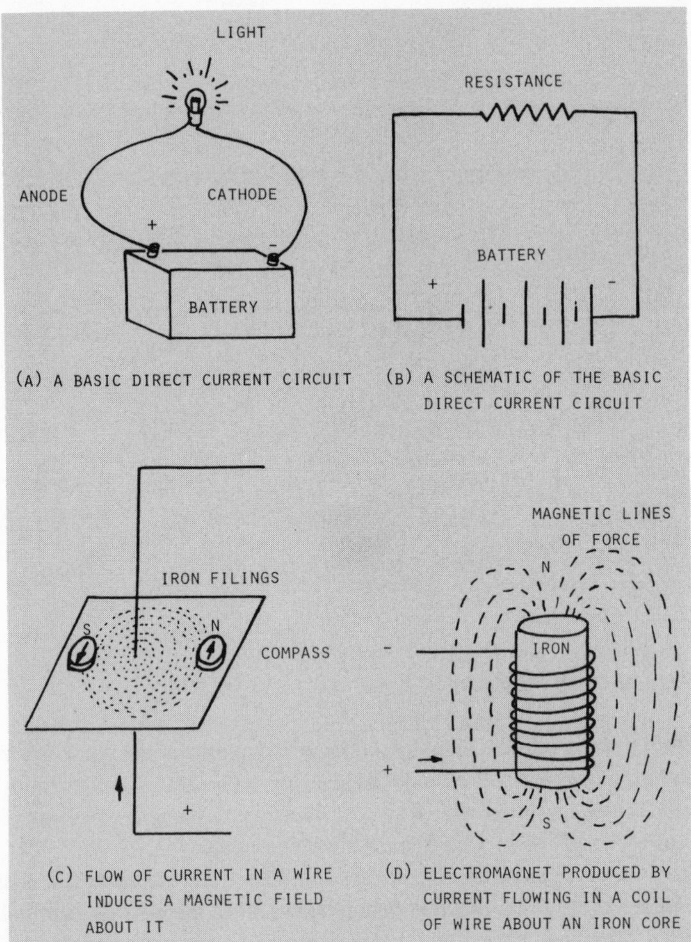

Figure 3.1. Some fundamental concepts concerning the flow of electricity are illustrated.

second (cps), or *Hertz* (Hz) in modern usage, where a cycle includes two reversals: i.e., from (+) to (−) and back again to (+).

When an electric current flows in a wire, it produces a magnetic field about the wire as shown in Figure 3.1c. When the wire is wound into a coil and a core of soft iron is inserted in the coil, the coil and iron will concentrate the weak magnetic field of the wires into a strong magnetic field whenever electric current flows through the wire. This system is an electromagnet and is shown in Figure 3.1d. What kind of current is required to make an electromagnet, ac or dc?

Conversely, when a wire is passed through a magnetic field, a current is induced to flow in the wire. This relationship between magnetism and electricity is the underlying principle of motors and generators.

When acoustic (sound) energy impinges on a diaphragm which is mechanically connected to a wire that cuts across the magnetic field of a permanent magnet, the vibration of the diaphragm causes the wire to move in the magnetic field. This movement in turn induces a current to flow in the wire, and the induced current varies directly with the number of vibrations or frequency of the acoustic energy. This is the principle of the *dynamic microphone*. Generally speaking, when a device converts one form of energy to another form, in this case sound to electrical energy, it is called a *transducer*.

The preceding has been introduced in its most simplistic manner and more detailed discussions may be found in any physics textbook.

3.2. INTRODUCTION

In this chapter we examine some of the characteristics of communications systems that carry *baseband signals*. Baseband signals are signals that are at originating frequencies such as those produced by terminal equipment, microphone pickups, vocal chords, musical instruments, etc. Baseband signals may also be referred to as the signals input to modulation equipment. This will be covered in more detail in later chapters.

We start with the most elementary kind of signaling system; namely, that of the direct current (dc) telegraph. In reality these systems are virtually obsolete, and have been replaced by more efficient alternating current or high-frequency systems using modulation methods. The dc systems, however, can be more readily visualized and comprehended by the layman. The concepts of (1) baseband signals, (2) signal waveforms or shapes, (3) distortion effects on the transmission, and (4) the capacity of a communications channel all can be demonstrated in the simpler dc system as a prelude to their discussion in the context of present-day communications.

Concepts of the operations of communications equipment are also presented in this introductory chapter.

3.3. DIRECT CURRENT TRANSMISSION

Samuel Morse, in 1844, demonstrated a telegraph system for the transmission of information which was to become universally accepted. The early system consisted of a single wire with the ground as the return path. (In 1836, Steinheil had demonstrated that the earth could replace one wire of a transmission path.) Figure 3.2 shows a simple single-battery, closed-circuit type system. In the idle

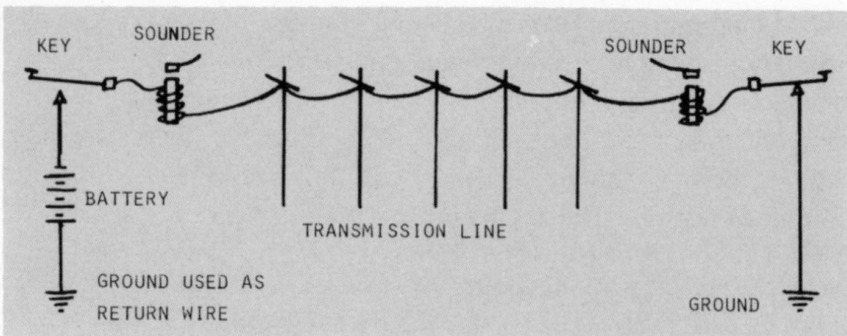

Figure 3.2. Closed-circuit telegraph system. The sounder operates as an electromagnet producing audible clicks.

condition all the keys are closed and current is flowing. Signaling to other stations is done by opening the circuit at the keying instrument. These signals originated by the keying instrument are an example of *baseband signals*.

Figure 3.3 illustrates an open-circuit telegraph system where all the keys are open and no current flows during the idle condition. Each station requires a battery. Operating the keying instrument at one station, while the other station keeps its key open, causes current to flow in the form of pulses and operate the sounder to emit the "clicks" corresponding to the dots and dashes of Morse code.

These systems are examples of *neutral* or *unipolar* signal (so named because they represent one bit by the presence of current and zero bit by its absence) circuits, and are but one of the many ways of representing information by electrical signals.

3.3.1. Relay Operation

The sounder in these systems illustrates the function of the *relay*. When current flows in a wire, it induces a magnetic field around the wire, and thus by

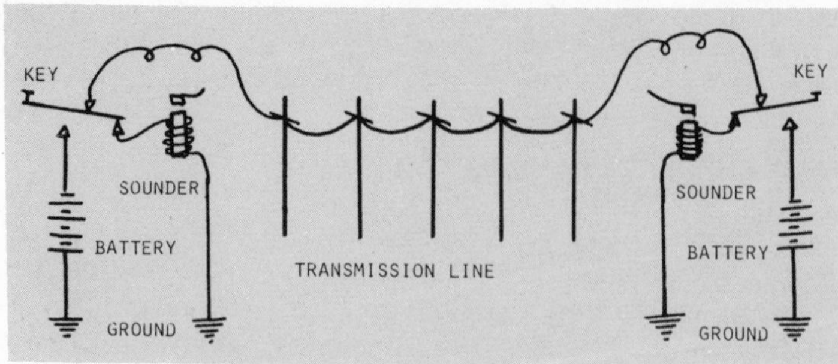

Figure 3.3. Open-circuit telegraph system.

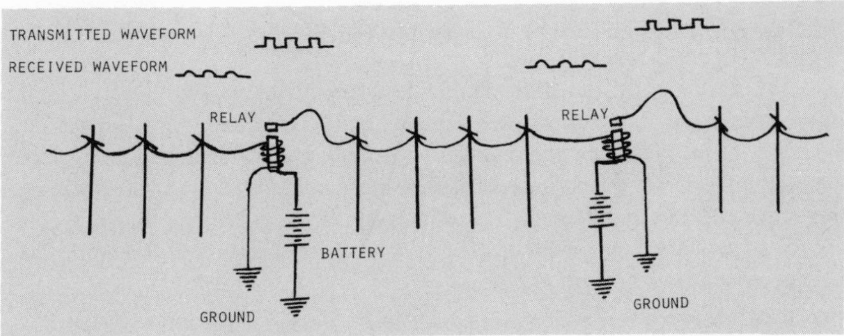

Figure 3.4. Use of relays as regenerative repeaters increases the distance of transmission.

coiling the wire, this magnetic field is intensified. An iron core, inserted in the coil, concentrates the lines of force of the magnetic field, which then attracts a piece of metal giving a "click" sound. This is the principle of the familiar electromagnet already introduced. By attaching the metal to a spring, a series of "clicks," representing the elements of a code, can be transmitted by operating the keying instrument. By having the metal key function as a contact to an electric circuit, we have what is known as the *relay*.

3.3.2. Repeaters

As we shall shortly learn, signals do not travel over long distances without being subjected to distortion effects and losses, and so one important use of a relay is to use it as a *repeater* (a term for any device that retransmits, or repeats, a signal). From the above discussion, and using Figure 3.4, we see how a signal can be "recreated" free of any distortion effects by using the relay. Such devices are called *regenerative repeaters,* because they reconstruct the signal before repeating it, and they are used in today's digital transmission systems. Repeaters that are used in analog circuits are called *amplifiers,* as they increase the energy of the original signal. However, amplifiers also increase the strength (or level) of any distortion present in the signal. Thus, by expanding the simple idea of the relay, we can understand the concept of the regenerative repeater, and provide an extension of this to the amplifier.

3.3.3. Signal Sampling

In present day equipment the keying instruments and relay sounders have been replaced by mechanical components and electronic circuits which provide for greater efficiency and reliability. The transmitter (which corresponds to the keying instrument) still generates and transmits square-shaped pulses representing the symbols 1 and 0. In telegraph systems, the terms "mark" (1) and "space" (0) are frequently used.[1]

The receiver, on the other hand, does not continuously "listen" to the signal coming in, but rather takes samples of the incoming signal at periodic intervals. More precisely, the receiver, operating under the control of its clock which is *phased* (or synchronized) with respect to the incoming wave, samples this wave at some point in the pulse interval. If the wave amplitude is at, or above, some value, known as the *decision threshold,* the symbol is recorded as a 1, otherwise it is recorded as a 0.

3.4. BASEBAND SIGNAL WAVEFORMS

The use of current–no current to represent symbols is known as *neutral,* or *single current,* signaling. The use of currents in opposite directions (polarities), where the decision threshold is zero, is known as *polar,* or *double-current,* signaling. In systems with neutral or polar signaling there is no change in signal level when the symbols are repeated. Sometimes it is desirable to have a definite separation between repeated symbols and this is the object of *return-to-zero* types of signaling. The signal returns to zero current between symbols. These and other waveforms are shown in Figure 3.5.

Another type of signaling uses the zero interval as a third symbol to separate the information symbols and is known as *polar return-to-zero* signaling. This type of signaling can be operated asynchronously and is sometimes referred to as self-clocking because the receiver clock can be made to reset itself to proper phase according to the incoming signal.

When alternating polarity pulses are used for 1 symbols and no pulse for 0 symbols the signaling is known as *bipolar return-to-zero*. This type of signaling is used where it is desired to reduce the transmission of dc or low-frequency components because the symbols can be represented using relatively little current.

Sometimes encoding the information in terms of signal transitions is advantageous. A transition in polarity may be used to indicate a 0 and no transition indicates a 1. The waves may be inverted in polarity without loss of information since such systems have no sense of absolute polarity. The detection process in the receiver is known as *differential detection* and requires synchronous operation.

An inverse type of differential encoding uses polar pulses to indicate the transitions of an information wave. The maximum rate at which transitions can be transmitted is a function of the pulse length. This type of signal does not have any dc components. It can be used in asynchronous transmission and is sometimes referred to as a *dicode* signal. The average power varies directly with the density of transitions of the information wave.

In data communications we can think of these current and no-current states as pulses representing the information bits "0" and "1." A pulse representing a

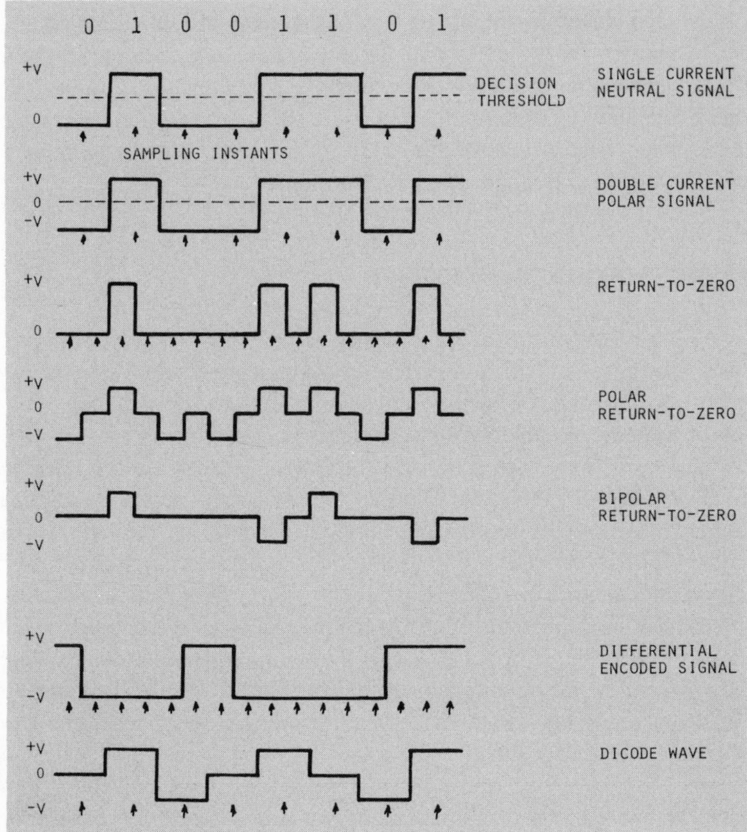

Figure 3.5. Some examples of baseband signal waveforms. The receiver samples the incoming signal one or more times to determine its value.

"1" bit is known as a mark, and the zero bit is known as a space. These terms originated with the early Morse telegraphy systems.

In summary, the main categories of baseband signals are:

1. Neutral signals: The mark is an applied voltage and the space is a no-voltage condition.
2. Polar signals: The mark and space are represented by different voltage levels, such as $+V$ volts for a mark and $-V$ for a space. There is always a voltage on the line.
3. Return-to-zero signals: The voltage returns to zero during the time interval of transmitting a mark pulse. This is used to provide a definite separation between consecutive pulses.
4. Differential signals: The detection of a change in voltage level indicates a mark or a space. Such systems have no sense of polarity.

These illustrated waveforms are but a few of the many different kinds that exist today. The reasons for the variety of baseband waveforms are (1) to facilitate detection of errors due to current loss, polarity violations, etc., (2) to aid the receiver in maintaining synchronization by assuring that sufficient transitions exist even when long strings of the same bit are sent, and (3) to reduce the amount of dc (or zero frequency) signal transmitted.

3.5. ASYNCHRONOUS TRANSMISSION

One of the early forms of transmission is known as a start-stop, or *asynchronous,* transmission, which is exemplified by teleprinter (or Teletypewriter®) equipment. For this type of operation the equipment receives a steady mark and remains in a quiescent state. When the receiving teleprinter's current changes from a mark to a space, the equipment becomes ready to receive information pulses. On the basis of this "start" pulse, the sampling instants are aligned (or synchronized) to properly receive the subsequent pulses. In the case of baudot code, five information pulses are transmitted for a character of information. This was shown in Figure 2.4. A "stop" pulse is then transmitted which puts the equipment back in a quiescent state. In the case of older teleprinter equipment using baudot code, the stop pulse was of longer duration (1.42 to 1.5 times as long) than any of the information or start pulses. This allows the equipment to go back to the quiescent state and align itself for the next start pulse when consecutive bits of code are transmitted.

Modern asynchronous transmission typically employs only bits of equal duration with one start bit and either one or two stop bits delimiting the information bits of the character. For example, ASCII (American Standard Code for Information Interchange) uses one start, seven character, one parity, and two stop bits, a total of eleven bits for asynchronous transmission (see Figure 2.4).

It should be noted that the equipment operates at the transmission rate and then remains in the quiescent state rather than maintaining some average rate. Whether the characters are keyed in at the rate of one character every ten seconds or at ten characters every second, the transmission of each character occurs at the speed of the equipment. The pulses of each character travel down a communication channel at a speed of approximately 100,000 miles per second.

3.6. BASEBAND SIGNAL DISTORTION

Computer terminals, and similar equipment, transmit baseband signals by applying voltage and causing current to flow on transmission lines. The generated signals are initially square wave pulses. As the current flows down the line, the pulses become distorted with increasing distance. This is shown in Figure

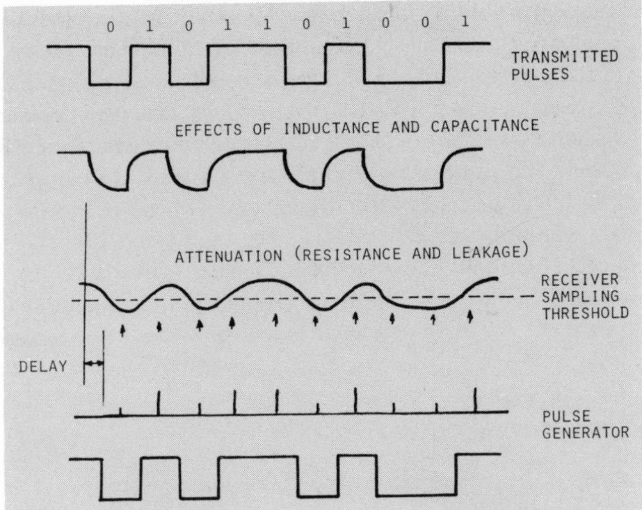

Figure 3.6. Distortion of baseband signals.

3.6. There are four effects operating simultaneously. These are (1) resistance, (2) inductance, (3) capacitance, and (4) leakage. In addition there is a propagation delay due to the transmission speed of the signal figured at 100,000 miles per second. Because of these effects, signals cannot be sent over any appreciable distance without using repeaters (cf. page 45). Currently the distance limitation is 2,000 to 4,000 feet of cable run between terminal devices and communication controllers.

3.6.1. The Effect of Resistance

Resistance (R) to current flow, usually shown as the symbol -ᐱᐱᐱ-, is the result of friction and shows up as heat which is especially evident in power lines and devices such as light bulbs, space heaters, etc. The units of resistance are typically given in ohms (Ω). In data transmission, the effects of line resistance shows up primarily as *attenuation* of the signal, i.e., reduction in signal strength. The resistance of transmission lines varies with *frequency* as well as with distance. Baseband systems typically operate at low frequencies, for which distance is the most important factor.

3.6.2. The Effect of Inductance

Inductance is the property of a circuit to oppose any changes of current flow in a transmission line and is usually represented by the symbol -ℓℓℓ- When a current of electrons starts to flow along any conductor, a magnetic field starts to expand from the center of the conductor. The lines of magnetic force (flux) move outward, through the conducting material itself, and then continue into the air. As the lines of force sweep outward through the conductor, they induce a voltage (emf) in the conductor itself which is always in a direction opposite to the direction of current flow. The effect is to oppose the immediate establishment of maximum current. This effect is only temporary, for when the current reaches a steady value, the lines of force will no longer be moving or expanding and a counter voltage will no longer be produced. The same effect occurs, in reverse, when current ceases to flow. The effect of inductance then is a slowdown of the buildup and dropoff of the square pulses or a rounding of the square shapes. This resistance to current flow in an ac circuit is known as *inductive* reactance.

3.6.3. The Effect of Capacitance

Capacitance is the property of a circuit to oppose any changes in the voltage levels and is usually indicated by the symbol ⊣ ⊢. The effect of capacitance on transmission lines which pass varying dc voltage baseband signals is to have a varying dc current flowing in the opposite direction trying to equalize the signal voltage. This effect lasts longer than inductance and also causes distortion of the pulses, rounding the square shapes. Line capacitance varies with wire diameter, type and thickness of insulation, and air space between conductors. It is also influenced by surrounding wires and other metallic shields, as well as weather conditions. Mutual capacitance between two wires varies very little with frequency and temperature.

3.6.4. The Effect of Leakage

Leakage is a term used to describe losses in the transmission line due to current flowing across or through insulators, or due to changes in the electric or magnetic fields (known as dielectric or magnetic hysteresis losses). The amount of leakage varies with frequency, environmental conditions, and the type of conductor insulation. Another term used for leakage is *shunt resistance*.

3.6.5. Distortion Effects on Speed of Transmission

A transmission line, consisting of a very long pair of parallel wires suspended in air, is considered for the purpose of analysis to be a ladder network of equivalent circuits, as shown in Figure 3.7. (The length of each subsection is less than the wavelength of the applied frequency.) Each subsection circuit contains a series resistance, series inductance, shunt capacitance, and shunt resistance.

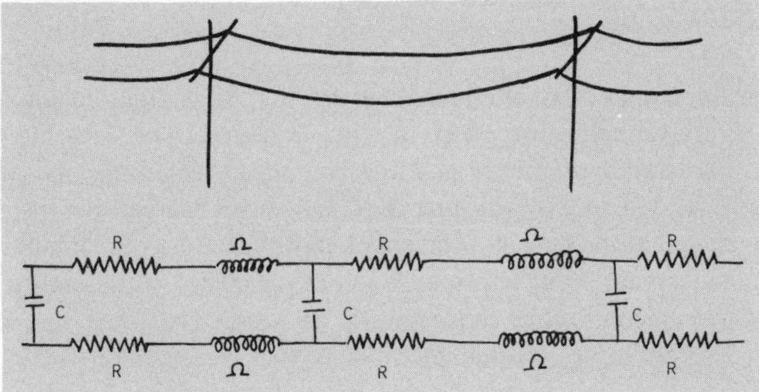

Figure 3.7. A transmission system can be thought of as series of circuits. (R = resistance, Ω = inductance, C = capacitance.)

Because of the interaction of these effects, when too many pulses per second are transmitted they become indistinguishable, as shown in Figure 3.6. A train of pulses transmitted down a line could appear lengthened or shortened when they are received. This is known as *bias distortion.* Adjustments in the level of the sampling threshold can increase or decrease the bias distortion.

3.7. ANALOGY FOR CAPACITY

An analogy to the communication transmission line would be, perhaps, sending message signals along a flexible garden water hose by means of a plunger. At one end, the person would transmit by alternately pushing and pulling the plunger in and out of the hose, thus sending pressure pulses to a receiving plunger operating a pressure gauge at the other end. If the hose was a rigid steel pipe and the fluid in it was absolutely incompressible, the movement of the receiving plunger would follow the movement of the transmitting plunger exactly and the pressure readings would plot to a square-shaped curve. If the fluid had no *viscosity* and the plunger were frictionless, the pressure pulses represented by the pushes and pulls could be transmitted at very high speeds. In reality, however, the garden hose is elastic and the fluid is slightly compressible, so that the receiving plunger does not exactly follow the transmitting plunger. If we plotted the received pressure values, the resulting curve would appear similar to that in Figure 3.6. In addition, there is the effect of viscosity and friction, so that the plunger cannot move at limitless speed. In fact, if one were to increase the number of pushes and pulls, then the pulses at the receiving end would become indistinguishable. These limitations roughly illustrate the effects of induction and capacitance of a transmission line.

3.8. LOADING

When telegraphy was attempted on the first submarine cables (circa the 1850s) a direct limitation on speed was encountered. The early investigators found that the central conductor and a return sheath acted like the plates of a Leyden jar (i.e., a capacitor) in that they had to be charged before the signal could be received at the far end. The shunt capacitance was the inhibiting factor in that one had to wait until the response to one signal had sufficiently died down before another recognizable pulse could be sent. This was the advent of bandwidth limitation (cf. Chapter 5).

In 1855 Kelvin showed that the maximum operating speed of a transmission line with negligible inductance and leakage is inversely proportional to the line resistance, the capacitance, and the square of the length of the line. In other words, if it is desired to send telegraph signals at a given rate, then the line cannot exceed a certain length. If transmission is to be made over great distances then some means of regenerating the deteriorating signal must be used.

Heaviside, in 1887, proposed that a balance of resistance multiplied by capacitance be made with the product of inductance and leakage for transmission lines. In practice the value of the product of resistance and capacitance can be made very small, but still it is very large compared to the unadjusted value of the product of inductance and leakage. To balance the line, leakage could not be increased without diminishing the signal, so that inductance is the only parameter that can be increased. In the early 1900s it was found that inductance could be added by winding magnetic tape or wire around the central conductor and thus increase the operating speeds by a factor of eight to ten.

For land lines in the telephone plant, *loading coils* were found to be more suitable than the continuous method in reducing the transmission loss. [Loading improves the signal attentuation and phase distortion characteristics (cf. Chapter 8). The addition of inductance to the line results in a higher line impedance and a lower velocity of propagation and thus is no longer used in certain types of wire circuits.] The main purpose of loading in today's wire circuits is to overcome the effect of capacitance and to keep the attentuation more or less constant over a range of frequencies.[2–4]

3.9. LOW-PASS FILTER

The addition of inductance to a cable causes it to assume the characteristics of a *low-pass filter,* in which attenuation of a signal increases very rapidly above certain frequencies. These frequencies are known as *cut-off* frequencies.

While this effect is undesirable in transmission lines, we shall see later the importance of having filters in communications systems. *Filters* are electronic circuits that allow certain frequencies to pass through and severely attenuate all other frequencies. We have low-pass, band-pass, and high-pass filter circuits.

3.10. SUMMARY

In this chapter some of the basic concepts of data transmission were introduced using the aritifice of a direct current transmission system. The notion of the *repeater* and in particular the *regenerative repeater* was described using dc transmission systems. The idea of an amplifier was introduced. The concepts of *baseband signals* and *signal sampling* at the receiver were discussed.

Asynchronous transmission was described. The influence of signal distortion on signal speed was discussed, with the main point being that the problem of determining what message was sent lies with the receiver. The idea of a *filter* circuit was presented. These concepts lay the framework for describing present-day communications channels using signals of varying frequencies.

PROBLEMS

1. Define the following terms:

baseband signals	attentuaion
transducer	filter
repeater	loading coils
neutral signal	amplifier
polar signal	mark and space
bipolar return-to-zero signal	alternating current (ac)
	direct current (dc)

2. What are some of the reasons for the variety of different baseband waveforms? What are some of the disadvantages of particular baseband waveforms?
3. In what way is a polar signal superior to the primitive dot–dash system invented by Samuel F. B. Morse?
4. What is the present distance limitation for transmitting baseband signals (as square wave pulses) between terminal devices and communication controllers?
5. What effects cause baseband signal distortion?
6. Why can a transmission line be considered as a filter?
7. What device is placed on a transmission line to overcome the distortion effects and increase the distance?

Chapter 4

Data Communications Fundamentals

4.1. INTRODUCTION

This chapter is perhaps more technical in detail than the other parts of this text. The objective for the reader, however, is not to become enmeshed in the detail, but to comprehend several important concepts. Namely, *what determines how fast information can be transmitted over a communication channel?* To understand this, it is necessary to have a clear idea of *frequency* and *bandwidth*. Frequency and bandwidth, in turn, lead to the concept of a *band(width)-limited signal*.

Next, two important concepts for the ideal communication channel are presented: *signal sampling* to avoid intersymbol *interference,* and the *Shannon–Hartley* relationship for *errorless coding* in a channel with noise. It can be shown that the capacity of a communications channel is related to the bandwidth, signal strength, noise level, and the channel error rate. This chapter serves as a prelude to the succeeding chapter on modulation.

4.2. FREQUENCY

All periodic phenomena can be described in terms of frequency. Recall that in Chapter 3, frequency was defined for alternating current. We now extend this concept. Frequency is a term used to indicate the rate of oscillation of the instantaneous amplitude of an electromagnetic wave. Frequency is expressed in units of Hertz (Hz). The older form was cycles per second. The relationship between wavelength λ in meters and frequency f in Hertz is expressed by $c = \lambda f$, where c is the velocity of propagation of radio (and light) waves in space, approximately 3×10^8 meters/second (m/s).

Naturally occurring phenomena such as light, radio, x-rays, gamma radiation, etc., can be depicted relative to each other on a chart of the electromagnetic spectrum as shown in Figure 4.1. The portion of the total electromagnetic spectrum that is of interest for telecommunications is shown in Figure 4.2. The

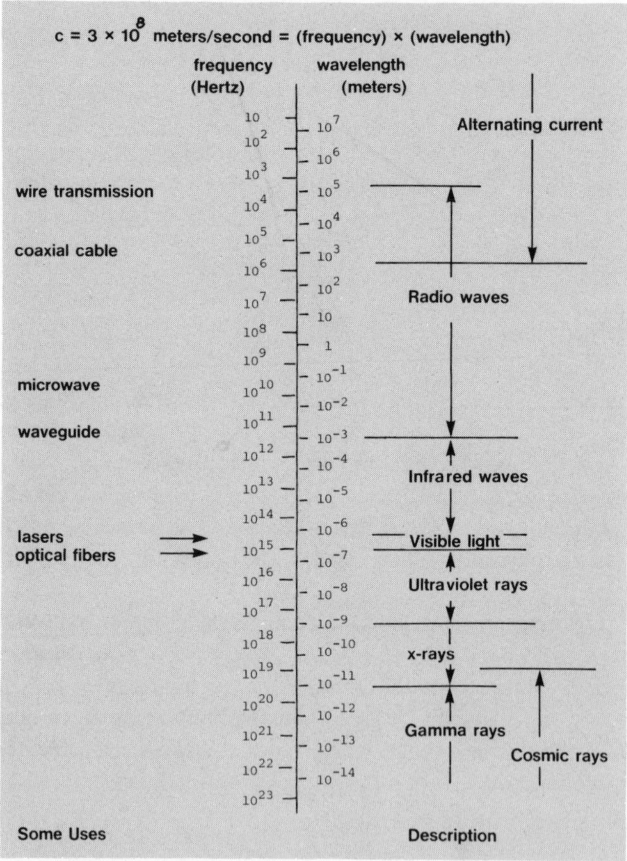

Figure 4.1. The electromagnetic spectrum is shown on a scale of frequency and wavelength. Some naturally occurring phenomena at various frequencies are described to the right. Some applications at their approximate frequency ranges are shown to the left of the scale.

BAND	CLASSIFICATION	USAGE	FREQUENCY	(WAVELENGTH)
			3 KHZ	(100,000 METERS)
4	VLF MYRIAMETRIC	LONG-DISTANCE COMMUNICATIONS		
			30 KHZ	(10,000 METERS)
5	LF KILOMETRIC	BROADCASTING RADIO NAVIGATION		
			300 KHZ	(1,000 METERS)
6	MF HECTOMETRIC	AM BROADCASTING COAXIAL CABLE TRANSMISSION		
			3 MHZ	(100 METERS)
7	HF DECAMETRIC	RADIO TELEPHONY SHORT-WAVE RADIO		
			30 MHZ	(10 METERS)
8	VHF METRIC	FM BROADCASTING TELEVISION MOBILE RADIO		
			300 MHZ	(1 METER)
9	UHF DECIMETRIC	TELEVISION TROPOSPHERIC SCATTER MICROWAVE, RADAR		
			3 GHZ	(.1 METER)
10	SHF CENTIMETRIC	SATELLITE RELAY MICROWAVE MICROWAVE, RADAR MULTICHANNEL TELEPHONY		
			30 GHZ	(.01 METER)
11	EHF MILLIMETRIC	WAVEGUIDE		
			300 GHZ	(.001 METER)

Figure 4.2. The telecommunications spectrum shows the different bands of frequencies that are allocated for various purposes by the ITU (International Telecommunications Union). In the United State's the FCC assigns the frequencies for different uses. [Note: 10^3Hz = 1 kHz (kilohertz), 10^6 Hz = 1 MHz (megahertz), 10^9 Hz = 1 GHz (gigahertz), 10^{12} Hz = 1 THz (terahertz).]

telecommunications spectrum is partitioned and named by frequency and wavelength by agreement of the member countries to the International Telecommunications Union (ITU).

Mechanically generated periodic phenomena such as acoustic waves (sound) or electric pulses representing digital signals can also be described in terms of frequency.

4.3. BANDWIDTH

Figure 4.3. shows the speech spectrum as the average energy output by the human voice at different frequencies. The energy output is given in units of

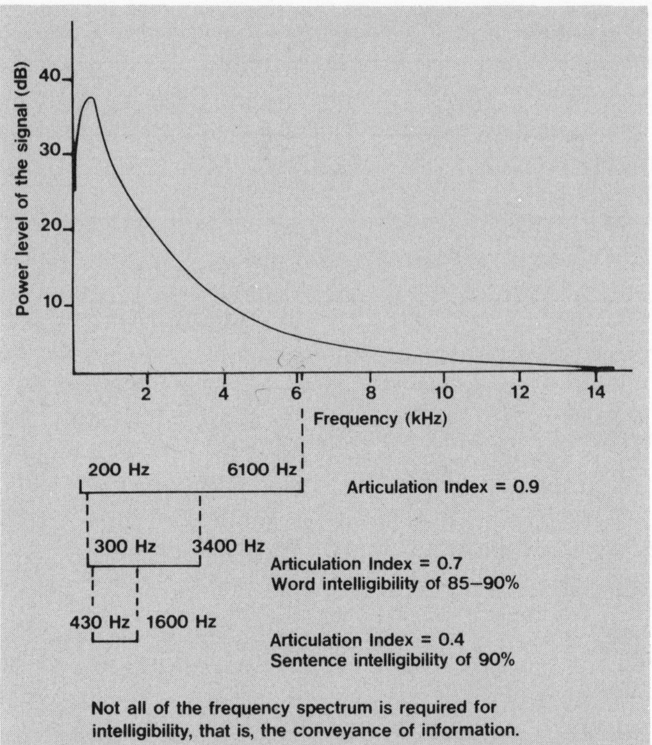

Figure 4.3. Idealized long-term average speech spectrum showing the power levels at different frequencies for an average speaker at a distance of one meter. Also shown is the effect on intelligibility of reducing the frequency range of speech. Note that the higher frequencies contribute little to intelligibility, but give speech its tonal qualities, timbre, etc.

decibels (dB), defined in Section 7.6. From this figure it can be seen that the lower frequencies of the voice contain the most power. Power diminishes quite rapidly with increasing frequency. The average person speaking would have a speech spectrum that is a subset of Figure 4.3 and characterizes the "quality" of his voice. (A voiceprint!)

When a person listens to a full symphony orchestra he might appreciate the "full" range of sound that he hears. Similarly when the music is picked up on a microphone that has a sensitivity range of 0 to 15,000 Hz and is recorded on high fidelity equipment, only the most discerning listener can detect a reduction in quality due to the loss of those sounds above 15,000 Hz (or 15 kHz). Most people would not notice the difference.

Now, if this same music were to be transmitted by a sound system whose frequency range is 0 to 5000 Hz, such as an AM radio broadcast, most people *would* be able to detect a reduction in the quality of the music. If one equates the quality of the music with the amount of information transmitted, then it appears that this amount increases with an increase in the frequency range used for the transmission.

The capacity of a communications channel is, in fact, related to the range of frequencies in which transmission takes place. This range of frequencies is known as the *bandwidth* of the channel. Bandwidth should not be confused with the frequency of transmission.

A channel whose bandwidth is 4 kHz (i.e., 4000 Hz) may transmit at a midchannel frequency of 4 kHz, in which case transmission occurs from 2 to 6 kHz; or it may transmit at a midchannel frequency of 400 kHz, in which case transmission occurs from 398 to 402 kHz.

Baseband signals are describable in terms of bandwidth. For example, as shown in Figure 4.3, the audio bandwidth for music or speech is 30 Hz to 20,000 Hz, and the bandwidth for intelligible speech is 200 Hz to 6100 Hz. Telephone speech has a bandwidth of 300 Hz to 3400 Hz. This means that the microphone in the telephone handset only picks up the frequency range of 300 Hz to 3400 Hz and the remainder of the audio frequency range is not picked up. More precisely, it is said that the unwanted frequencies are attenuated or filtered out. In the United States, the bandwidth for a telephone or voice channel is arbitrarily taken to be 4 kHz even though the actual transmission range is from 300 to 3400 Hz.

4.3.1. Uses of Bandwidth

Another illustration of a familiar use of bandwidth comes from United States broadcast transmission. In Table 4.1 the headings AM and FM correspond to the amplitude and frequency modulation broadcasts picked up by radio receivers. The baseband bandwidth is the output of the microphone pickup, or the output of a video camera in the case of television broadcasts. The size of the channel bandwidth results from the modulation method used as promulgated by

Table 4.1. Examples of Bandwidth from Broadcast Transmissions

	AM	FM	Television	
Baseband bandwidth	5 kHz	15 kHz	0.25 MHz	audio
			4.5 MHz	video
Channel bandwidth	10 kHz	200 kHz	6.0 MHz	
Broadcast band	535-1605 kHz	88-108 MHz	54-216 MHz	470-890 MHz
Number of channels	107	100	12 VHF	
			70 UHF	

Federal Communication Commission Rules and Regulations, which will be discussed in the following chapter. The channel bandwidth is the range of frequencies used in the transmission. The broadcast band (AM, FM, shortwave, TV, etc.) is the range of frequencies allocated by the Federal Communications Commission (FCC) in the United States. The number of available transmitting channels in a broadcast band is found by dividing the channel bandwidth into the size of the broadcast band.

As can be seen in Table 4.1, if an AM station was broadcasting at, say, 750 kHz, then the receiving radio would be tuned to that frequency and receive the signal from 745 kHz to 755 kHz. Likewise on the FM band, a tuned station broadcasting at 92.1 MHz would be received over a bandwidth from 92.0 MHz (megaHertz or 10^6 or million Hertz) to 92.2 MHz.

4.3.2. Radio-Frequency (RF) Transmission Characteristics

From a consideration of Table 4.1 and from personal experiences, several characteristics that are applicable to all communications systems become apparent: (1) To carry the same amount of information, FM requires a disproportionately large bandwidth when compared with AM. Furthermore, larger bands seem to be available at higher frequencies. (2) AM radio stations can be received at extremely long distances at night, and then they seem to "fade" during daylight hours. Since there are about 4500 AM radio stations in the United States, this fading attribute and transmitter power limitation seems to allow them all to "fit" in the 107 channels allocated to AM broadcasting. (3) AM radio reception is severely interfered with during a lightning storm, while FM seems to be undisturbed. The reason for the FM resistance to interference is the modulation and detection method used. (4) FM and television broadcasts are "line of sight," i.e., the receiver antenna must "see" the transmitting antenna. Line-of-sight transmission and reception is characteristic of higher frequencies. Furthermore, these higher frequency signals can be reflected off solid objects such as mountains and buildings, and they are attenuated by weather conditions such as fog, rain, and snow. These characteristics of commercial transmissions are discussed in subsequent chapters.

4.4. ANALOG SIGNAL CHARACTERISTICS

Electrical pulses that are rectangular or square shaped, as those we saw in our baseband signal representations (cf. Figure 3.5), can also be described in terms of frequencies. It is in this description that several seemingly paradoxical concepts are encountered because time-varying phenomena are described in frequency units which contain reciprocal time units.

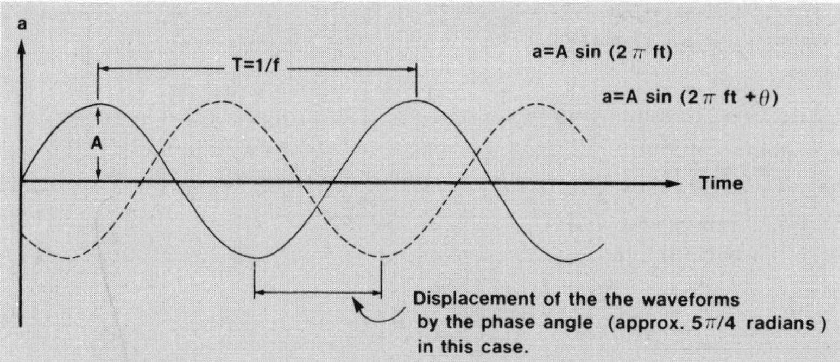

Figure 4.4. A spectral line is a waveform at a single frequency *f*. A second waveform at the same frequency but with a phase difference θ is shown as a dashed line. *a* is the instantaneous amplitude, *A* the maximum amplitude, and *T* the time for each cycle.

A single frequency of transmission, known as a spectral line (or a pure tone), may be represented by a sine function [equation (4.1) below] shown in Figure 4.4. In this equation, which can also be described as an analog waveform, the instantaneous *amplitude* a, or level (strength) of the signal is a function of time t, the frequency f, and the *phase* angle θ (theta). The maximum amplitude is A. From the figure

$$a = A \sin(2\pi ft + \theta) \tag{4.1}$$

there are f peaks occurring every second, which graphically illustrates the phrase, "the frequency is f hertz (or cycles per second)." The length of the wave can be computed as $\lambda = c/f = 3 \times 10^8/f$ meters. As f increases, the length of the wave becomes smaller, giving rise to such terms as shortwave or microwave radio.

Analog Phase Angles

Figure 4.4 shows two waves with the same frequency f but displaced from each other in time so that their peaks do not occur simultaneously. The waves are said to be different in *phase* from each other. The phase difference is measured in angular units such as radians, where 2π radians = 360°. The term $2\pi ft$ occurring in all of the following equations is in units of radians, viz. 2π(radians/cycle) f(cycles/second) t(seconds) yields $2\pi ft$ radians. Two waves of the same frequency but differing in phase by 360°, or 2π radians, are identical. The time for one cycle of the sine wave is $1/f$ and is equivalent to a phase difference of 2π radians. Two sine waves differing in time by Δt have a phase difference of $\theta = 2\pi f\Delta t$ radians or a time difference of $\theta/2\pi f$ seconds.

4.5. **MATHEMATICAL REPRESENTATION OF ELECTRICAL SIGNALS

In a direct current telegraph circuit, the transmitted signal can be considered as a sequence of similar rectangular pulses of electrical potential. These pulses occur at time intervals that are multiples of the duration of the shortest pulse (code element), as shown in Figure 4.5. Any periodic function (subject to certain mathematical conditions) is representable by a Fourier series of the form

$$E(t) = \frac{a_0}{2} + \sum_{n=1}^{\infty}[a_n \cos(nft) + b_n \sin(nft)] \tag{4.2}$$

where

$$a_0 = \frac{f}{\pi}\int_{-\pi/f}^{\pi/f} E(t)\, dt$$

$$a_n = \frac{f}{\pi}\int_{-\pi/f}^{\pi/f} E(t) \cos(nft)\, dt$$

$$b_n = \frac{f}{\pi}\int_{-\pi/f}^{\pi/f} E(t) \sin(nft)\, dt$$

The term *E(t)* is the instantaneous amplitude of the signal as a function of time.

If a time scale is arbitrarily chosen so that the function is symmetric about

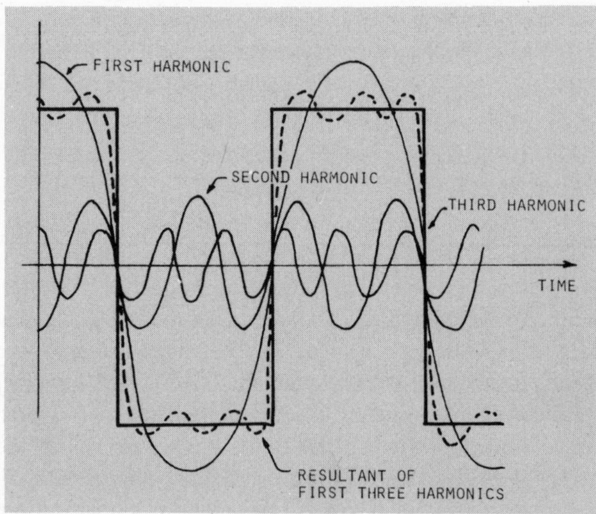

Figure 4.5. A train of binary 010101 . . . pulses can be approximated as closely as one desires by adding more and more harmonics according to Fourier's theorem.

the origin, then $b_n = 0$. Assuming that there is a regular repeated pulse with a pulse repetition period of T (seconds/cycle), a pulse width of S (seconds and an amplitude A (as shown in Figure 4.5) then the coefficients become

$$a_0 = \frac{2}{T}\int_{-S/2}^{S/2} E(t)\,dt = \left(\frac{2A}{T}\right) t \Big|_{-S/2}^{S/2} = \frac{2AS}{T}$$

$$a_n = \frac{2}{T}\int_{-S/2}^{S/2} E(t)\cos\left(\frac{2\pi nt}{T}\right) dt = \left(\frac{2AS}{T}\right)\frac{\sin(\pi nS/T)}{(\pi nS/T)} \tag{4.3}$$

$$E(t) = \frac{AS}{T} + \sum_{n=1}^{\infty} (2AS/T)\sin(\pi nS/T)\cos(nft)/(nS/T) \tag{4.4}$$

This analysis of the elementary pulse wave form into cosine wave components shows that the representation can be made in terms of frequencies ranging from zero to infinity. These component frequencies are referred to as *harmonics* of the basic frequency f. The amplitude contribution of each of these harmonics, $(2AS/T)[\sin(\pi nS/T]/(\pi nS/T)$ follows a $(\sin x)/x$ envelope as shown in Figure 4.6, where $x = \pi nS/T$. We note that there are no components at precisely $1/S$, $2/S$, $3/S, \ldots$.

When a particular pattern of pulses of duration nT seconds is continuously repeated, the harmonics become concentrated at frequencies that are multiples of $1/nT$. Assume a train of binary pulses of 1010101 . . ., where $S = T/2$; then equation (4.4) becomes

$$E(t) = A\left[\frac{1}{2} + \frac{2}{\pi}\cos(ft) - \frac{2}{3\pi}\cos(3ft) + \frac{2}{5\pi}\cos(5ft) - \ldots\right] \tag{4.5}$$

where the component frequencies are the fundamental plus the odd harmonics.

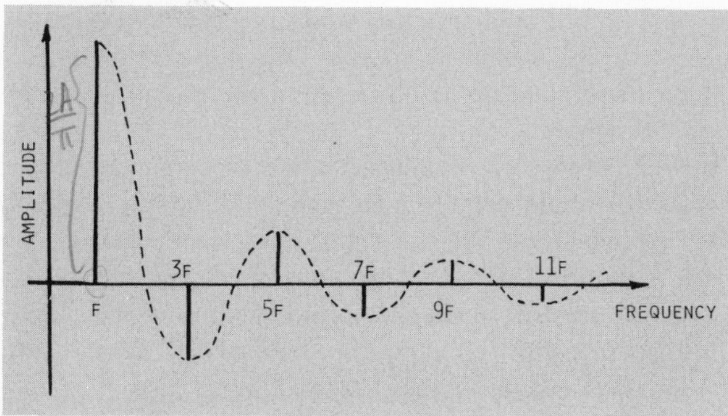

Figure 4.6. The spectral components are shown by plotting the harmonics of Figure 4.5 on frequency coordinates. The locus of their points follows a (sin x)/x envelope which is shown as a dashed curve.

Figure 4.5 shows how the addition of higher frequency harmonics approximates the rectangular wave form with a smaller deviation.

If the distance between pulses is increased so that a repetitive pattern of 10000 . . . is transmitted, then $S = T/5$ and equation 4.4 becomes

$$E(t) = (AS/T) + \frac{2A}{\pi} \sin\left(\frac{\pi}{5}\right) \cos(nft) + \frac{A}{\pi} \sin\left(\frac{2\pi}{5}\right) \cos(2nft) + \ldots \tag{4.6}$$

If the pattern were increased to a single pulse, i.e., a one followed by an infinite string of zeroes, $E(t)$ would be a constant-amplitude function.

If a transmission rate of 3000 bps is assumed and the pulse wave is f Hz, then, when the bit pattern is 101010 . . ., the transmission is $2f$ bps, where $f =$ 1500 Hz. When the bit pattern is 1000010000 . . . the transmission is $5f$ bps, where $f =$ 600 Hz. An examination of equations (4.5) and (4.6) shows that for the bit rate of 3000 bps we have two spectral lines at $2f$ bps and five spectral lines at $5f$ bps to the first crossover point on the $(\sin x)/x$ curve. If one random bit were transmitted in a pattern of nf bps, then there would be n spectral lines to the first crossover.

Thus to reproduce the signal waveform exactly at the receiver, the transmission line must carry all the frequency components without change of relative amplitude and phase. But this is unnecessary in practice. The energe conveying the essential message is concentrated in the lower part of the frequency spectrum (base frequency f and the harmonics to the first crossover point), and the higher-frequency components may be discarded without destroying the message.

From the mathematical analysis the following is observed: (1) When the pulse width is a smaller fraction of the repetition frequency then there are more spectral lines, and (2) in a limiting sense, when the bit pattern is irregular instead of strictly repetitive, the number of spectral lines will also be large. The more numerous are the transmitted spectral lines, the more recognizable (i.e., easier to reconstruct) is the signal.

The bandwidth of frequencies contains the number of spectral lines allowed for transmission that would reproduce the signal. An infinitely wide bandwidth would exactly reproduce the original signal, but would be very wasteful. A bandwidth that is too small would not generate a recognizable signal. Technology ever strives to use the smallest possible bandwidth that would give the highest probability of correctly reproducing the original signal at the receiver. For data transmission it will be shown that a signal rate of n bps could be recovered in a receiver if the channel bandwidth was $n/2$ Hz.

Further discussion of this material may be found in many suitable texts where References 1–4 are but a small sample.

4.6. THE NYQUIST INTERVAL AND CHANNEL CAPACITY

Computer terminal equipment with the capability of sending at a rate of n bps can produce pulse trains similar to the neutral baseband signals shown in Figure 3.6. These machines are said to have a frequency bandwidth ranging from 0 Hz, when a long string of consecutive "1" bits are sent, to $n/2$ Hz when a series of alternate "1" and "0" bits are transmitted. The 0-Hz frequency is referred to as the dc component. This is shown in Figure 4.7a.

Theoretically, a single pulse can be sent through an ideal low-pass filter with a cut-off frequency F_c. This means that all the signals at frequencies below the cut-off frequency are allowed to pass through the filter while all others are attenuated to zero. This is shown in Figure 4.7b. Sending a pulse through such a filter results in the energy being spread out in frequency with time as shown in Figure 4.7c. The main energy is preceded and followed by waves of energy. The amplitudes of these waves fall to zero at equally spaced intervals separated in time by $1/(2F_c)$ seconds.

In Figure 4.7c, it can be seen that the energy curves are shown *prior* to the instant the impulse is applied, i.e., the output appears before the input is applied. Such behavior is physically impossible and hence the filter is nonrealizable. Fictitious though they may be, ideal filters are conceptually useful in the study of communications systems.[3]

Applying this principle, if the terminal transmits pulses at a steady rate of 100 bps, then its bandwidth is 50 Hz. Furthermore, if these pulses are transmitted through an ideal low-pass filter whose cut-off frequency F_c is 50 Hz, then the waves of energy from pulses will fall to zero at intervals of 1/100 second. The energy in all the waves of the separate single pulses will combine, but there will not be any interference between successive pulses at the $1/(2F_c)$ (=0.01 seconds) instants, which are called the zero crossings.

If one considers the passage of a train of pulses spaced in time by $1/(2F_c)$ seconds, as shown in Figure 4.8, then the energy in all the waves of the different single pulses will combine; but there will be no interference between successive pulses at the $1/(2F_c)$ instants which are the zero crossings.

Thus if the received data are sampled at these precise instants, it is possible to determine whether or not a pulse is present even though at every other instant the energy of the pulses are run together. The interval of time between the samples $[1/(2F_c)]$ is known as the Nyquist interval.

The significance of this is that if a communication channel is sampled at a rate at least twice the highest baseband frequency at which the message transmission occurs, then the samples will contain all of the information of the original message. From the example above, the transmission bandwidth is 50 Hz. So, if the channel is sampled 100 times per second, i.e., twice the bandwidth, all the information of the message will be obtained.

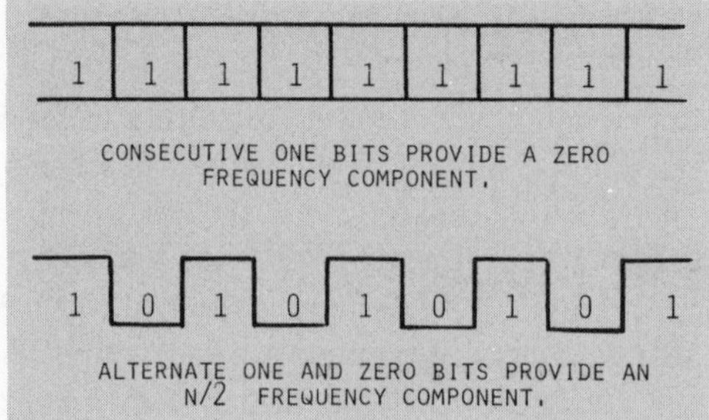

Figure 4.7a. Machines transmitting pulse trains at a rate of N bps are said to have a frequency bandwidth from 0 Hz, when consecutive "1" bits are sent, to $N/2$ Hz when alternate "1" and "0" bits are sent.

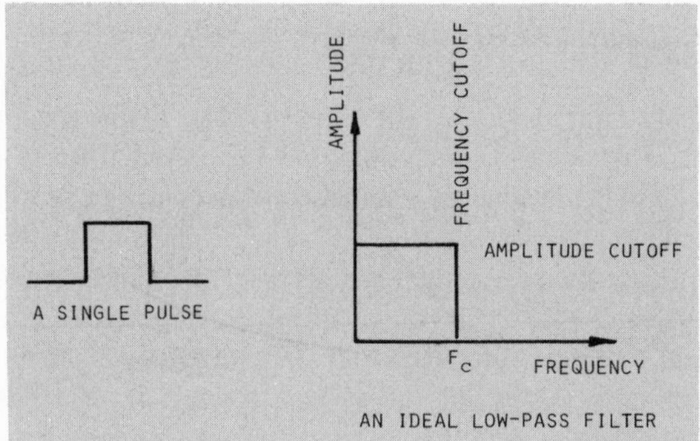

Figure 4.7b. A single bit pulse is transmitted through an ideal low-pass filter, which is an electrical circuit that allows all the energy below a cut-off frequency F_c to pass through while attenuating everything else. The filter is said to be ideal when the frequency attenuation is sharp as shown.

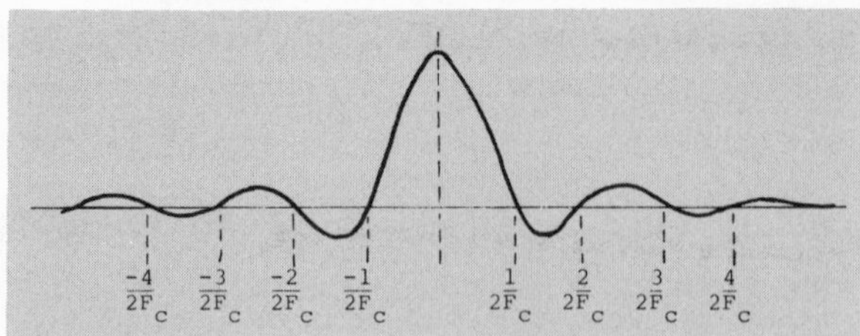

Figure 4.7c. A single bit passing through an ideal low-pass filter results in the energy being spread out in frequency with time where the amplitudes of these energy waves falling to zero at equally spaced intervals separated by $1/(2\ F_c)$ seconds.

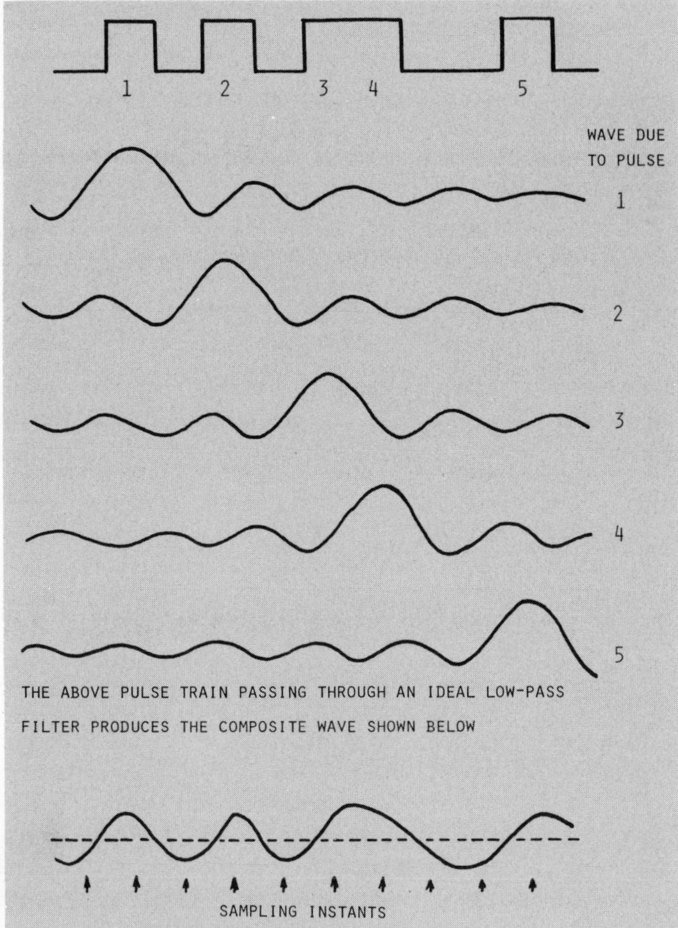

Figure 4.8. Transmission of pulses without intersymbol interference. When a bit-pulse train is passed through an ideal low-pass filter, the composite wave shown at the bottom is produced. If samples are taken at equally spaced intervals of $1/(2\ F_c)$ then it is guaranteed that the wave falls below the decision threshold when no "1" bit pulses were transmitted. The signaling pulse rate is at twice the cut-off frequency F_c of the low-pass filter.

Another way of stating the above is that a bandwidth B Hz can carry $2B$ different symbols per second without intersymbol interference. These symbols are referred to as signal elements, signal pulses, or baud. For instance, a bandwidth of 3000 Hz can have a maximum signaling speed of 6000 baud. If on a channel of B Hz one transmits symbols that can have one of two separate values or levels, then a single bit could be used to represent those symbols and the capacity of the transmission channel is $2B$ bps. Continuing with this reasoning:

Symbols having one of 4 separate levels require 2 bits per symbol and a channel capacity of $4B$ bps.

Symbols having one of 8 separate levels require 3 bits per symbol and a channel capacity $6B$ bps.

Symbols having one of 2^n separate levels require n bits per symbol and a channel capacity $2nB$ bps.

If $L = 2^n$ is the number of signal levels, then $n = \log_2 L$ and $2nB = 2B \log_2 L$ = capacity of noiseless channel of bandwidth B. This is the Nyquist relationship and is given by the equation

$$C = 2B \log_2 L \tag{4.7}$$

where C is the capacity in bits per second, $2B$ is the baud rate of the channel, and $\log_2 L$ is the bits per second per baud, i.e., the number of bits carried by each baud. The number of bits per baud is determined by the modulation method.

4.7. SHANNON–HARTLEY LAW AND CHANNEL CAPACITY

The capacity of a channel is defined as the maximum rate at which information can be transmitted over the channel. This maximum is taken from the rates of all sources that can be connected to the channel. Channel capacity was given significance by Shannon's coding theorem,[5,6] which, in nonrigorous terms, states that the output from any source of rate R can, with suitable encoding and decoding, be transmitted over a channel of capacity $C \geqslant R$ with arbitrarily small error. This theorem is an existence theorem and consequently does not provide a rule for finding an ideal method of matching, or encoding, the source to the channel. Shannon's theorem also shows that it is not necessary to increase the redundancy of the messages transmitted in order to reduce the probability of error. The price that one pays is a long time before the intelligence of a message is completely specified and the encoding procedure can start.[7]

In 1948, Shannon (based upon preliminary work by Hartley) rigorously showed that the capacity of a channel whose inputs are restricted to signals within a frequency bandwidth of B Hz with an average signal power of S (watts), and having an internal source of mean *Gaussian* noise with a mean power of N (watts) is given by

$$C = B \log_2(1 + S/N) \tag{4.8}$$

The capacity C is given in bits per second.

A communications channel, whether it be leased or switched, represents a financial investment. It should be the goal of system designers to obtain as great a benefit as possible from the money invested, which in this case means maximizing the information transfer rate of the system. In this regard, the Shannon–Hartley law [equation (4.8)] has several important implications. First, it gives the absolute best that can be accomplished given the channel parameters—the channel's maximum capacity with a zero probability of error. Second, for a specified information rate, equation (4.8) shows how bandwidth could be exchanged for power or signal-to-noise ratio. Third, it shows how the number of signaling levels given by Nyquist's law [equation (4.7)] that can be distinguished is limited by the signal-to-noise ratio.

For a telephone voice channel with a bandwidth of 3100 Hz (i.e., 300 Hz to 3400 Hz) and a signal-to-noise ratio of 30dB, the Shannon–Hartley capacity would be 30,880 bps. This is calculated as follows:

$$\begin{aligned}
30\text{ dB} &= 10 \log_{10}(S/N) \\
(S/N) &= 10^3 = 1000 \\
C &= B \log_2(1 + S/N) \\
&= 3100 \log_2(1 + 1000) \\
&= 3100 \times 3.32 \times \log_{10}(1001) \\
C &= 30{,}880 \text{ bps}
\end{aligned}$$

This figure represents the ultimate challenge to the designers of communications equipment. The number of signaling levels required to achieve this rate is approximately 32, which is another way of saying the modulation method should give us five bits per baud. This is asking a lot from today's technology!

Present systems achieve a rate of up to 10,800 bps on voice channels. This is not surprising. Because of diminishing returns in attaining higher fractions of capacity, little effort will be expended toward this goal in the future. There are also both practical and theoretical obstacles to increasing the capacities. The Shannon–Hartley law considers only Gaussian noise. There are, however, other kinds of noise and other impairments encountered (which are discussed in Chapter 8) that provide severe constraints on actual equipment design. Finally, Shannon's proof is only an existence proof. No recipe is provided, and even with unlimited equipment availability, no one *knows* how to construct a channel to achieve data speeds near capacity with vanishingly small error rates. The challenge of the Shannon–Hartley law will be with us for a long time to come.

PROBLEMS

1. Define the following terms:

frequency	signal amplitude
wavelength	phase angle
spectral line	Nyquist interval
harmonic component	intersymbol interference

2. What is the Nyquist relationship for an ideal noiseless channel? What is the baud rate of such a channel? What determines the number of signal levels that can be carried by each baud (i.e., bits per second per baud)?
3. What is the minimum sampling rate of a communication channel to insure that all of the information carried by that channel can be retrieved?
4. Explain in general terms how the Fourier series is related to data communications.
5. What is the Shannon–Hartley law? Discuss with respect to the practical vs theoretical capacities of a telephone voice-grade channel.

Chapter 5

Modulation Methods

5.1. WHAT IS MODULATION?

A signal created by any device such as a microphone pickup, a transducer, a computer terminal, etc., may be in either analog or digital form as seen in Figure 5.1. Analog signals have continuously varying amplitudes while digital signals consist of discrete pulses. These signals, whether digital or analog, are called baseband signals. In Chapter 3 it was shown that baseband signals cannot be transmitted for any appreciable distance over a communication link. These signals suffer distortion effects which are in large measure due to the presence of low-frequency components in the signal. A process known as *modulation* is used to allow communication to take place more efficiently over longer distances.

More exactly, modulation is a process whereby the characteristics of a carrier signal, that is usually at a higher frequency, are altered (i.e., modulated) by the *instantaneous amplitude* of the baseband signal. The device which performs the modulation is the transmitter. A device known as the *receiver* demodulates the received signal to recover the original baseband signal.

5.2. WHY THE NEED FOR MODULATION?

Modulation is used to improve the efficiency of transmission. Low-frequency signals require extremely large antennas for direct electromagnetic

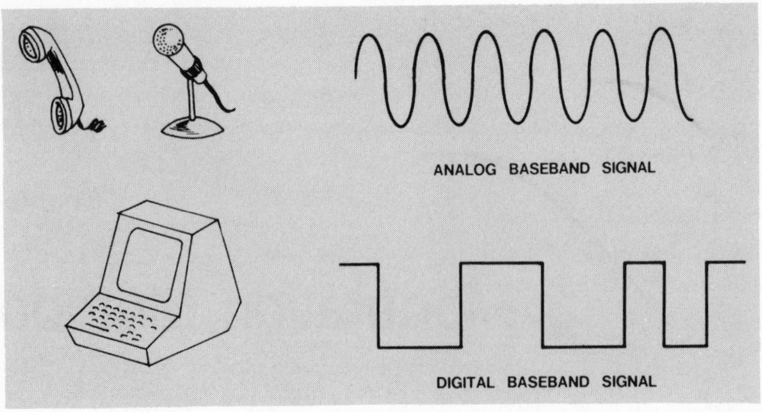

ANALOG BASEBAND SIGNAL

DIGITAL BASEBAND SIGNAL

Figure 5.1. Baseband signals can be generated in either a digital or an analog form.

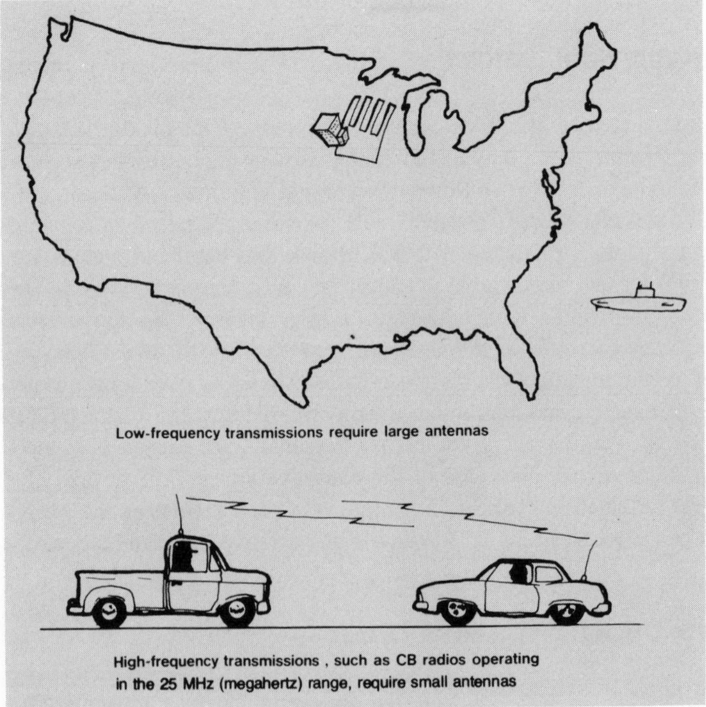

Figure 5.2. Antenna size is inversely related to the frequency of transmission.

radiation (e.g., for radio transmission). By utilizing the frequency translation property of modulation, these signals can be imprinted upon a higher-frequency carrier signal, thereby reducing the size of antennas required as in Figure 5.2. Furthermore, many baseband signals contain a direct current component that cannot be transmitted over appreciable distances because of resistive losses (cf. Chapter 3).

This leads to the notion of using modulation to overcome transmission channel noise and distortion effects. Some modulation methods are more resistant to particular types of noise than others. Perhaps the most common example is that of FM radio (i.e., frequency modulated). Its reception is not hampered by atmospheric disturbances, such as lightning, to the degree that AM radio (i.e., amplitude modulated) is affected. This is illustrated in Figure 5.3.

Modulation is also used to allow the simultaneous transmission of several subchannels over a communications channel by a process known as *multiplexing*. This is accomplished by imposing the baseband signal of each subchannel on a different frequency of the transmission channel. Telephone conversations, as shown in Figure 5.4, are a common example of translating baseband signals to different frequencies for transmission on one channel.

Finally, modulation allows the transmission of a large number of signal levels as coded bits of information. In discussing Nyquist's law (equation 4.6) we saw that the capacity of a communications channel can be increased by

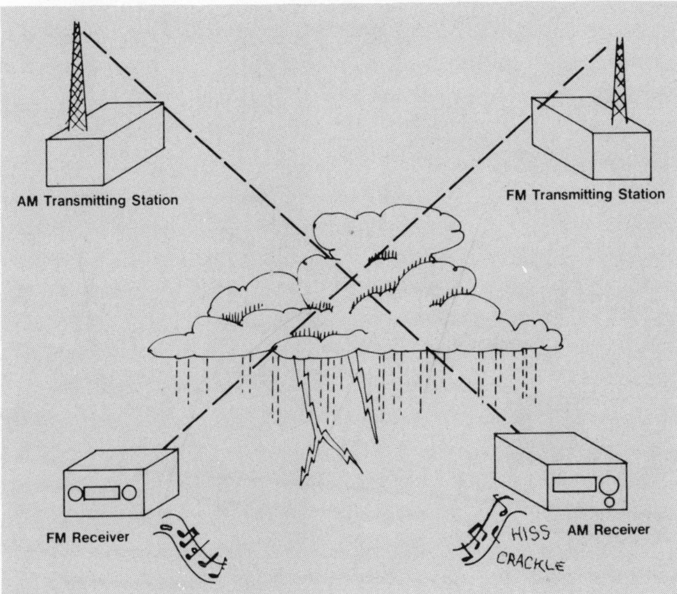

Figure 5.3. Modulation can be used to overcome atmospheric noise.

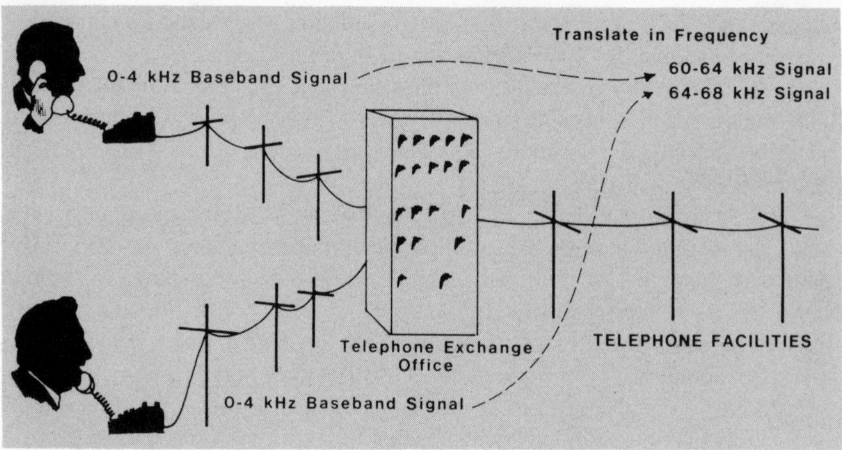

Figure 5.4. The frequency translation characteristic of modulation can be used for multiplexing signals.

increasing the number of bits carried by each pulse. This can be accomplished by using combinations of different modulation methods, especially when the baseband signals are digital data. This will be discussed in more detail later in this chapter.

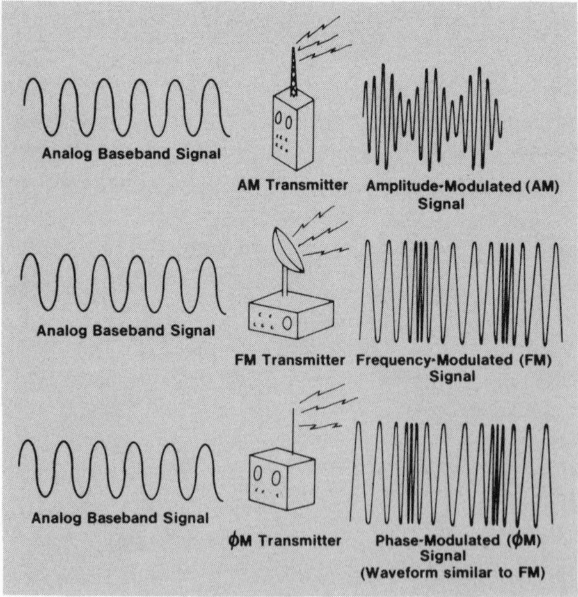

Figure 5.5. Analog modulation methods for an analog baseband signal.

5.3. THE MODULATION PROCESS

The modulation process alters the characteristics of a carrier signal. When the carrier is an analog signal (cf. Figure 4.4), the characteristics that can be altered are:

1. The carrier's *amplitude* for amplitude modulation (AM).
2. The carrier's *frequency* for frequency modulation (FM).
3. The carrier's *phase angle* for phase modulation (ϕM).

These analog modulation methods are illustrated in Figure 5.5.

The carrier can also be a periodic train of pulses as in a digital waveform. In this case the process of digital modulation alters characteristics that are discrete in nature. There are two ways to accomplish this. First, there is *pulse modulation* where the characteristics of the carrier pulses are altered directly by the baseband signal. The resulting signal may be pulse amplitude modulated (PAM), pulse duration modulated (PDM), pulse position modulated (PPM), or pulse frequency modulated (PFM). The various pulse modulation methods are shown in Figure 5.6.

The second method of digital modulation is known as *pulse code modulation* (PCM). This modulation process involves a symbol conversion and therefore

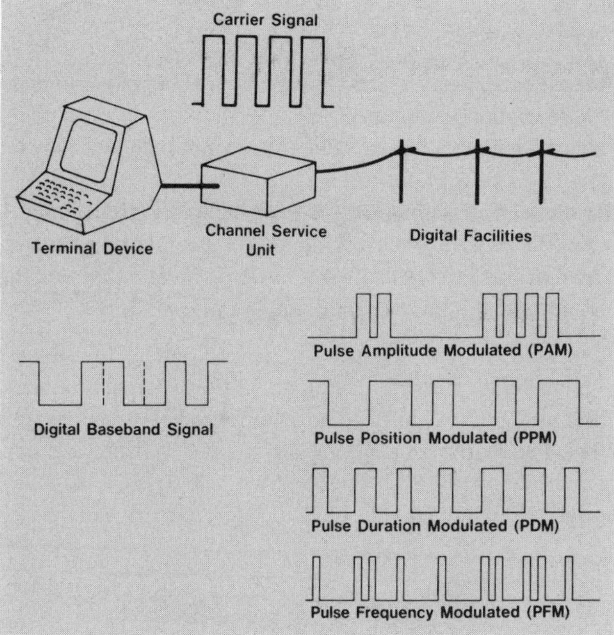

Figure 5.6. Digital modulation methods for a digital baseband signal.

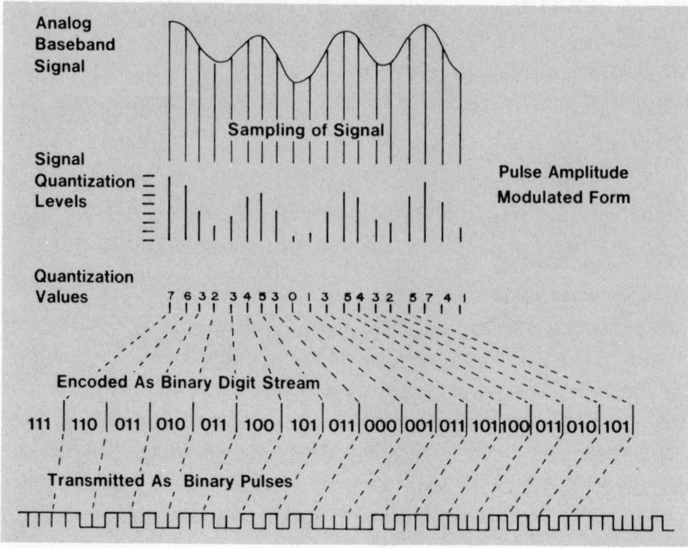

Figure 5.7. Pulse-code modulation applied to an analog baseband signal.

differs from the previous methods. Several distinct steps are involved. Figure 5.7 illustrates these steps.

1. The baseband signal is sampled at a high enough rate to insure that all of the information is obtained.
2. For each sample, a digital value of the amplitude is obtained by a process known as *signal quantization*.
3. The digital value obtained for each sample is transmitted in its binary form. The receiver recovers the original signal by a reverse process. A variant of this method is known as *delta modulation,* which is discussed in Reference 1, pp. 387–389.

The remainder of this chapter will cover each of the above modulation methods in more detail. Table 5.1 summarizes the different modulation methods. It should be noted that modulating an analog carrier signal requires a modem device. When the output is a digital signal, the transmitting device is more commonly referred to as a channel service unit (CSU), digital service unit (DSU), digital transmitter, digital modem, etc., such as shown in Figure 5.6.

5.4. AMPLITUDE MODULATION

One of the earliest and most common modulation methods is amplitude modulation (AM), in which the amplitude of a carrier signal is altered by lower-frequency baseband signals. In the basic process, amplitude modulation yields a modulated signal (i.e., the carrier) that is twice the bandwidth of the baseband signal (i.e., the modulating signal). This modulated signal consists of three components: the original carrier, and the lower and upper *sideband signals*. Each sideband is the same bandwidth as the bandwidth of the baseband, which is why the modulated signal is twice the bandwidth of the baseband. This is shown in Figures 5.8 and 5.9. These figures show signal spectra, that is, signal strengths vs. frequency ranges.

5.4.1. Double Sideband Amplitude Modulation (DSB-AM)

Figure 5.8 shows speech, whose frequency components are from 30 to over 18,000 Hz, being picked up by a microphone at a radio station. The output of the microphone is a speech baseband signal of from 30 to 5000 Hz, which is input to an AM transmitter tuned to transmit a 750 kHz channel signal. This type of transmission is known as double-sideband transmitted carrier (DSBTC-AM). It is perhaps the most common type of transmission used for commercial radio broadcasting in the United States.

The important characteristics of DSBTC-AM are:

1. The sidebands have the same bandwidth as the original modulating signal.
2. The identical intelligence, that is, the amount of information carried by the modulating signal, is contained in each sideband as mirror images of each other.

Table 5.1. Various Modulation Processes

Analog modulation
Amplitude (AM)
Frequency (FM)
Phase (ΦM)
Digital modulation
Pulse modulation
Pulse amplitude (PAM)
Pulse duration (PDM)
Pulse position (PPM)
Pulse frequency (PFM)
Coded modulation
Pulse code modulation (PCM)
Delta modulation (DM)

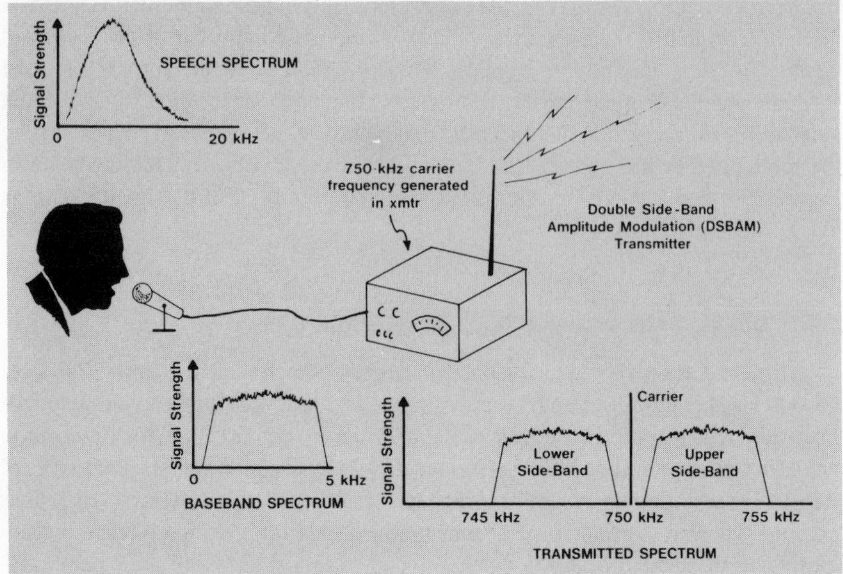

Figure 5.8. Amplitude modulation produces two sideband signals.

3. The frequency component signals in the upper sideband appear identical to the modulating signal, but they are inverted in the lower sideband.
4. The power distribution of the modulated signal is directly related to the distribution of power in the modulating signal.

5.4.2. Other Forms of Amplitude Modulation

Since a substantial amount of the total power transmitted in DSBTC-AM carries no information, the amount of wasted power can be reduced by eliminating the carrier from the modulated signal. This form of modulation is called *double-sideband suppressed-carrier* (DSBSC-AM). Because of the elimination of the carrier signal, all zero crossings (transitions from + to − voltage) of the

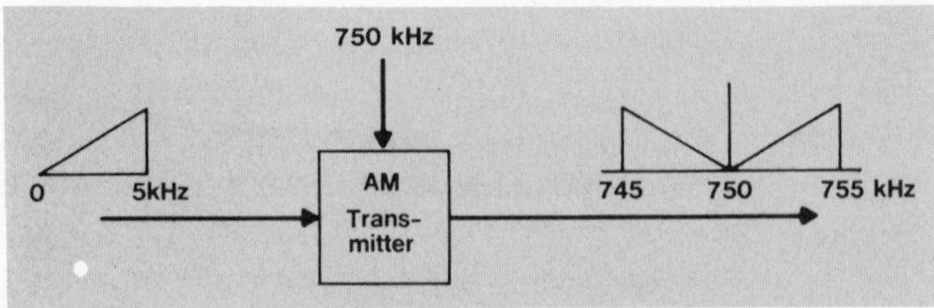

Figure 5.9. A schematic representation of the amplitude modulation process.

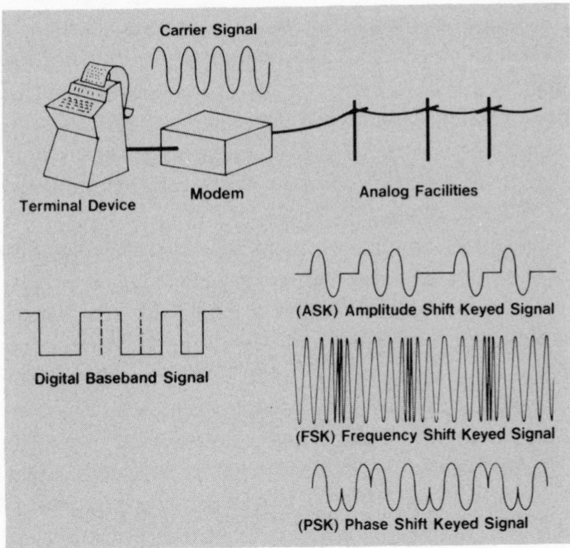

Figure 5.10. Analog modulation applied to a digital baseband signal.

message wave will result in phase reversals in the modulated waveform. The DSBC-AM receiver needs more complex circuitry to detect these phase reversals in order to properly demodulate the signal. Thus we have a tradeoff between transmission power efficiency and receiver complexity, for DSBTC signals require greater power, but at the same time they require simpler receiver circuitry. This simpler circuitry is the reason that most of today's commercial AM broadcasting is of the DSBTC type.

Both DSBTC and DSBSC require a transmission bandwidth that is twice the baseband bandwidth because of the requirement that both sidebands be transmitted. By suppressing the transmission of one of the sidebands as well as the carrier, we would expect both to reduce the signal power and to improve bandwidth usage. This type of system is known as *single-sideband suppressed carrier* (SSBSC-AM, or more simply SSB). The receiver circuitry is moderately complex, as it must generate a strong carrier of the correct reference phase (i.e., it must reproduce the carrier) in order to properly demodulate the signal. SSB signals inherently contain quadrature components (i.e., some component signals vary in phase by 90° because of the nature of this modulation technique). Therefore if the reference carrier signal that is generated at the receiver varies in frequency from the original carrier, quadrature distortion occurs. Voice transmission systems are not greatly affected by quadrature distortion, hence the popularity of SSB systems in the amateur and private radio sectors.

In order to use SSB for digital data transmission, a good, reliable source of reference-carrier frequency must be provided. A common technique for transmitting digital baseband data containing low-frequency or dc components is to first modulate a subcarrier (i.e., a carrier of lower frequency) using DSB-AM or frequency or phase modulation (described below) and then to use SSBSC-AM to translate the signal to the desired carrier frequency. This is typically accomplished in the multiplex terminals of frequency division multiplexed systems (cf. Chapter 6).

A more convenient modulation method is to compromise between DSB modulation, which can be used easily for data signals but is wasteful of bandwidth, and SSB modulation, which is bandwidth-efficient but cannot tolerate the low-frequency components of data signals. Such a compromise is *vestigial-sideband suppressed carrier* (VSBSC-AM) modulation. This method involves passing a DSB signal through a bandpass filter which allows one sideband plus a vestige (approximately 30%) of the other sideband to pass through and be transmitted. The demodulation circuitry is not as complex as that required for SSB systems, and furthermore, VSB is fairly tolerant of equipment distortions in the manner of DSBTC systems. Thus, VSBSC-AM has been used extensively for wideband transmission of data signals (at rates greater than 19.2 kbps). In addition, VSBTC-AM has become a standard for television transmission where the carrier is transmitted at a separate frequency.

5.5 AMPLITUDE MODULATION OF DIGITAL DATA

Up to now we have described amplitude modulation in which the modulating wave is analog. The modulating wave can also be digital data to be transmitted as rectangular pulses. The simplest amplitude modulation technique for digital data is *amplitude-shift keying* (ASK), where the carrier amplitude is switched between two or more values, usually on and off, to represent binary signals. The resultant modulated wave then consists of analog pulses or ''marks'' representing the binary digit 1, and ''spaces,'' representing the binary digit 0. This is shown in Figure 5.10. The price of this simplicity is excessive bandwidth and wasted carrier power, and therefore it is not used extensively in digital transmission systems.

5.6. FREQUENCY MODULATION OF ANALOG SIGNALS

Frequency modulation (FM) is a process whereby the amplitude changes of a modulating wave are used to vary the instantaneous frequency of a carrier from its unmodulated value. The amplitude of the modulated signal remains constant as shown in Figure 5.5. Because of its resistance to noise, FM is currently used for commercial high-fidelity broadcasting in the United States. It should be pointed out that it is the detection process in the receiver that provides the noise resistance by maintaining a signal of constant amplitude. Frequency modulation, along with phase modulation, is sometimes referred to as angle modulation.

The spectrum resulting from frequency modulation is much more complex than the equivalent amplitude modulation spectrum, with many more sideband components. Unlike AM, the FM carrier signal contains information from the baseband signal and thus the transmitted carrier signal cannot be discarded.

In AM, the amplitude of the carrier is directly affected by the amplitude of the modulating signal (viz., the loudness of speech into a microphone). In FM, on the other hand, the amplitude of the modulating signal results in *greater variations* of the carrier frequency from the assigned or center frequency,

5.6.1. Broadcast Frequency Modulation

For United States FM broadcasting, the FCC rules permit the carrier to deviate a maximum of 75 kHz on each side of a center frequency, thus allowing a *total swing* of 150 kHz. This rule allows the transmission of a sufficiently loud signal without using an excessive amount of frequency spectrum. This means that if two tones have the same strength, then they will be transmitted with the same deviation of the carrier from the center frequency, regardless of their frequencies.

In FM, the swinging of the carrier from one frequency to another generates a great number of sidebands in proportion to the amount of swing. Theoretically an infinite number of sidebands is produced by an FM transmitter, but only the first few are strong enough to be significant. The number of significant sidebands can be mathematically determined by using Bessel functions. See Reference 2, pp. 36–39, or Reference 3, pp. 226–228 for further discussion.

The FM bandwidth requirements are very large compared with AM. For example, a 15 kHz baseband bandwidth with 75 kHz allowable frequency deviation requires a 200 kHz channel bandwidth for transmission.

5.6.2. Applications of Frequency Modulation

The primary application of frequency modulation, other than commercial broadcasting, is for radio frequency (RF) transmissions on multiplexed microwave systems. The frequencies are in the gigahertz (GHz) range (from 1.5 to 15 GHz) and the bandwidths are in the megahertz (MHz) range (from 4 to 6 MHz). FM requirements for extremely large bandwidths can be met in these kinds of transmission systems.[4]

5.7. FREQUENCY-SHIFT KEYING

For data communications, frequency modulation is used in low-speed asynchronous applications in a form known as *frequency-shift keying* (FSK). In this modulation method the frequency of the carrier is altered to one of two frequencies. One frequency represents a mark, or a one bit, and the other frequency represents a space, or a zero bit. Figure 5.10 illustrates FSK for digital data.

Typically the frequency assignments for origination/answer channels at speeds up to 300 bps are

E–W transmission	mark	1270 Hz	F1M
	space	1070 Hz	F1S
W–E transmission	mark	2225 Hz	F2M
	space	2025 Hz	F2S

The last column gives the symbols used to describe each type of transmission, the M and S corresponding to mark and space. All of these frequencies are within the bandwidth of a voice channel. Because there is a separation of frequencies, the channel can be operated in a full-duplex (FDX) mode. It is, however, rarely done at such low speeds with the channel operation being in the half-duplex (HDX) mode.

Some equipment has been designed to operate at speeds of 1200 bps or higher using FSK modulation over a voice-channel bandwidth of 300 to 3400 Hz. These modems use a mark frequency of 1200 Hz and a space frequency of 2200 Hz with a centering frequency of 1700 Hz. The operation must be half-duplex (HDX) because there is not enough usable bandwidth available for another channel. Other mark/space frequencies can be used with improved system performance.[5]

5.8. PHASE MODULATION

Phase modulation (ϕM) is the process in which the phase of a carrier wave is varied in proportion to the instantaneous amplitude of the modulating signal. ϕM is similar to FM, and both are examples of angular modulation methods. The phase modulated wave appears similar to the FM modulated wave, as shown in Figure 5.5. Analysis of the phase modulation process is similar to but more complex than FM.

5.9. PHASE MODULATION FOR DIGITAL DATA

Phase modulation has been successfully applied to the transmission of digital data by the technique known as phase-shift keying (PSK). In PSK the phase angle of the carrier is directly altered by the value of the digital signal. For binary transmission we would have

$$\text{"0" bit} \qquad \theta_c = 0°$$
$$\text{"1" bit} \qquad \theta_c = 180°$$

where the instantaneous amplitude is

$$a_c = A_c \sin (2f_c t + \theta_c)$$

Two-bit codes called *dibits* can be transmitted in this manner, using 4-phase-PSK modulation (written as 4ϕ-PSK). An example is shown in Table 5.2. In fact, as shown in the same table, up to eight phase angles can be detected in the received signal, giving a coding for three binary bits at a time.

Two phase-relation patterns are most commonly used, one in which phase changes are all some multiples of 45°, the other in which all changes are odd multiples of 22½°. When multiples of 45° are used, there is a possibility that a series of pulses could be produced without a phase change, while the pattern using 22½° always provides a phase shift. This is the format originally used in all Bell-system-compatible 4800 bps modems.[6]

5.10. WHY USE PHASE MODULATION?

Phase modulation, in the form of multilevel phase-shift keying (PSK), is the preferred process when transmission at high data rates is desired. There are

Table 5.2. Possible Phase-Angle Values for Multilevel Phase-Shift Keying

Bits transmitted	Signal levels	Possible phase-angle values (degrees)	
00	0	0	45
01	1	90	135
10	2	180	225
11	3	270	315
000	0	0	22.5
001	1	45	67.5
010	2	90	112.5
011	3	135	157.5
100	4	180	202.5
101	5	225	247.5
110	6	270	292.5
111	7	315	337.5

several reasons why phase modulation is preferred to frequency modulation even though the techniques are similar. One important reason is that phase modulation is applied directly to the carrier signal and does not require modulation of the carrier oscillator as in frequency modulation. Thus, in systems where a highly stable carrier frequency is required, such as in limited bandwidth communications systems and in telemetry systems, phase modulation is preferred over other forms of modulation.

In digital communications systems, a stable carrier frequency at the transmitter eases the problem of recovering the carrier at the receiver, and this has led to the use of phase modulation in such systems. Finally, multilevel phase-shift keying gives better spectral efficiency (i.e., more bits per hertz of transmitted bandwidth) than does frequency-shift keying (FSK) modulation.

5.11. COMBINATIONS OF MODULATION METHODS

Modem designers have devised many ingenious schemes for putting many bits into each baud, or signal pulse. Typically these involve combinations of modulation methods. Figure 5.11 illustrates some methods of using combinations of modulation methods. Two methods will be discussed.

5.11.1. Quadrature Modulation

Quadrature modulation, also known as two-phase–two-level amplitude modulation, is a process of transmitting dibits in a single-sideband system. This is accomplishied by encoding and decoding two independent bit streams using single-sideband amplitude modulation (SSB-AM) on the same carrier frequency, but with the carriers differing in phase by 90° (i.e., in quadrature) from each other. The signals are sent out together, that is, in the same frequency bandwidth, without interfering with each other. The receiver can demodulate the two streams using envelope detection. In order to transmit dibits, two independent data streams must be created from the single input stream. This is done by transmitting alternate bits on alternate data streams (see Reference 2, pp. 138–141).

5.11.2. Quadrature Amplitude Modulation (QAM)

Data transmission at 9600 bps over a voice channel can be accomplished by packing four bits into each pulse and transmitting at 2400 baud using a technique known as quadrature amplitude modulation (QAM). This method can be described as a combination of phase modulation and amplitude modulation in which 12 values of phase and three values of amplitude can produce 16 possible signal states. Figure 5.12 shows the possible signal states, with each representing

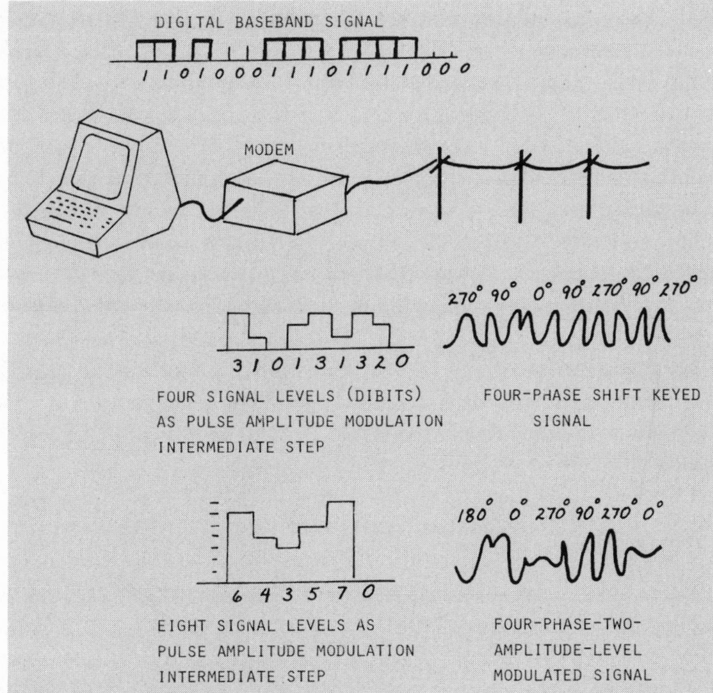

Figure 5.11. Combinations of modulation methods are used to achieve higher bit rates.

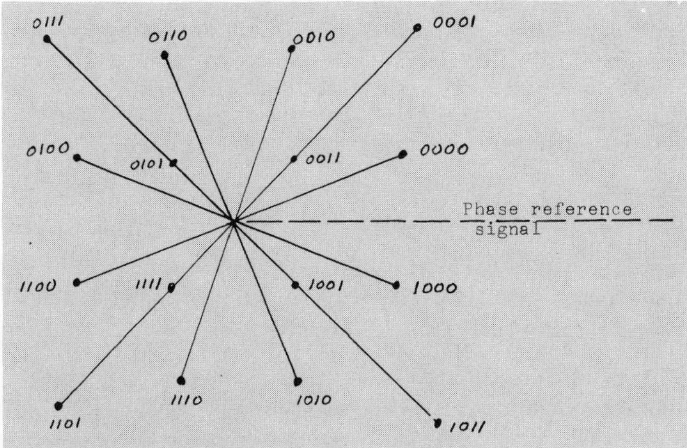

Figure 5.12. Quadrature amplitude modulation produces sixteen signal states from a combination of twelve phase angles and three amplitude levels.

a four-bit *Gray-coded* binary number. Each phase is given in relation to an absolute phase reference signal. Figure 5.13 shows the values of the Gray code. Four of the phase angles are associated with two amplitude levels which are different from that of the other eight, so that if a pulse assumes one of these phases, its amplitude either increases or decreases.[7]

These sixteen signal levels can be achieved in a number of different ways and still be known as QAM. Two principal schemes are known as 4 × 4 QAM (8-phase 2-level) and CC1TT v. 29 (proposed) (8-phase 4-level). The reaşon for having different schemes is (1) to facilitate decoding in the demodulation process and (2) to provide immunity to signal distortion due to phase jitter and harmonic distortion.[8]

The Bell system 209A data set is an example of a modem that uses QAM. The serial stream of binary data is grouped four bits per baud and a 1650 Hz carrier is modulated with a transmission rate of 2400 baud to produce a 9600 bps throughput.[9]

5.11.3. The Duobinary Method

Another transmission scheme is related to an old telegraph technique known as "doubling the dotting speed." GTE Lenkurt has refined this scheme and called it the *duobinary technique*. It was used primarily in the GTE Lenkurt 26D modem equipment. The transmitter sends three kinds of output signals: positive, indicating a mark; negative, indicating a space; and zero, indicating a reversal of the previous value. The actual bandwidth of the channel is f_B and has a Nyquist rate of $2f_B$ bps in a binary type of channel. The claim is made that the duobinary technique doubles the signaling speed to $4f_B$ bps.

It can be shown that this system requires sampling at transition points where three levels are possible. In other words, the receiver interprets a ternary code

	Binary code	Gray code
0	0000	0000
1	0001	0001
2	0010	1001
3	0011	1101
4	0100	0101
5	0101	0111
6	0110	1111
7	0111	1011
8	1000	0011
9	1001	0010
10	1010	1010
11	1011	1110
12	1100	0110
13	1101	0100
14	1110	1100
15	1111	1000

Figure 5.13. For the Gray code, shown on the right, successive numbers differ by only one digit. In straight binary coding, anywhere from one to all of the digits must change in order to produce the next number in sequence.

and thus does not contradict Nyquist's theory which does not allow ternary sequence-dependent coding of binary signals.

It has been determined that the system fails due to intersymbol interference where the bit rate reaches $2f_B/0.700 = 2.857$ times the bandwidth in Hertz. Straight ternary signaling at a rate of $2f_B$ three-level choices per second gives $2f_B \log_2 3 = 3.170 f_B$ bps. Thus, it can be said that the true Nyquist rate in bits per second is not attainable by doubling the dotting speed (see Reference 2, pp. 125–127).

5.12. SUMMARY OF ANALOG MODULATION

Some comparisons of the various modulation methods are given in Table 5.3. FM equipment is reasonably simple, performs well in the presence of noise, and can be used for asynchronous transmission and therefore is perhaps the most widely used method for data speeds up to 1200 bps. In addition, FM is used in wideband transmission systems operating in the microwave range where the available bandwidths are large. AM is used in combinations with other methods primarily because of its poor noise tolerance. Phase modulation finds greatest application in bandwidth limited situations such as 2400 to 9600 bps speeds on a voice channel. Phase modulation has good noise tolerance, but the receiver equipment is the most complex.

5.13. PULSE-MODULATION PROCESSES

All of methods so far described use an analog carrier. In pulse-modulation systems the unmodulated carrier is a series of regularly recurrent pulses instead of a continuous wave. In pulse modulation some parameter of each pulse is

Table 5.3. Summary of Modulation Methods for Digital Transmission

Method	Equipment complexity	Bits per Hz of bandwidth	Tolerance-to-noise distortion
DSBTC-AM	1	1	Poor
SSBSC-AM	3	2	Poor
VSBSC-AM	4	2	Good
FSK (FM)	2	1	Good
PSK (ϕM)	5	2-4	Good

altered, or modulated, by a particular value of a sample of a baseband signal. These pulse parameters may be pulse amplitude, pulse duration, pulse position, or pulse frequency.

Note that an important phrase was used in describing pulse modulation, namely, the "value of a sample." In analog modulation the characteristics of the carrier are directly altered by the baseband signal. In pulse modulation, the baseband signal has to be sampled, its value determined, and then that value is applied to the pulse carrier. Thus, if the baseband signal is a continuous wave, it must be sampled at a rate to insure that all the values derived from the samples and transmitted over the carrier will allow the receiver to reconstruct the signal without any loss of information. Visualize the analogous process of reading a number of data points from a graph and then using these data points to plot a new graph which when superimposed on the original graph will not show any deviation (provided, of course, the same coordinate system is used).

The rate of sampling comes from Nyquist's law [equation (3.7)], which assures that if samples are taken at a rate that is *at least* twice the value of the highest significant signaling frequency in the bandwidth, then all the information of the original message will be obtained. For example, a message on a voice channel such as a telephone call is said to be *bandlimited,* i.e., to contain the highest frequency, at 4 kHz. (This is by convention, even though actual speech is transmitted from 300 to 3400 Hz.) If at least 8000 samples of the received signal are taken each second, then none of the message information will be lost. Figure 5.14 illustrates some of the different kinds of pulse-modulation methods that can be used to transmit analog signals. More detailed discussion of pulse-modulation systems may be found in Reference 1, pp. 267–387.

5.13.1. Pulse Amplitude Modulation

If the baseband signal is sampled at regular intervals as described above, then we can obtain the value of the instantaneous amplitude of this signal for every sample taken. In the modulation technique known as pulse amplitude modulation, this value is used to alter the amplitude of a pulse carrier for transmission. (Figure 5.14 shows the different types of pulse modulation methods.) This type of modulation is usually an intermediate step in processing signals in time division multiplex terminals.

5.13.2. Pulse Duration Modulation

Another form is pulse duration modulation (PDM), which may also be referred to as pulse length modulation or pulse width modulation. The value of the instantaneous sample of a baseband modulating signal is used to produce pulses of varying duration as shown in Figure 5.14. In practice, the leading edge of the pulse occurs at fixed time intervals and the trailing edge occurs with variable

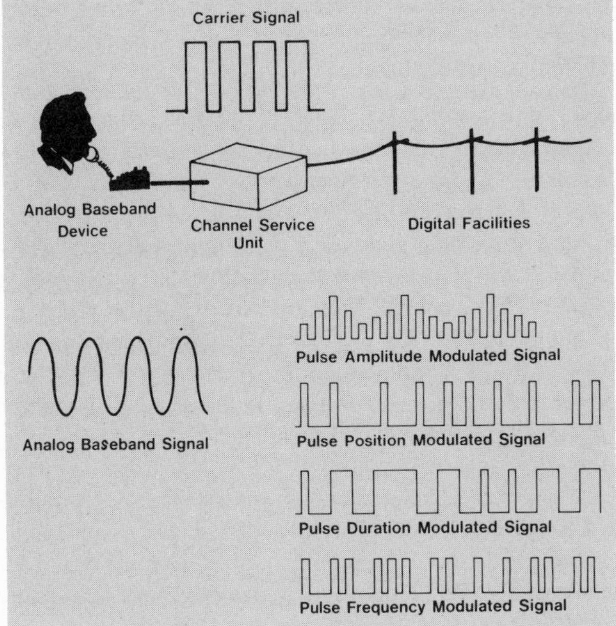

Figure 5.14. Pulse modulation processes applied to an analog baseband signal.

spacing. Thus pulses of long duration require expenditures of additional amounts of energy with no additional information-carrying capability. Pulse duration modulation is used primarily for the generation and detection of another form of pulse modulation, namely, pulse position modulation, which is discussed below.

5.13.3. Pulse Position Modulation

In pulse position modulation (PPM), the value of each instantaneous sample of the baseband signal is used to vary the carrier pulses relative to their unmodulated time of occurrence. This form of modulation is more suitable for transmission than PDM because of lower power requirements. The circuitry for generating PPM signals is not as complex as that required for the other methods of pulse modulation.

5.14. PULSE CODE MODULATION

All of the modulation methods discussed previously, whether pulse modulation or analog modulation, have involved *direct* representations of the baseband or modulating signal in the carrier or modulated signal. Pulse code modulation

(PCM), on the other hand, is an entirely different form of modulation in that a conversion of symbol representation (coding) is used. The process of generating a PCM signal from an analog baseband involves the following distinct steps:

1. Samples of the modulating signal are obtained at a rate that is at least the Nyquist rate, that is, at a rate at least twice the highest frequency in the modulating signal. For example, if a voice channel whose bandwidth is 4000 Hz were the modulating wave, then the Nyquist rate would be 8000 samples per second.

2. The value of the amplitude for each sample is determined by a process that is not unlike PAM (pulse amplitude modulation). This process is known as *signal quantization*. For example, if the maximum possible range of the sample amplitudes (from the largest plus value to the largest negative value) were to be represented by one of 128 values, then some combination of seven bits ($2^7 = 128$) could be used to represent the sample value. By this process, the continuous value range of the signal has been discretized exactly as in an analog-to-digital (A/D) converter.

3. The sample value obtained is then represented by a group of bits in a binary form. For example, if the previously determined sample amplitude were 67 (out of a possible 128), then the representation of this value would be 1000011.

4. These groups of bits are transmitted as digital (discrete amplitude) pulses. The bipolar waveform is usually used. (See Figure 3.5.)

Figure 5.15 illustrates these steps for pulse code modulation using an analog baseband signal. From the figure note that the quantization levels are *not* of the same size. This allows greater discrimination of the low-amplitude signals (i.e., the weaker signals) into distinct quantization levels. This process is known as companding and is discussed in Chapter 6.

5.15. DEMODULATION OF RECEIVED SIGNALS

The method used in the receiver to demodulate the incoming signals and to recover the transmitted baseband influences the modulation process. Remember, the signal going out over the channel is subjected to noise and distortion effects. The demodulation process must display a certain amount of immunity to these deleterious effects. A second approach to this noisy channel problem is to introduce redundancy into the message as a part of the coding process. This is described in Chapter 13. Voice transmissions are very tolerant of noisy channels because of the large amount of redundancy that exists in natural languages. Data transmission, on the other hand, is greatly affected by channel distortions because of the limited amount of redundancy that is used. Therefore the demodulation pocess is more important in data transmission than it would be in voice transmissions.

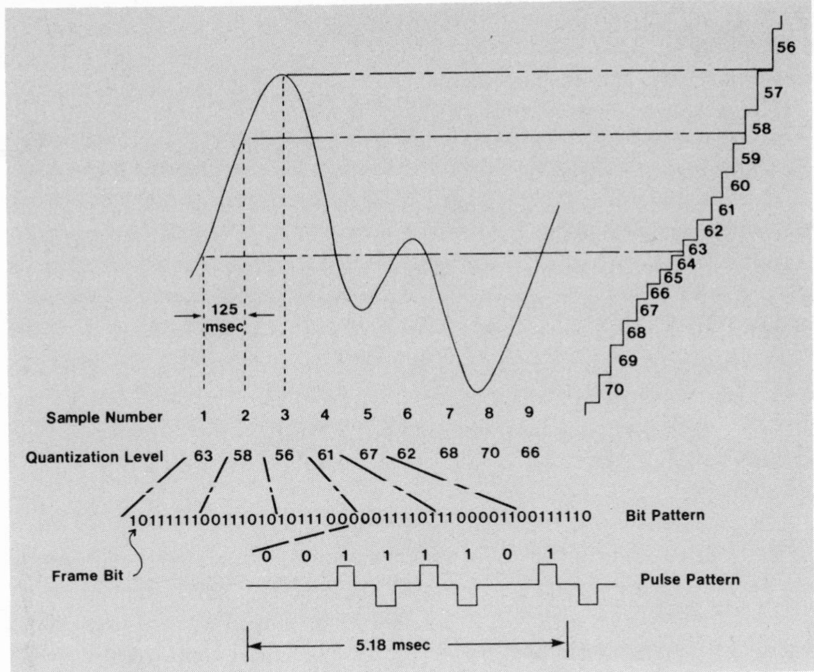

Figure 5.15. Pulse code modulation using seven-bit quantization.

There are three basic approaches to the demodulation of the received signal. They are known as *coherent detection, envelope detection,* and *differential detection*. The differences between these methods are primarily whether the incoming signal itself is used in the demodulation process or whether a locally generated signal must be added to the incoming signal. These methods are dependent on the type of modulation used.

5.15.1. Detection of the Received AM Signal

The most common demodulation method for DSBTC-AM systems is *envelope detection,* which requires a very simple circuit. In addition to being used in most commercially sold AM radio sets, envelope detection is used for television video signals that are vestigial-sideband-plus-carrier. For two-level amplitude-shift keying (ASK), envelope detection can be accomplished by simple *rectification* of the received signal. Rectification converts all of the signal to positive polarity by multiplying the received wave by -1 if the wave is negative, and $+1$ if the wave is positive. Envelope detection is not used in SSB-AM and VSB-AM data transmission systems because the zero-crossings of the binary signals cannot be preserved. When sidebands are not symmetric about the carrier, the envelope shape differs from the modulating signal because of the presence of quadrature components, and thus envelope detection results in distortion (see Reference 2, p. 138). Envelope detection also gives poor results when used to demodulate mlutilevel AM signals. The problem lies in decoding the lower amplitude levels (see Reference 2, p. 160).

Very few modems use envelope detection. Some of the early modems were the AN/TSQ data system using DSBTC-AM at 750 bps, the A1 data system (in the SAGE system for continental air defense) using ternary level VSB-AM at 1600 bps, and the Rixon Sebit using VSB-AM at 2500 bps. All of these modems were custom-made for specialized types of data communications.

To detect SSB-AM and multilevel AM the method of *synchronous detection* is used. The receiver uses a locally generated carrier signal to reinsert the missing carrier frequency with the incoming signal. This method is also known as *coherent detection,* but this term is applied more frequently to describe phase demodulation.

In practice some suppressed carrier systems transmit a small amount of carrier from the transmitter. This transmitted pilot carrier-signal component is then used to synchronize the generation of the receiver's carrier frequency for the demodulation process. Such a system is known as *homodyne detection*. Thus, in essence, any systems that use a locally generated carrier signal (at the receiver) are referred to as being either synchronous, coherent, or homodyne detection.

5.15.2. Detection of Frequency-Modulated Signals

The FM signal is a carrier wave varying in freuqency in accordance with the amplitude of the baseband modulating wave. At the receiver the line noise and interference outside the frequency band of interest are removed by a bandpass filter. Then an electronic circuit known as a limiter removes any residual amplitude modulation introduced by the bandpass filter and any in-band noise. The limiter output is passed to the FM demodulator as a square wave. There are two general types of circuits used for frequency demodulation. One of these derives a baseband component directly from the time rate of zero crossings and is known as a zero-crossing, axis-crossing, or cycle-counting detector. This circuit generates pulses of fixed length and height at each zero crossing and integrates the pulse train in a low-pass filter. The method is simple and well suited to cases where the frequency shift is large.

The other detection method involves passing the limiter output to a frequency-selective network which introduces an amplitude variation proportional to the instantaneous frequency. This is then rectified and filtered to recover the baseband signal.

5.15.3. Detection of Phase-Modulated Signals

The two principal methods for demodulating a phase-modulated signal are coherent detection and differential detection. With ϕM the major problem is determining the proper phase angle of the incoming signal. The easiest method is to provide a local signal (at the receiver) of known phase that is used as a reference to which the received signal is compared. This method, known as *coherent detection* (CD), requires circuitry with a high degree of precision and is thus an expensive procedure.

The less expensive process is to compare the phase of the present sample with the phase of the previous sample. This method, known as *differential detection,* does not require highly accurate reference tones and is fairly insensitive to many kinds of channel distortions. Differential detection, however, has a higher error rate than coherent detection (because of a reduced signal-to-noise margin). In addition, differential detection tends to double errors. If the first error occurs because of some channel disturbance, chances are good that the following symbol will also be in error. Systems relying on simple parity for error detection will fail to detect such doubled errors.

5.15.4. Modem Design Choices

For the transmission of data over analog circuits the selection of modulation methods has been determined to a great extent by past experience. The range of variation in voice channel circuits with regard to available bandwidth and nonlinear distortion directly influences the modem designs. The maximum symbol rate (in baud) is limited by the available bandwidth. The number of signal levels (bits per baud) that can be used and still attain satisfactory error rates depends on the nonlinear distortion and phase jitter which is discussed in Chapter 8.

For data speeds of 600 bps or less on narrow-band FDM systems and data speeds of 1200–1800 bps on the full voice channel, FSK is the method universally used. For 2400 bps, DPSK (differentially encoded phase-shift keying) has become a worldwide standard. The standard rates for voiceband modems above 2400 bps are 4800, 7200, and 9600 bps. In this range, current modems use PSK, VSBSC-AM, QAM, or combinations of both PSK and AM.

Chapter 6

Multiplexing and Transmission Media

In this chapter the technique of multiplexing communications channels is described. This process involves the carrying, by one communication channel, of a number of smaller-capacity communication channels. The two principal methods of accomplishing this are *frequency-division multiplexing* (FDM) and *time-division multiplexing* (TDM).

The second part of this chapter is concerned with the various physical forms that constitute a communications channel. These are often referred to as transmission *media* or communication *links*. They include everything (wires, circuitry, antennas, etc.) between the transmitter and receiver; that is, between modems. Bear in mind that when communications services are leased from a common carrier, all of the required links are transparent to the user. It is only when a private system is being considered that the nature and type of link becomes important.

6.1. BACKGROUND OF MULTIPLEXING

In the early days of communications, separate transmission lines were required for each channel. This was first true for telegraph and then for voice channels on telephone lines, and eventually resulted in many wires being strung on poles, especially in urban areas. We can remember photographs of city streets

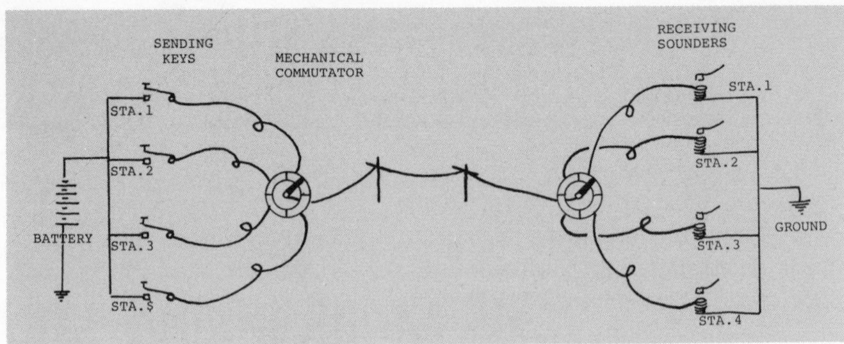

Figure 6.1. Multiplexing telegraph signals on a single wire.

virtually laced with telephone wires. These crowded conditions led to the ideas of *carrier telephony,* which is now known as multiplexing. The idea was to carry many communication channels over one transmission line, and thus reduce the number of lines required. It was first operational in 1918 and has now grown to systems carrying thousands of voice channels.

Multiplexing telegraph communications on a single wire can be visualized with the use of a mechanical armature which samples the input from several different sources and sends them one after another as shown in Figure 6.1. The main problem with this device is in maintaining synchronization at the receiving end. With the development of telephone usage, an early technique of multiplexing involved sending telegraph signals over telephone lines. This was called superposing, where a phantom circuit was derived by using the midpoint of transformer wires.[1] This gave the effect of an extra pair of wires without causing interference with telephone conversations. Modern telephone voice channels transmit a bandwidth of 300 to 3400 Hz. To transmit a number of these bandwidths simultaneously, some means must be used to keep them apart so that they do not interfere with each other. The two methods that are commonly used are called *frequency-division multiplexing* (FDM) or *time-division multiplexing* (TDM).

6.2. FREQUENCY-DIVISION MULTIPLEXING

Frequency-division multiplexing (FDM) is a technique of dividing a channel's frequency spectrum into a number of smaller frequency bands or subchannels as shown in Figure 6.2. The modulation process is used to translate these subchannels to their assigned frequency band from their baseband frequencies. The receiver, in turn, demodulates these subchannels back to their basebands. This process is illustrated in Figure 6.3.

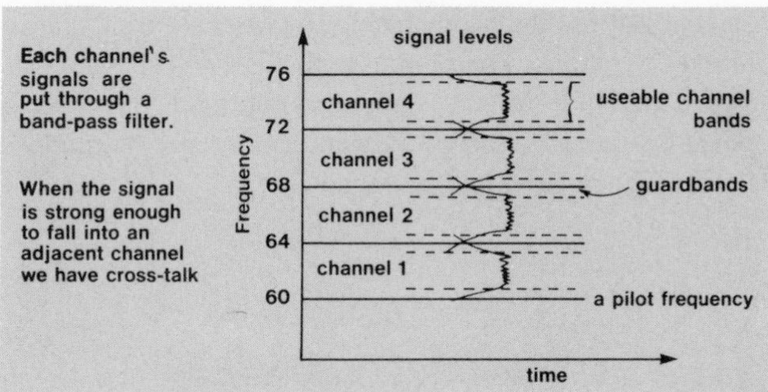

Figure 6.2. Frequency-division multiplexing assigns certain frequencies to each channel.

On of the early applications of FDM was for multiplexing a number of low-speed teleprinter devices on a leased voice channel. Typically an ASR-33 Teletype® operates at 110 baud requiring a frequency bandwidth of 170 Hz. The maximum available bandwidth of a leased voice channel is 3100 Hz, and thus it would be theoretically possible to divide this range into eighteen 170-Hz subchannels. As shown in Figure 6.2, the frequencies of the subchannels are separated by a *guard band*. These guard bands are required because the bandpass filters do not sharply attenuate the signal, but they gradually diminish the signal

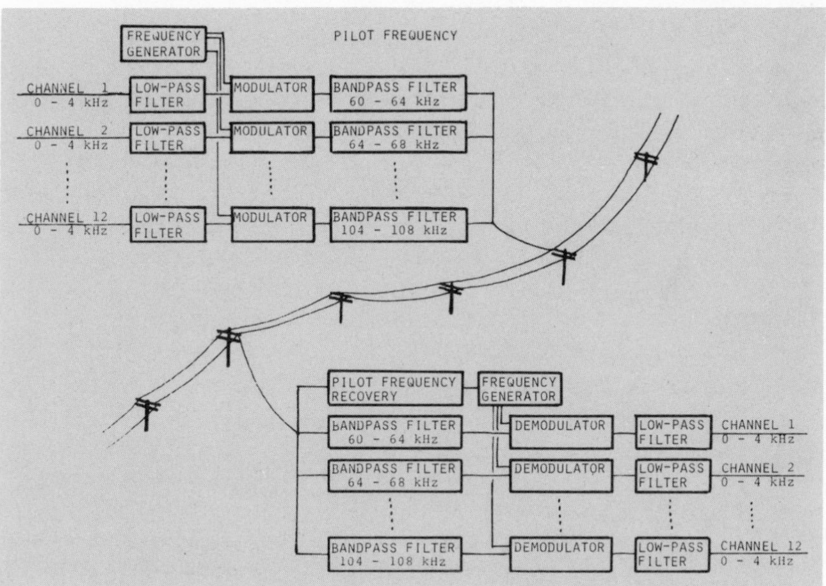

Figure 6.3. Frequency-division multiplexing of voice channels.

strength at the edges of the frequency band. Thus a guard band compensates for the nonideal filter operations. Therefore, the number of 110 baud channels generally permitted is twelve to fifteen. With higher-speed devices such as ASR-37 Teletypes, which operate at 150 baud, fewer channels can be multiplexed since each channel's frequency band will be larger.

6.3. FDM IN CARRIER SYSTEMS

Another use of FDM is in carrier systems. A number of voice channels are multiplexed in various ways for transmission over various communications media. In order to head off the proliferation of different FDM schemes, standards were established by the Consultative Committee on International Telephony and Telegraphy (CCITT). Not surprisingly, many of the FDM methods used by AT&T

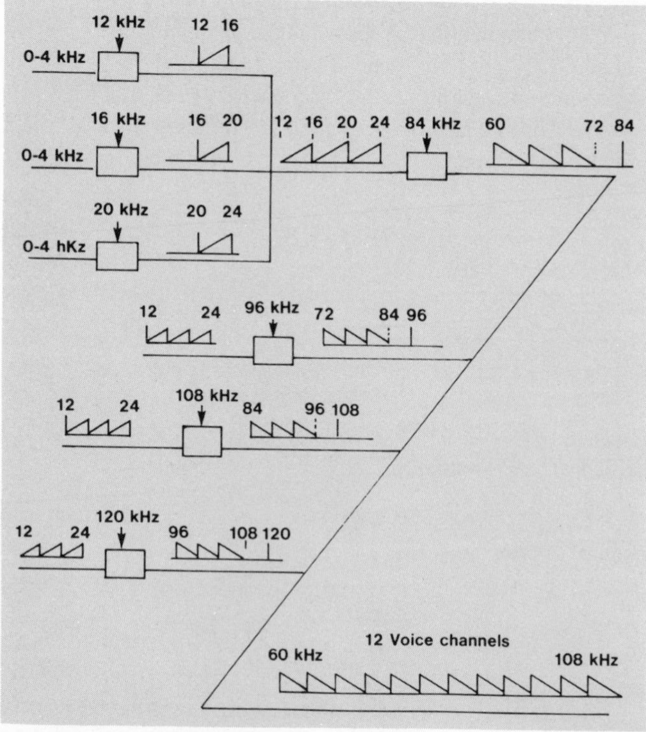

Figure 6.4. Formation of a standard CCITT channel group by two modulation steps using SSBSC-AM. While this method is more economical in terms of filter design, adding a modulation step adds noise to the system.

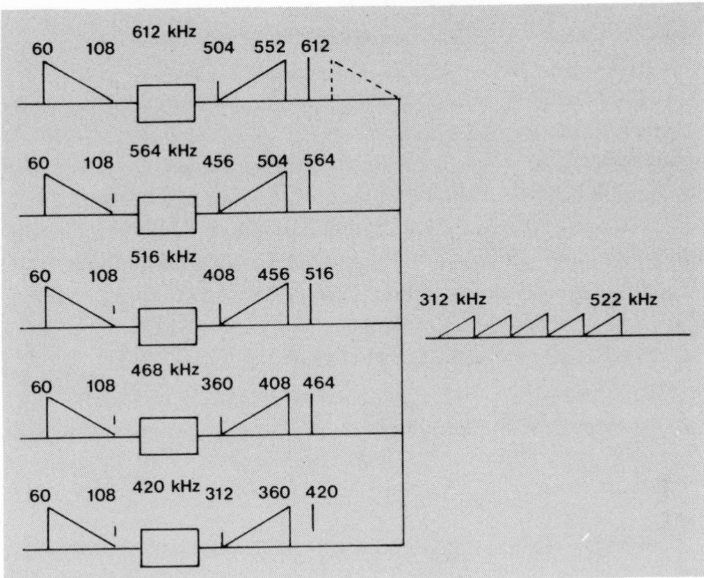

Figure 6.5. Formation of a standard CCITT channel supergroup from five channel groups carrying 60 voice channels using SSBSC-AM.

were adopted as standards. The standards are in fact recommendations for best combining the voice channels and for determining what the resulting multiplexed channel frequencies will be. The recommendations basically involve a system of groupings as follows:

- 12 voice channels make up a basic channel group
- 5 channel groups make up a basic supergroup
- 5 supergroups make up a 300 channel mastergroup, or
  10 supergroups make up a 600 channel mastergroup

Various numbers of mastergroups may be used to create either supermastergroups or jumbogroups.

The CCITT recommendations for the formation of the basic channel group is shown in Figure 6.4. Note that the method prescribes the frequencies to which each voice channel is to be translated, the modulation method (in this case SSBSC-AM), and which sideband will be retained. Figures 6.5 and 6.6 show the CCITT recommendations for the formation of the supergroup and the basic mastergroup using FDM. Figure 6.7 shows the FDM organization used by the Bell System in its carrier systems. A more detailed discussion may be found in References 2 and 3.

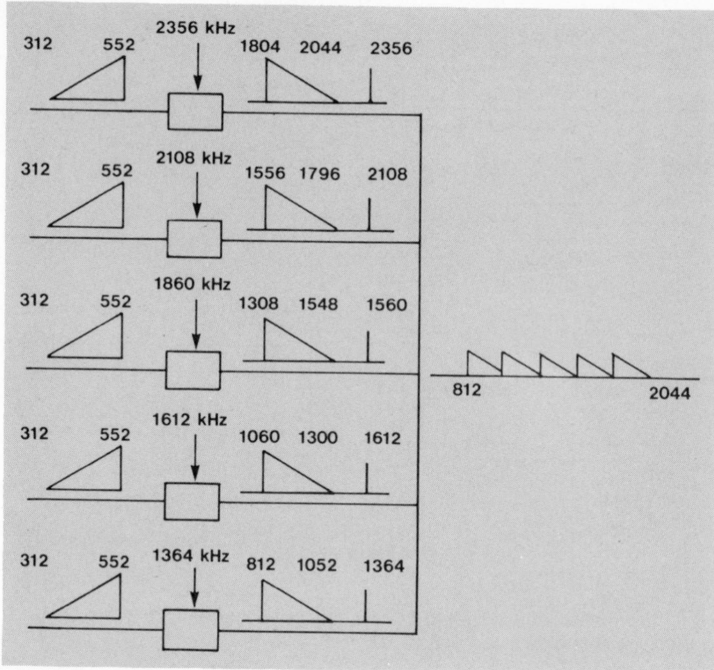

Figure 6.6. Formation of a standard CCITT channel basic mastergroup from five supergroups carrying 300 voice channels.

6.4. FDM APPLICATIONS

Current technology is progressing away from using frequency-division multiplexing in favor of time-division multiplexing techniques. The requirements of guardbands limit the maximum aggregate throughputs on leased voice grade channels to 2000 bps.

Applications where FDM is cost effective involve (1) the use of low-speed asynchronous terminals, (2) the use of FDM devices that also perform the modem functions, and (3) FDM devices that can drop or insert channels at intermediate points on multidropped lines. In this regard no distinction can be made from using separate leased lines except in the reduced channel costs.

6.5. TIME-DIVISION MULTIPLEXING

The technique of time-division multiplexing (TDM) involves interspersing several input signals, which are all bandlimited by lowpass filters, to the same bandwidth as the transmission channel. These input signals are sequentially sampled at the transmitter by a rotary switch, or *commutator* device. This is similar in concept to the mechanical commutator shown in Figure 6.1 for the telegraph system, but in modern devices this is all accomplished electronically. At the receiver a similar rotary switch, the decommutator, or *distributor*, separates the samples and distributes them to a bank of lowpass filters which in turn reconstruct the original messages. Synchronization of the distributor with the commutator is the most critical aspect of TDM systems. Figure 6.8 illustrates the TDM system for a number of voice channels.

The sampling switch must make one complete revolution in $S \leq 1/(2 \times$ channel bandwidth), getting one sample from each input signal. If the transmission channel is a 4-kHz bandwidth voice channel, then the commutator must make one revolution at least every 125 microseconds (μs), or 125×10^{-6} s. If there are M inputs, the time spacing for each input is S/M which is called a *frame*. Thus if there are 12 input signals to be modulated on a voice channel, then with TDM each input signal is sampled every 125 μs over a sample interval of 10.42 μs.

There are a number of varieties of TDM systems involving both pulsed and analog systems. Each input signal can provide a bit or character for interleaving, and the framing technique can be either fixed or variable. The input signals can

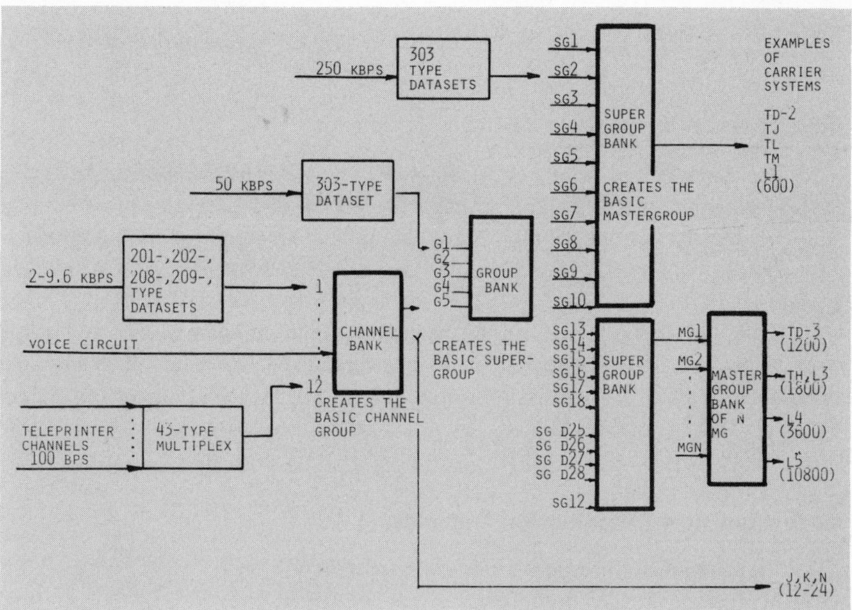

Figure 6.7. The frequency-division multiplexing hierarchy used by the Bell system. Note that the basic mastergroup is formed from ten supergroups.

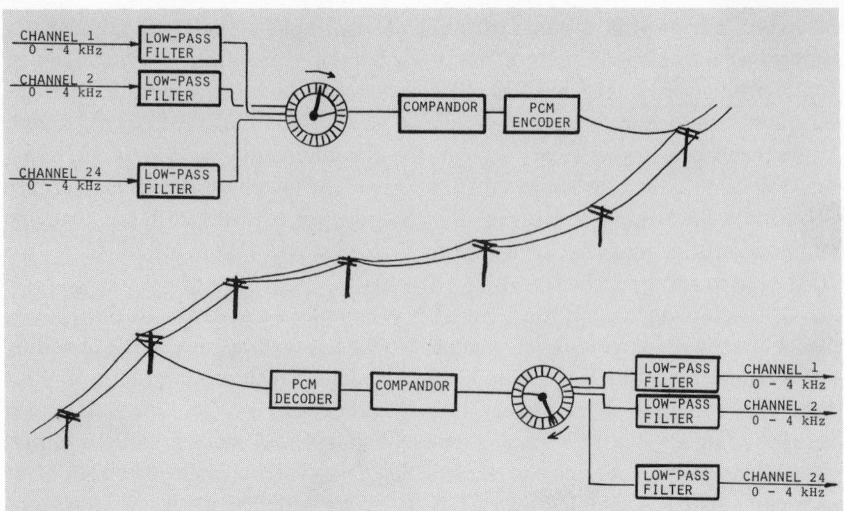

Figure 6.8. Time-division multiplexing illustrated by a simplified diagram. The sampling gates, which act like a commutator, are kept in synchronization by the frame bits in the message.

be converted to PAM, PDM, PPM, or PCM and transmitted with or without carrier modulation.

6.5.1. Asynchronous Time-Division Multiplexing

The fixed-frame approach is referred to as *asynchronous time-division multiplexing*. In this method a frame consists of one data element (either a bit or a character) from each input signal along with any required timing information. Each input signal always occupies the same frame whether there is any data or not.

Currently, these devices are incorporated into the modem design to provide subchannels of 1200, 2400, and 4800 bps for 4800, 7200, and 9600 bps line speeds. Since these devices use the entire bandwidth, they are more efficient than FDM devices. These devices are discussed in Reference 4.

6.5.2. Statistical Time-Division Multiplexing

The variable-frame approach is called statistical time-division multiplexing (STDM) (or statistical multiplexing).

In this approach, control information must be provided in addition to timing information to indicate whether a particular input channel signal is present. The advantage of this approach is that blank or null data need not be transmitted for those input signals devoid of data. In situations where data is being manually keyed in, the variable-frame approach offers the possibility of handling two to four times more input channels than with the synchronous time-division multiplexor.

These devices require buffers to hold the data from the input channels, elaborate addressing and control circuitry, and allowance for delays under heavily loaded conditions. Since the basic assumption is that each particular subchannel operates at a small fraction of the time, the statistical time-division multiplexor will not operate if all the channels were subjected to heavy traffic at one time. Much of the theoretical work relating to statistical multiplexing has been done by W. Chu.[5]

6.5.3. TDM Carrier Systems

One of the most common TDM carrier systems is the T1-carrier, whose transmission rate is 1,544,000 bps derived from 24 voice channels using pulse code modulation (PCM). There exists a TDM hierarchy involving multiplexed T1 lines. This is shown in Figure 6.9, with output lines T2 = 6.3 megabits/second (Mbps), T3 = 45 Mbps, and T4 = 274 Mbps. These signals are carried on twisted wire-pair cable, coaxial cable, or waveguides.

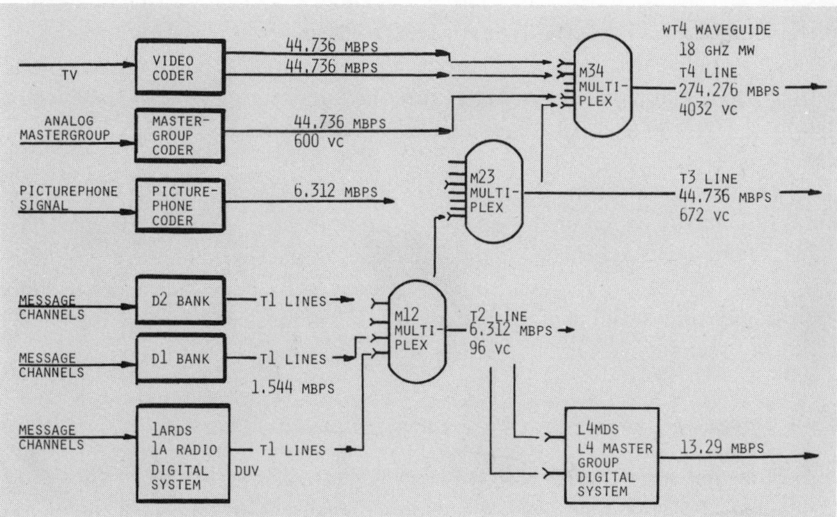

Figure 6.9. A time-division multiplexing hierarchy used by the Bell system.

6.6. COMPARISON OF THE TWO METHODS

FDM and TDM accomplish the same goals although their methods are entirely different. From a theoretical viewpoint, TDM has no advantage over FDM, but from a practical viewpoint TDM is superior to FDM in two respects.

First, TDM devices are simpler to construct. In TDM, bit multiplexing is less expensive while character multiplexing is more efficient. TDM synchronization is only slightly more demanding than suppressed carrier modulation FDM devices. FDM requires subcarrier, or intermediate-modulating, bandpass filters for each input signal, while TDM only requires the commutator and distributor.

Second, TDM is more channel efficient than FDM since TDM uses the entire channel bandwidth. For the transmission of digital data, the aggregate bit rate is approximately 2000 bps for FDM devices and 9600 bps for TDM devices. FDM requires guardbands to reduce interchannel crosstalk, and this in turn reduces the available channel bandwidth for data transmission.

Table 6.1 illustrates how low-speed devices may be multiplexed on voice channels. References 6–9 discuss some of the economics of multiplexed systems.

6.7. COMMUNICATION-CARRIER SYSTEMS

Communication links that are organized or arranged in a particular way by common carrier companies (i.e., the telephone companies) are known as *carrier systems* and are prefixed with some designation to indicate their arrangement (viz., J-carrier, L3-carrier, T1-carrier, etc.). These systems are multiplexed according to published standards of frequency allocations. They are available as off-the-shelf items from a number of manufacturers for private communication systems. The characteristics of a number of these carrier systems are given in Table 6.2.

As can be seen from Table 6.2, these carrier systems consist of different kinds of communication links—open-wire pairs, twisted wire-pair cable, coaxial cable, microwave radio relay, submarine cable, tropospheric scatter radio, high-frequency (HF) radio, communication satellites, waveguide, and more recently optical fiber cables. Some of the features of each of these will be described in the following sections. A general discussion may be found in Reference 10.

6.7.1. Open-Wire Pairs

From the early 1800s, bare wires strung between poles were used as live conductors. Poles with crossties suspending copper or copper-coated steel wires from glass insulators (known as open-wire pairs) carried the telegraph messages across the early American West and more recently carried telephone conversa-

Table 6.1. Low-Speed Devices Multiplexed on a Voice Channel

Standard terminal devices	Words per minute	Baud rate	Code used	Code bits	Asynchronous character length (bits)	Number of channels derived by TDM on a voice-grade line	
						2400 bps	4800 bps
TTY-28	100	75	Baudot	5	7.42	27	45
TTY-33/35	100	110	ASCII	8	11	27	45
IBM 1050/2740	148	134.5	6-bit transcode	6	9	18	27
TTY-37	150	150	ASCII	8	10	18	36

Table 6.2. A Summary of Different Carrier Systems

Name	Year in service	Modulation	Frequency range[a] (MHz)	Number of voice channels per circuit	Description	Total system: Number of circuits	Total system: Number of voice channels	Repeater spacing (miles)	System length (miles)
Open wire pairs									
A (Bell)	1918	SSBSC	0.005-0.025	4	BN-2-wire	16	64	—	—
B (Bell)	1920	SSBTC	0.006-0.024	3	EQV-4-wire	—	—	—	—
C (Bell)	1924	SSBSC	0.002-0.031	3	EQV-4-wire	16	48	160	2000
D (Bell)	1926	SSBSC	0.003-0.010	1	EQV-4-wire	—	—	—	—
E (Bell)	1928	SSBSC	0.005-0.150	1	VF-switch	—	—	—	—
G (Bell)	1936	DSBTC	0.008-0.012	1	2-wire	—	—	—	—
H (Bell)	1937	SSBSC	0.004-0.010	1	EQV-4-wire	—	—	—	—
CCITT		SSBSC	0.036-0.140	12	EQV-4-wire	—	313	50	1600
J (Bell)	1938	SSBSC	0.036-0.143	12		16	192	50	1500
ON		SSB	0.040-0.264	12		—	—	6	—
Paired cable									
K (Bell)	1938	SSBSC	0.012-0.060	12	Nonloaded	48	268	17	1500
CCITT		SSBSC	0.012-0.060	12	Subgroup A	—	—	19	1500
N1	1950	SSBSC	0.044-0.260	12		—	—	—	200
N2	1962	DSBTC	0.044-0.260	12		—	—	—	200
N3	1964	SSBSC	0.172-0.268	24		—	—	—	200
CCITT		SSBSC	0.012-0.204	48	Star or quad cables	—	—	—	—
Coaxial cable									
L-1	1941	SSBSC	0.060-2.79	600		6 + 2	1800	8	4000
L-3	1953	SSBSC	0.312-8.28	1860		18 + 2	16,740	4	4000
L-4	1967	VSB	0.564-17.55	3600	6-LMG	18 + 2	32,400	2	4000
L-5	1974	VSB	3.12-60.5	10,800	15-LMG	20 + 2	108,000	1	4000
CCITT		SSB	0.316-12.4	540	Plan 1A	—	—	3	1550

CCITT		SSB	0.312–12.4	420	Plan 1B	—	—	3	1550
CCITT		SSB	0.312–12.3		Plan 2	—	—	—	1550
Submarine cable									
SB (TAT-1)	1956	SSBSC	0.024–0.168	36		2	72	39	2500
SD (TAT-3)	1963	SSBSC	0.108–1.05	128		1	128	20	3500
SF (TAT-5)	1969	SSBSC	5.64–5.88	720		1	720	10	4000
SG (TAT-6)	1976	SSBSC		4000		1	4000	6	4000
Tropospheric scatter radio									
DMEW	1961	FDM/FM	0.4–2.0	240		2	480	—	—
EMT	1965	FDM/FM	0.4–2.0	120		2	240	—	—
DEW East	1962	FDM/FM	0.4–2.0	72		2	144	—	—
UR Spain	1962	FDM/FM	0.4–2.0	24		2	48	—	—
Microwave radio relay									
TJ	1958	FDM/FM	K	600	Short-haul	3 + 3	—	25	250
TL-1		FDM/FM	K	240	Short-haul	3 + 3	—	25	250
TL-2		FDM/FM	K	600	Short-haul	3 + 3	—	25	250
TM-1	1966	FDM/FM	C			4 + 4	—	25	250
TD-2	1948	FDM/FM	C	600		10 + 2	6000	29	4000
TD-3	1967	FDM/FM	C	1200		10 + 2	12,000	29	4000
TH-1	1961	FDM/FM	C	1860		6 + 2	14,880	29	4000
TH-3	1969	FDM/FM	C	1800		6 + 2	14,400	29	4000
TN-1	1974	FDM/FM	K	1800		10 + 2	10,800	29	1000
ARA6	1980	FDM/FM	C	6000		7	42,000	30	4000
Communication satellites									
INTELSAT I	1965	FDM/FM	C	240		2	240	—	—
INTELSAT II	1966	FDM/FM	C	240		1	240	—	—
INTELSAT III	1968	FDM/FM	C	1200		2	1200	—	—
INTELSAT IV	1970	FDM/FM	C	300		12	3600	—	—
INTELSAT IVA	1975	FDM/FM	C	300		40	6000	—	—
INTELSAT V		FDM/FM	K						

[a] Frequency range: C band includes frequencies from 3.7 to 6.8 GHz. K band includes frequencies from 10.95 to 20.2 GHz.

tions. By the 1920s the cities were becoming enmeshed in wire as shown in Figure 6.10. Today open-wire pairs have all but vanished from the city scene, but they occasionally can be seen in rural areas.

Open-wire pairs have attenuation coefficients of 0.04 to 0.1 dB/mile at 1 kHz. This means that amplifier repeaters are needed every forty to fifty miles for long-distance transmission. Perhaps the most serious disadvantage to open-wire pairs is the *crosstalk* distortion that occurs when there are many pairs strung on the poles. Crosstalk is the phenomenon of one wire picking up (i.e., listening to) the transmissions on adjacent wires.

The telephone companies organized these open-wire pair links as carrier systems complete with amplifiers to carry up to 12 voice telephone channels in a frequency-division multiplexed manner. The maximum frequency used was under 300 kHz.

6.7.2. Twisted Wire-Pair Cables

As the number of open-wire circuits strung on poles and rooftops in the large cities reached the saturation point, methods had to be found for compacting

Figure 6.10. A street scene in New York City before and after the advent of underground exchange cables. (Courtesy of Bell Labs.)

Figure 6.11. Twisted wire-pair cables. (Courtesy of Bell Laboratories Record 1978.)

the wires into overhead or underground cables. Initially the wires were placed in pipes and sealed against moisture with paraffin or asphaltum. The use of lead, heated to plasticity, extruded over a core of conductors with dry paper as insulation comprised the beginnings of the modern telephone cable.

Today the network of lines which interconnect approximately 125,000 communities in the United States includes over 40 million miles of wire on over 300,000 miles of route, with over 90% of the wires in cable and the remainder open wire. For the rest of the world the percentage of long distance furnished by cable ranges from nearly 100% in a few countries to a very low figure in less populated regions. Technological advances have made possible the increase in the number of wire pairs in a full-sized local cable from a maximum of 50 in 1888 to over 2000 today. Figure 6.11 shows a typical wire-pair cable.

If crosstalk was a problem in open-wire systems, then placing many wire pairs in close proximity should increase the crosstalk problem! In actuality, this problem was reduced by a simple artifice. A type of long-distance cable, common in the United States, uses conductors 36 mils (0.091 cm) in diameter and weighing 20 lbs per mile (No. 19 AWG gauge). In making this cable, two wires are first twisted together to form a pair, and then a quad is formed by twisting two pairs together. By alternating the direction of the twists in each pair, crosstalk is diminished to the point where it is not a problem.[11] In European toll cables, four conductors are usually twisted together to form a spiral four or a star quad. In either case the quads are grouped together and enclosed by a sheath of thin layers of aluminum and steel covered with polyethylene.

Typical wire-pair cable systems in the United States are the K-carrier and the N-carrier, which are designed to carry 12 voice channels over distances of 20–200 miles. As in an open wire system, wire-paired cable operates at frequencies under 300 kHz.

6.7.3. Coaxial Cable

As the frequencies increase, the flow of electric current in a metal conductor confines itself to a shallow zone on the surface, increasing the effective resistance of the wire. This phenomenon is known as the *skin effect,* and the depth in the metal to which the field penetrates is called the skin depth. It is possible to define a surface resistivity which is proportional to $(f/c^2s)^{1/2}$, where f is the frequency of the applied electromagnetic field, s is the bulk conductivity of the metal for steady currents, and c is the velocity of light.[12] The net effect of this relationship is to place a limit on how high a frequency can be transmitted over wire systems. Higher frequencies are desirable because large bandwidths can be used, thus increasing the capacity of the link.

To get around the problem of the skin effect, the coaxial cable was developed. This cable can be described as consisting of all ''skin'' with a center conductor, as seen in Figure 6.12. Coaxial cables can transmit at much higher frequencies than wire pairs. A coaxial cable consists of a copper tube forming the outer shield and a centrally supported smaller tube, rod, or wire. The center conductor is supported by some insulating material.

The major advantage of using coaxial cables is the reduction in channel noise and the elimination of crosstalk distortion. Furthermore, because higher frequencies may be used, many voice channels may be carried on a coaxial cable in a multiplexed mode. Coaxial cable systems have been devised to carry anywhere from 1800 to 10,800 simultaneous telephone conversations. Such systems are among the highest-density transmission media in common use today. The coaxial cable systems, when they are built by AT&T in the U.S., are known by the designation L-carrier system.[13] Table 6.2 summarizes the L-carrier systems.

The advantages of a coaxial cable system may be summarized as:

1. Huge capacity at low cost.

2. The self-shielding property of coaxial units prevents interference from external signals, allowing many units to be placed in a single cable sheath and permitting many cable routes to intersect at a common point.

3. Since cable loss is a smooth function of frequency, traffic capacity can be increased whenever new technology permits amplifiers with greater

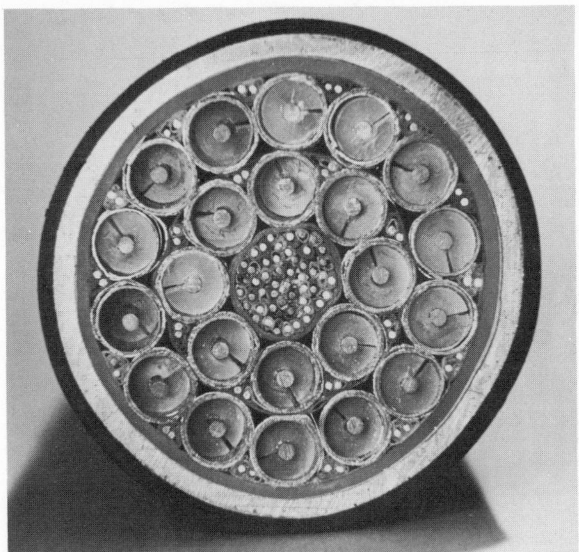

Figure 6.12. A cross section of a 22-tube coaxial cable. A repeater spacing of one mile permits 10,800 voice channels to be carried over one tube. (Courtesy of AT&T.)

bandwidth. Such increases in capacity are economically attractive since a large fraction of the cost of a system is in the installed cable, right of way, and buildings.

6.7.4. Microwave Systems

The radio counterpart of the coaxial cable system is the microwave relay system, which carries thousands of voice channels over long distances. Since microwave radio operates at high frequencies, the signals follow a straight line or "line-of-sight" path. This means that the transmitter can use a parabolic antenna to "aim" its signal in the direction of a similar antenna at the receiver. These antennas have different shapes as seen in Figure 6.13, but they are all capable of being "aimed" or pointed in a particular direction.

Microwave radio operates in the frequency range of 1.7 GHz to 15 GHz (1 gigahertz = 10^9 Hz). At these frequencies systems are provided with sufficient bandwidth to carry from 2400 to 2700 voice channels or one television channel. Microwave systems constructed by AT&T have the designations TD-, TL-, and TH-carrier systems, as indicated in Table 6.2. In these systems, the channels are first frequency-division multiplexed (FDM) using SSBSC-AM modulation for the channel frequency translations. Then, this FDM signal is transmitted using frequency modulation (FM) in the GHz band.

Figure 6.13. A microwave radio relay station. (Courtesy of AT&T.)

A microwave signal suffers the following distortions:

a. Attenuation or absorption by solid objects such as earth and by rain, fog, snow, etc.
b. Reflection from flat conductive surfaces such as water or metal buildings.
c. Diffraction by solid objects and refraction by the atmosphere.

A typical system consists of antenna towers (50–200 feet high) spaced approximately 20–30 miles apart which are referred to as *hops*. The height is needed to compensate for the earth's curvature. At the site of each tower, there is a *radiolink repeater*. This can be either a regenerative repeater or an amplifier. Using a regenerative repeater, the signal is fully demodulated to its baseband, at which time channels may be added or dropped. The signal is then used to modulate the transmitter across the next hop. If an amplifier is used, the signal is simply amplified and transmitted to the next hop.

The growth of microwave systems both for common carrier and private communication system uses is shown in Tables 6.3 and 6.4. Additional discussions of microwave systems can be found in References 14–16.

Table 6.3. Industrial Microwave Market (12)

	Market (millions of dollars)				
	1976	1977	1978	1979	1980
Terrestrial communications (microwave radios)					
Specialized common carrier	5.6	6.5	6.7	8.4	9.8
Industrial/private communications	33.4	35.0	36.1	37.6	39.0
CATV	10.0	8.9	7.8	6.8	6.8
Independent telcos	26.7	26.8	31.2	33.3	35.7
Bell Telcos—non-W.E.[a] purchases	16.0	17.3	18.6	19.9	21.3
Total non-W.E. microwave market	91.7	94.5	100.4	106.0	112.6
W.E. sales to Bell Telcos	90.8	97.9	105.6	113.0	120.9
Total	182.5	192.4	206.0	219.0	239.5
Microwave equipment used in satellite communications systems					
INTELSAT	10.0	8.0	8.0	8.0	8.0
US DOMSAT	18.0	15.0	15.0	12.0	10.0
MARISAT	8.0	8.0	10.0	10.0	10.0
Other nation's earth stations	30.0	32.0	35.0	35.0	40.0
Total	66.0	63.0	68.0	65.0	68.0
Microwave equipment in satellites	24.0	20.0	20.0	20.0	16.0
Total	90.0	83.0	88.0	85.0	84.0

[a]W.E. = Western Electric.

Table 6.4. Number of Microwave Sites Constructed[12]

	1976	1977	1978	1979	1980
Specialized common carrier	100	80	120	150	175
Industrial private systems	880	920	950	990	1025
CATV	450	400	350	300	250
Independent telcos	445	480	520	555	595
Bell telcos	1780	1920	2070	2215	2370
Misc. (CCTV, MDS)	55	45	45	45	45
Total	3710	3845	4055	4255	4460

6.7.5. Submarine Cable

Extremely reliable and secure communications spanning large bodies of water could be achieved by using submarine cable. The first submarine cable used for telegraph transmission was laid across the Atlantic Ocean in 1858 and had a spectacular but short life. Because the cable did not have any repeaters, distortion was a severe problem. Messages of less than 100 words took as long as sixteen hours to transmit. This first cable lasted but two weeks when its insulation failed and it went dead forever.

Submarine cable is constructed to withstand the high pressures of deep waters. Typically the conductor is made of copper, stranded or having a central wire surrounded by spirally wound strips. The insulation is molded over this. Then continuous inductance loading is provided in the form of a thin ribbon or thread of highly permeable nickel-iron alloy wound around the conductor. Then layers of brass tape, more insulation, and armor sheathing are used. In areas where there is much ocean fishing activity, extra armor is used, so that these cables may weigh as much as 30 tons per nautical mile.[17]

In modern submarine cable systems, repeaters are used to increase the number of voice channels that can be carried. These are constructed with a high degree of reliability. Figure 6.14 shows such a repeater.

In spite of the spectacular advances made by other forms of communication links, the submarine cable is not obsolete. In fact, in October 1975, a French cable ship began laying TAT-6, the largest capacity telecommunications cable ever to span the Atlantic Ocean (from Green Hill, Rhode Island, to St. Hillaire de Riez, France, a distance of 3402 nautical miles). The entire cable system, called TAT-6, is owned by an extraordinary number of international partners including AT&T, ITT World Communications, RCA Global Communications, Western Union International, and the telecommunications administrations of sixteen European countries.[18]

Table 6.5 shows some of the transatlantic submarine cable systems in exis-

Figure 6.14. A repeater for a submarine cable has to withstand high pressures and provide long reliable service. (Courtesy of AT&T.)

tence. There were some 140 separate cable systems in the world in 1975. Submarine cables are continuing to be installed for two major reasons: (1) they provide an alternate or diverse circuit path for intercontinental communications, thereby insuring the availability of circuits, and (2) submarine cable circuits are an inexpensive way to provide secure communications. During the period from 1965 to 1973 the number of total worldwide cable circuits increased from 2,000 to over 18,000.[19] This is expected to increase to over 40,000 by 1985.[20]

6.7.6. Radio Systems

Two kinds of radio transmission systems are often used in communication systems: high-frequency radio and tropospheric scatter radio.

Table 6.5. Submarine Cable-Communication System

	TAT-1	TAT-3	TAT-5	TAT-6
Date installed	1956	1963	1969	1976
Capacity (voice channels)	48	128	845	4000
Repeater spacing	38.7	20	10	5.1
Top frequency	164 kHz	1.1 MHz	5.9 MHz	30 MHz
Distance (miles)	2200	3500	4000	3400

High-frequency radio, or HF, is radiofrequency transmission in the 3 to 30 MHz frequency range that has certain propagation characteristics suitable for long-distance transmission. It is primarily used for short-wave, worldwide broadcasting. The HF signal is characterized by a skywave component and a groundwave component. The groundwave follows the surface of the earth and can provide useful communications up to 400 miles (640 km)—particularly over bodies of water. The skywave component can provide reliable transmissions (90% path reliability) at distances up to 4000 miles (6400 km).

HF radio using skywave transmission depends upon reflection from the ionospheric layer of ionized gas above the earth. The signal depends upon the frequency, and the reliability varies with time of day, geography, season, and the sunspot cycle.

Tropospheric scatter is a method of transmitting ultrahigh-frequency (UHF) signals beyond the line-of-sight or "over-the-horizon" by utilizing the refraction and reflection phenomena in a section of the atmosphere called the troposphere, which exists from sea level up to a height of 35,000 feet (11 km) (Reference 3, p. 264). UHF signals are scattered in a way that gives 99.9% or better signal reliability on hops up to 400 miles (640 km). By operating a number of hops in tandem distances of thousands of miles may be covered. A tropospheric scatter system uses parabolic type antennas similar to a microwave radio link. These systems cost more than a comparable microwave radio system.

Tropospheric scatter is used for communications to inaccessible sites. The drilling platforms in the North Sea located over 110 miles from nearest land are examples of such inaccessible sites.[21] Submarine cable was too expensive. The distance was too great for line-of-sight microwave radio. HF radio was considered inadequate—a sufficient number of circuits could not be obtained because of congestion. Thus a tropospheric scatter system was developed to carry 24 voice channels, allowing for data to be transmitted at 2400 bits per second over these voice channels at a maximum error rate of one bit in 10^5. Figure 6.15 shows how the system was implemented using a radiated signal in the 2.5 GHz band.

6.7.7. Communication Satellites

The use of satellites for communication purposes was considered one of the most spectacular events in the growth of communications technology of the early 1970s. As early as 1945, British electronics engineer (and science fiction writer) Arthur Clarke had suggested that if a satellite circled the world at 22,300 miles above the equator, it would take exactly 24 hours to complete one orbit. Said Clarke: "It would remain fixed in the sky of a whole hemisphere and, unlike other heavenly bodies, it would neither rise nor set." This idea was to wait but 18 years for technology to catch up with it.

The age of the satellite opened with the launching of the first *Sputnik* in

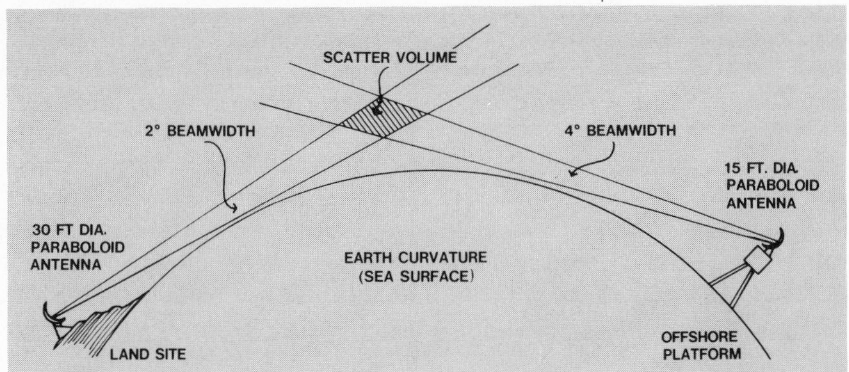

Figure 6.15. Tropospheric-scatter radio systems have a high degree of reliability for communications to isolated areas such as an offshore oil platform in the North Sea.

1957 by the Russians. *Score,* the first satellite to be used for voice communications, was launched by the United States Air Force on December 18, 1958. The satellite was equipped to transmit prerecorded messages conveying Christmas greetings to the world from President Eisenhower, upon receipt of certain signals. Score lasted only twelve days before its batteries became too weak for further use. A next significant step was project "moonbounce" in which microwave radio signals carrying live voice transmissions were bounced off the moon. These signals were transmitted and received intelligibly between scientists at the Bell Telephone Laboratories in Holmdel, New Jersey, and the Jet Propulsion Laboratories in Goldstone, California. The moon was used as a passive reflector some 250,000 miles distant. The transmission delay was about six seconds.

The Bell System's important role in satellite communications began on August 12, 1960, when a Thor-Delta missile launched Echo I, an inflated ten-story aluminized balloon, into an orbit about 1000 miles above the earth's surface. This was a prelude to the Bell System's historic Telstar satellites. With these it was proven that a broadband communications satellite could transmit telephone messages, data, and even television. On July 10, 1962, Telstar I was put into an elliptical orbit (apogee: 3531 miles, perigee: 592 miles). From that time the number of satellite launching increased greatly.

The launching of Syncom II in 1963 was significant in that it was the first geostationary satellite, making Clarke's prophetic words a reality. Figure 6.16 depicts the sequence of events for putting a geostationary satellite into orbit. Communication satellites are conceptually nothing more than microwave relay stations in the sky with two hops. The signal suffers a loss of almost 200 dB as it is radiated to and from the antennas.[22]

To effectively use communications satellites, multiple access is an oper-

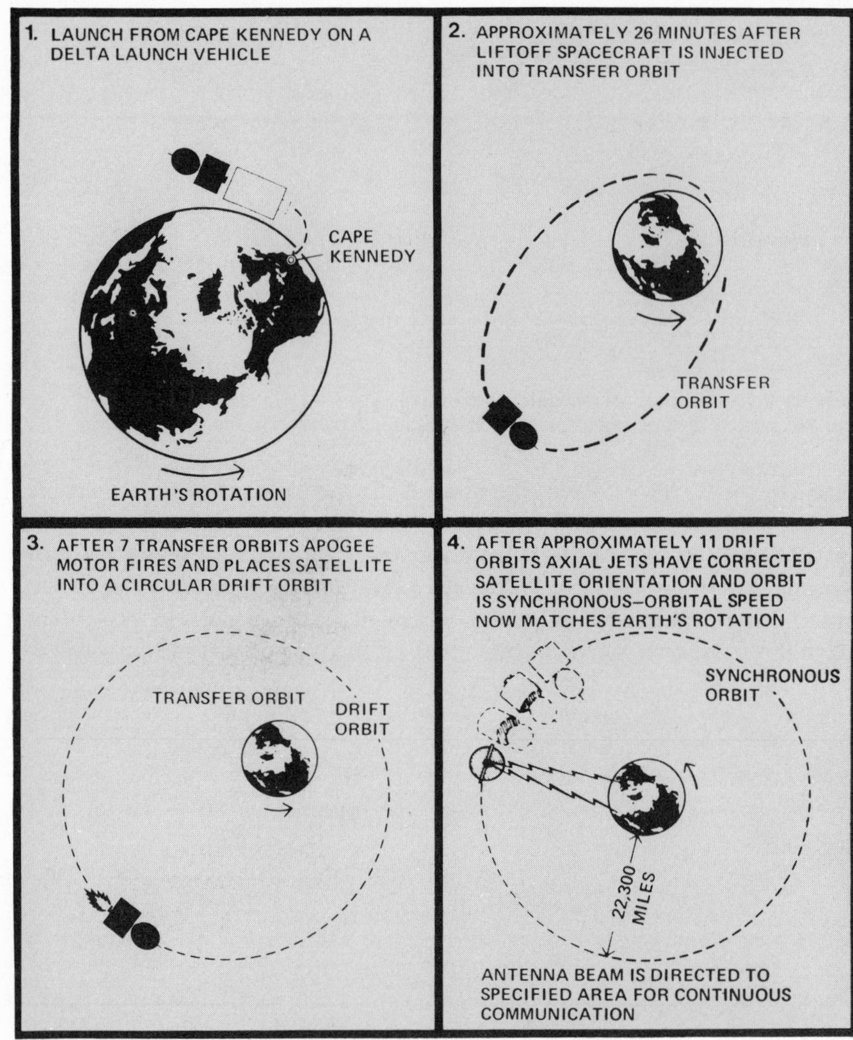

Figure 6.16. Putting a geostationary communications satellite into orbit. (From *Communication News,* Oct. 1973, reprinted with permission.)

ational requirement. Multiple access refers to the techniques which allow more than two earth stations to have simultaneous two-way (FDX) communications via one satellite. There are three basic multiple access (MA) techniques: frequency division (FDMA), time division (TDMA), and code division (CDMA). In frequency-division multiple access, the satellite frequency bandwidth is divided into a number of discrete frequency channels. Each earth station can use one or more channels. In time-division multiple access, an interval of the satellite time domain, called a frame period, is divided into a number of discrete time slots. Each earth station can use one or more time slots. In code-division multiple access each earth station has common usage of the full satellite bandwidth and time, but must use a coded waveform different from other earth stations.

Scheduling of multiple access can be accomplished in several ways: preassignment, time assignment, or demand assignment of the satellite channels.

Preassignment. Satellite channels are assigned permanently between the earth stations. The major drawback is that some channels become underutilized while at the same time adjacent channels may be at full capacity. Such situations occur during peak-hour traffic at different time zones on the earth's surface. Preassignment is suitable for heavy traffic earth stations with few destination points.

Time assignment. Satellite channels are assigned for various earth stations according to fixed time schedules based upon expected traffic patterns. This method somewhat alleviates the idle channel situation.

Demand assignment. Satellite channels are instantaneously assigned between two earth stations on demand based upon the actual traffic as it occurs. Studies have shown that this method uses from 50 to 90 percent fewer channels than the two previous methods, given the same total traffic. Demand assignment is suitable for earth stations having light traffic but serving many destinations.

Figure 6.17 shows the various domestic communication satellites that are in orbit over the Western Hemisphere. Figure 6.18 shows an RCA SATCOM II satellite in orbit. Power is produced from the two panels of silicon solar cells which are continuously pointed at the sun. The antennas are capable of "spot" beam transmission to a small region or of "broad" beam transmission to a wide geographic area on the earth's surface.

In the 1980s Western Union will launch a series of satellites known as Tracking and Data Relay Satellite System (TDRSS) to provide both commercial services and NASA (National Aeronautics and Space Administration) services. This satellite, shown in Figure 6.19, contains many different kinds of antennas covering different frequency bands. It is being built to handle a large amount of traffic. Four TDRSS satellites are planned (see Figure 6.20) to provide data relay services for up to 32 spacecraft as well as the ground stations. The Western Union service will contain 12 transponders as well as a 10^9-bps satellite-switched TDMA (time division multiple access) capability for voice video and data transmission.

Also in the 1980s the Satellite Business Systems (SBS), a joint venture of Aetna Life and Casualty, COMSAT General, and IBM Corporations, plans to offer a variety of satellite communication services. Earth stations will interface with interconnecting facilities to customer-provided, private branch exchanges (PBXs), foreign exchange (FX) lines, data terminals, and other equipment.

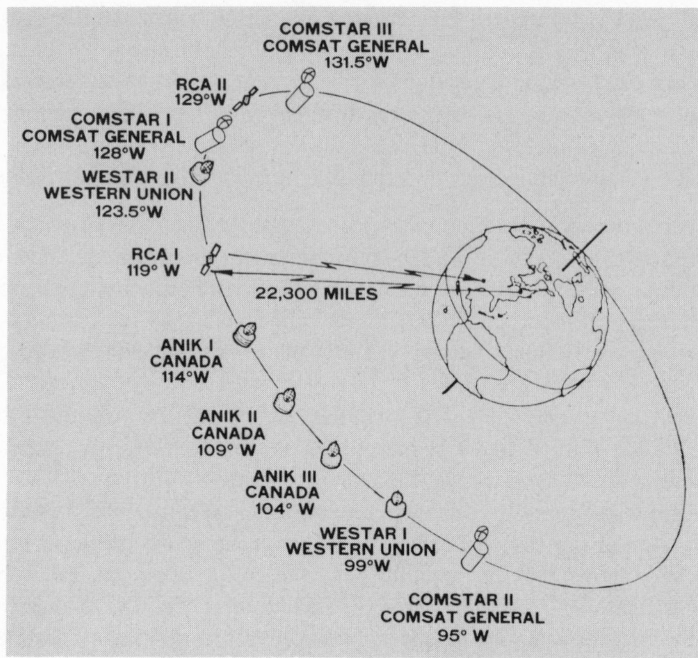

Figure 6.17. Communication satellites in orbit over the North American continent.

Figure 6.18. An artist's conception of the RCA SATCOM II satellite in orbit over the earth. (Courtesy of RCA American Communications.)

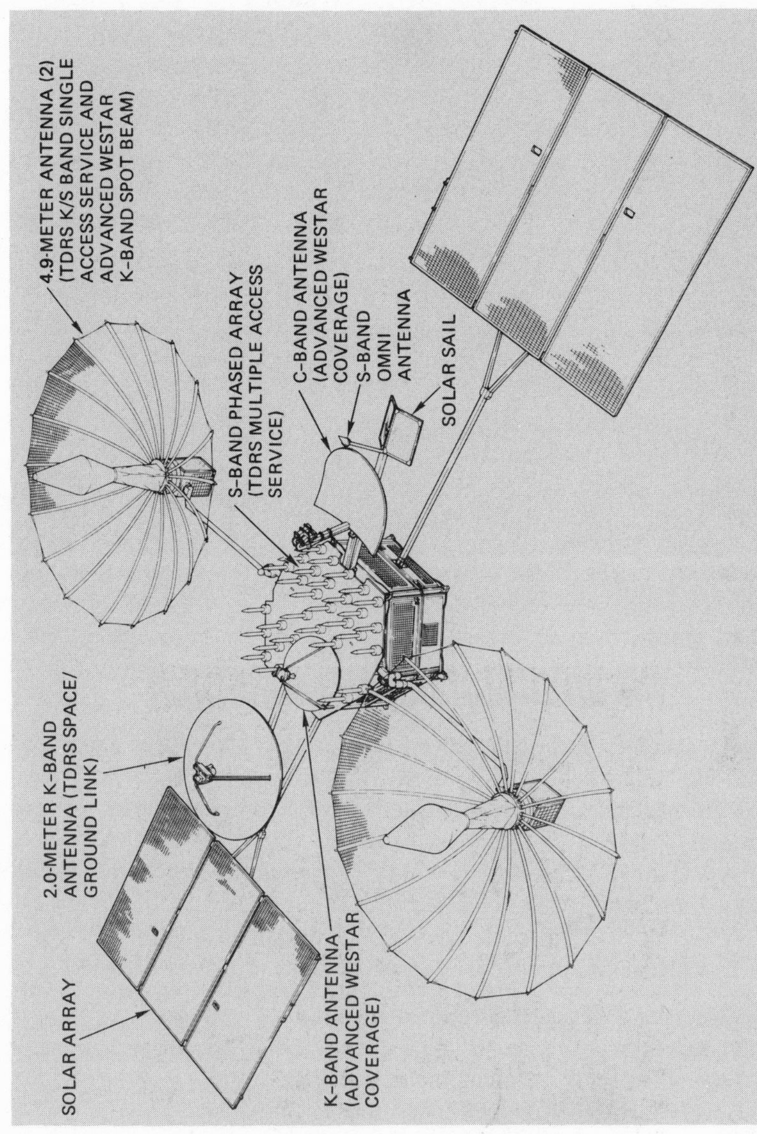

Figure 6.19. Tracking and Data Relay Satellite System (TDRSS) and Advanced Westar shared satellite is being developed by Western Union for NASA and is planned to be operational in the 1980s. (Courtesy of Western Union.)

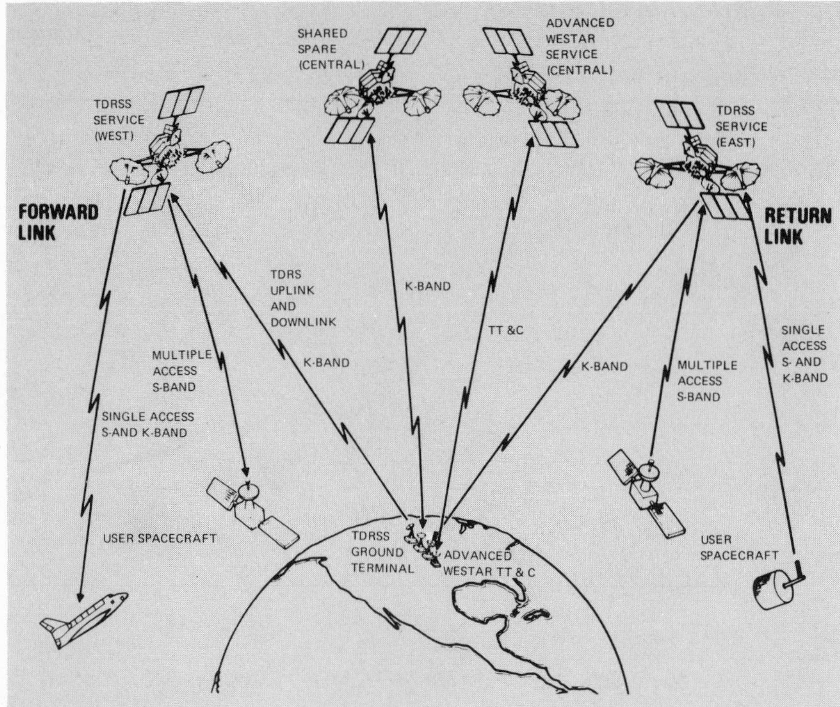

Figure 6.20. TDRSS/Advanced Westar Satellite system is planned for the 1980s. (Courtesy of Western Union.)

These earth stations can be situated on the customer's premises and may be connected via inplant cabling. Locations which are remote from earth stations will be interconnected via conventional terrestrial facilities available from common carriers.

Voice and other analog signals will be converted to a digital format at the originating earth station and converted back to analog at the receiving earth station. A variety of digital data rates from 2.4 kbps to 6.312 Mbps will be offered. It is planned to provide the following kinds of network services:

1. Voice and data conference arrangements
2. Multipoint distribution of digital data including document distribution
3. Teleconferencing including multipoint video
4. Hot-line and other priority connecting features
5. Network access control features

The satellite antennas will provide shaped beams to cover either the entire continental United States, most of the central U.S., or the eastern U.S., as three regions. The greatest benefits of using SBS will be for those customers that generate communications traffic at a number of locations geographically dispersed throughout the United States and whose requirements include the need for high-speed transmission services. The SBS system will provide direct access to a fully switched wideband communications network with minimum dependence on terrestrial facilities by utilizing small earth stations operating at 12 and 14 GHz located on the customer's premises close to his major traffic nodes.

A large nationwide corporation may require many earth stations to support its communications needs. By the use of demand assignment, the satellite acts as a concentrator that allows a large group of relatively low-intensity traffic earth stations to attain the trunk usage normally achieved with high-traffic points. Thus, all earth station locations benefit from traffic engineering advantages normally found on high-density toll-trunk routes. In terrestrial point-to-point communications systems, unused capacity on West Coast channels cannot be used in meeting East Coast traffic demand. By implementing continuous real-time reassignment of satellite capacity to meet the varying needs of the user, the SBS satellite networks can apply such capacity to the instantaneous traffic demands of that user without respect to location.

6.7.8. Waveguides

It is not practical to transmit microwaves over appreciable distances by means of open wires, mainly because of the loss of energy through radiation. A coaxial cable is used because it is self-shielded. However, as the frequency increases the losses also increase. These losses consist of the Joule (heat) loss in the inner and outer conductors and, possibly, dielectric leakage and reflection losses introduced by the supporting structure of the inner conductor. A detailed study of the losses in a coaxial cable reveals that the loss in the outer conductor is usually small in comparison to the others. Thus the possibility of transmitting waves of high frequencies within hollow tubes—reducing cost, weight, and losses—was considered at an early date in the application of electric waves.

It was not appreciated that metallic pipes could be used as a means of transmitting electric waves until 1933 when several patents were filed by G. C. Southworth of Bell Telephone Laboratories.

The principle of operation of a hollow waveguide is similar to that of acoustical speaking tubes in that the waves are confined within the walls of the tube by reflections from the smooth surfaces of conductors like copper, silver, or gold. Greater amounts of power can be transmitted with less loss than with coaxial cables. Transmissions must be limited to the microwave range, since one of the dimensions of any guide must be greater than one-half the wavelength. For example, microwaves cannot be used for power transmission since 60 Hz requires a waveguide dimension greater than 1550 miles.

6.7.9. Optical Fiber Systems

One of the more remarkable technological developments has been the rapid introduction of optical fiber (lightwave fiber) systems into telecommunication networks.[23,24] These systems consist of extremely small-diameter glass fibers which carry pulsed modulated light. The breakthrough came with the development of a process for making an ultrahigh purity glass by Corning Glass Works. Ordinary glass rods could not be used because they severely attenuate light passing through. For example, if light were shone into the end of a glass rod, then the attenuation could be seen as light escaping through the walls when viewed perpendicularly to the axis of the rod. Signal attenuation was reduced from 2 dB/m to 2 dB/km in the pure glass fibers. Lasers operating in a pulsed mode are used as the light source.

Techniques were developed to clad the fiber in a low-refractive resin material and encase several of these fibers in a practical cable. The cable contained 24 optical fibers, as shown in Figure 6.21, in a half-inch diameter. Each fiber carried 672 voice channels at a rate of 44.7 Mbps. The transmitter module used either a solid-state laser or LED (light-emitting diode). The receiver contained a tiny photodetector, known as an avalanche diode, that converts light pulses into electrical signals. These optical fiber systems were field tested by Bell Telephone Labs in Atlanta and Chicago in 1976 carrying voice, data, and video signals. These field tests demonstrated that the optical fiber transmission systems had a high degree of reliability with an outage of about 30 seconds per year. The percentage of one-second intervals that were error-free was 99.999% for digital

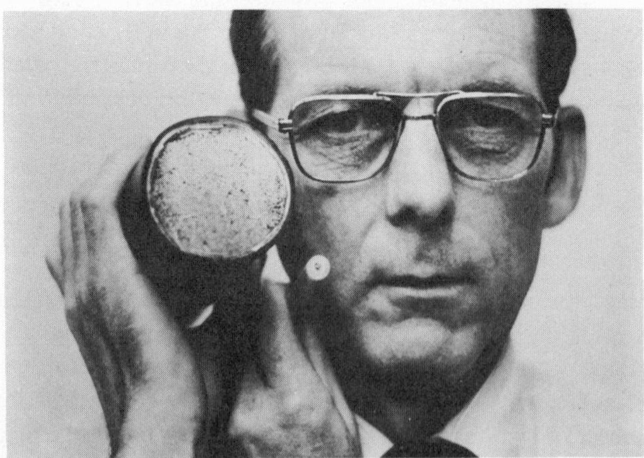

Figure 6.21. The half-inch-diameter lightguide cable on the right will carry over 15,000 voice channels, more than seven times the number carried by the conventional twisted wire-pair cable on the left. (Courtesy of AT&T.)

Table 6.6. Comparison of Some Existing or Proposed Metallic Cable and Possible Optical Fiber Digital Systems

System capacity		Metallic cable systems			Optical fiber systems		
Voice channels	Mbps	Cable type	Repeater spacing (km)	Cost per circuit (thousands of dollars)[a]	Fiber type	Repeater spacing (km)	Cost per circuit (thousands of dollars)[a]
30	2.048	Voice frequency	2	87	Step index	12–16	130
120	8.448	Screened pair 0.6–0.9 mm	3–4	41	Graded index	10–14	39
480	34.304	2.8 mm coax	2	23	Graded index	10–12	16
1920	140	4.4 mm coax	2	11	Graded mono or graded index	8–10	4.0
7680	560	9.5 mm coax	1.6–2	6	Mono mode	5–6	1.7

[a] Based on costs per voice-circuit-kilometer on routes of 50–100 km, ignoring multiplex equipment costs.

data communications. The major problem to be solved was splicing these cables in the field. This was accomplished by a mass splice technique that permitted joining all fibers to a tolerance of 0.0001 inches with no handling of individual fibers. The average signal loss was found to be about 0.5 decibels per splice, a result considered to be highly encouraging.

A single fiber can provide transmission bandwidths up to 20 GHz, thus providing the capability of carrying hundreds of thousands of simultaneous voice channels. Some of the other advantages of optical fiber cables over metallic cables are:

1. Small size and weight with a high strength
2. Low material cost—ordinary sand is the raw material
3. Large bandwidth with a small attenuation loss
4. Immunity to electromagnetic interference
5. Electrical isolation since glass is a nonconductor
6. Increased security of transmission due to difficulty of signal detection or interruption

Table 6.6 shows a comparison of some existing metallic cables and possible optical fiber digital systems. The relative costs between the two systems certainly shows great promise for optical fiber technology.

Chapter 7

The Carrier Telephone Plant

In this chapter, the facilities of the common-carrier system for voice communications are described. In the evolution of data communications, it was the adaptation of the public telephone network for transmission of digital data that molded the destiny of developments to come, as shall be described in Chapter 9.

When Samuel Morse transmitted his message "What hath God wrought" in 1844, introducing the era of long-distance communications, a historical chain of events was set in motion that led to the development of the Western Union Telegraph Company. Alexander Graham Bell, demonstrating the voice telephone in 1876, set in motion a similar chain of events leading to the Bell Telephone System of today. There were occasional excursions by the telephone and telegraph companies into each other's field, but voice telephony essentially remained the domain of the telephone companies and the telegraph system was Western Union's domain.

Under government regulation, the telephone system in the United States grew to be the finest message-switching facility in the world. Today, the telephone permeates every aspect of American social life, commerce, and industry. Thus when computer technology had advanced to the stage of teleprocessing, the choice was either to create new digital facilities or use the existing analog facilities of the telephone system. Economically, the path of least resistance favored the latter choice. It was this adaptation of a system designed for analog voice communications to digital data communications that created a number of difficulties. An understanding of these obstacles will give the reader a better working knowledge of the limitations of analog data communications and precisely how such facilities fit in the design of modern communications systems.

First, the nomenclature must be learned. A number of different terms (and acronyms) are used to describe essentially the same thing. By concatenating these words in various combinations, one can derive his own "buzz-word" lexicon. Some of the more common terms are given in Table 7.1.

7.1. TELEPHONE COMPANY (TELCO) ORGANIZATIONS

The largest telephone company in the world is the Bell System. It consists of several major organizations: American Telephone and Telegraph (AT&T), which operates the interstate network through its Long Lines Department; Western Electric Corporation, which is the manufacturing arm of the communications system; Bell Telephone Laboratories, the research and development (R&D) arm

Table 7.1. Some Common Telephone System Terms

Telco(s)	An acronym for the telephone company or companies; more specifically the Bell System, AT&T, GT&E, and members of the USITA. This is explained in more detail below.
Carrier	Refers to the company whose operations are regulated by the Federal Communications Commission.
Plant	Refers to the applicable telephone system equipment.
Switched	Describes the operation of establishing a connection through the dialing process
DDD	Direct distance dialing, a service of AT&T for establishing calls on its network. Also referred to as long-distance calling.
Public switched network	The telephone system in the United States.
Dial network	The telephone system in the United States.
Telephone	The device used for making voice telephone calls. It consists of an ear and mouth piece (E&M) and a dialing mechanism. It also can be referred to as a handset.
Sidetone	The talker's own speech is fed back to his ear through the handset as well as being transmitted through the system.
Rotary dial	The mechanism on a telephone for placing a call that operates in a rotary fashion, transmitting the dialed digits as sequences of pulses.
Touch-tone®	The mechanism on a telephone for placing a call that operates by pushbutton, transmitting pairs of tone signals.
Dataphone®	A service offered by AT&T for the transmission of digital data, usually over analog facilities.

of the system; and the Bell Operating Companies, each offering regional telephone and other communications services. Examples are Southwest Bell, Southern Bell, Ohio Bell, New York Bell, etc.

The next largest domestic organization is General Telephone and Electronic (GT&E), which primarily operates telephone and communications systems in the western United States and Florida. GT&E's research and manufacturing functions are performed by GTE Labs, the Lenkurt Electric Company, and the Automatic Electric Company.

The remainder of the telephone system is handled by regional area companies that are members of the United States Independent Telephone Association (USITA). There are approximately 2000 such companies.

7.2. INTERNATIONAL ORGANIZATIONS

These companies, sometimes known as International Record Carriers (IRC), provide intercontinental communications services. The major organizations are:

- ITT World Communications—a subsidiary of International Telephone and Telegraph (ITT) Co.
- RCA Global Communications—a subsidiary of Radio Corporation of America (RCA)
- Western Union International (WUI)—a subsidiary of Western Union
- TRT Telecommunications—this was formerly known as Tropical Radio and Telegraph Corp. (TRT)
- Cable & Wireless Ltd.—a British organization

These organizations provide voice, telegraph, and, more recently, data communications between continents. One of their principal functions is to provide compatibility between domestic and foreign communications formats.

7.3. FOREIGN TELECOMMUNICATIONS ORGANIZATIONS

In foreign countries telecommunications are monopoly operations that exist in one of three forms: a department of the government, a statutory corporation or state-trading corporation, or an incorporated, limited liability company.[1]

The government department is usually known as the Postal, Telegraph, and Telephones, or by some similar name. France, Germany, Switzerland, Holland, and all Eastern European countries have this type of organization, with the head of the organization being some minister of government.

The statutory corporation is presumably nongovernmental in organization, but it reports to a government minister. The United Kingdom Post Office

(UKPO) is an example of this type of monopoly structure. Italy has a similar setup, but with a state holding company interposed between the government and the operating company.

The incorporated, limited liability company has all the appearances of a commercial enterprise, but all of its shares are owned or controlled by the government. The Spanish National Telephone Company (CTNE) is an example of this type of monopoly.

World Telecommunications Directory, published by Frost and Sullivan (106 Fulton Street, New York, N.Y. 10038) contains detailed information about telecommunications services and tariffs around the world.

7.4. TELEPHONY TERMINOLOGY AND DESCRIPTION

7.4.1. Equipment Organization

The telephone plant has evolved over the years into a highly efficient message-switching system. The interface between the *subscribers,* which is another term for customers, and the entire system is at the telephone exchange office (EO), or end-office. It is here that the last four digits of a dialed number carry the signal over wire pairs, called loops, to the subscribers' premises, ending at what is referred to as a *terminating station*. The *tariffs* published by the telephone companies describe the different kinds of services that are provided.

At the terminating station there may be a switchboard, which exists either as *customer-provided equipment* (CPE) or carrier-provided equipment such as *PBX* (private branch exchange), *PAX* (private automatic exchange), or *PABX* (private automatic branch exchange), and which provides *extension* tones to various instruments located on the customers' premises. There may be one or more telephone instruments or data transmission terminals at the terminating station. When the telephone company exchange office contains the switchboard and the subscriber loops terminate with telephone instruments, the service is known as *centrex*. Circuits between two switching equipments are known as *trunks*.

The term *local exchange service* refers to providing telephone circuits within an area served by the *central,* or exchange, office. *Foreign exchange* (FX) service refers to providing telephone circuits to areas outside the local central office that can be accessed by a local number call.

The telephone exchanges contain the switching equipment that is the embodiment of the *public switched network,* whose primary purpose is to connect two (or more) subscribers. The older forms of such systems, known as magneto or common-battery systems, required an operator to handle all calls, through the use of a patchboard arrangement. The development of step-by-step, the cross-bar, the correed (cross-point tandem), and ferreed (No. 1 ESS*) electromechanical switching elements went hand-in-hand with the introduction of the rotary dial system. The introduction of electronically controlled logic and electronic switching elements (No. 4 ESS) coincides with the wider use of the pushbutton or Touch-tone® systems. These recent developments have virtually eliminated the need for operators. Further information on the switching equipment in the telephone plant may be found in References 2–5.

7.4.2. Message Toll Switching System

The dial network is also referred to as direct distance dialing (DDD), or the public switched network (PSN), or message toll service (MTS). This is the implementation of a complex switching system for handling calls on the North American continent.

The general toll-switching plan has evolved as a hierarchic structure to permit alternate-call routing in the United States, Canada, and Northwest Mexico. This geographic area is divided into about 150 numbering plan areas (NPAs). Each NPA is divided into a maximum of 800 telephone exchanges. Each telephone exchange is divided according to the individual numbers, of which there may be up to 10,000. This structure currently contains approximately 140,000,000 telephones. Sometimes this structure is referred to as the nationwide switching plan. The method of calling is known as the *closed numbering plan*. It uses a three-digit area code, a three-digit office code, and a four-digit station code, hence the system equipment "counts" the number of digits dialed to determine when the dialing is completed. The number of possible combinations is not a maximum because of restrictions on the use of certain digits for telephone company functions. For example, a zero as the first dialed digit means an operator call or an international call, while a "1" initiates a continental long-distance call. The use of other digits is reserved to differentiate between area calls and office calls as well as service type calls (such as information, etc.). Thus the total number of NPAs that are currently served is 152 instead of the 999 possible combinations. A map of the numbering plan areas and their codes may be found in any telephone directory.

The nationwide switching plan uses sets of five types of calling offices. The end office, or Class 5, is the exchange office which contains the loops to the subscribers' phones. The end office, in turn, connects to a *toll center,* a Class 4 office. This office is called a center if the operator handles the inward calls; otherwise, it is known as a toll point, or center. There are approximately 3000 toll centers in the United States. The toll center connects to a *primary center,* a

*ESS = electronic switching system.

Class 3 office. The primary center connects to a *sectional center,* Class 2, of which there are approximately 75 in the United States. The sectional center connects to the *regional center,* a Class 1, of which there are approximately 9. The Class 1, 2, and 3 centers are known as control switching points (CSP). There are interconnecting channels between these centers so that a call need not go in order among the class offices. Enough trunks are provided so that a DDD call can be made via one of several alternate paths, depending on the amount of traffic on the system. This is illustrated in Figure 7.1.

It must always be kept in mind that the telephone plant was designed for voice communications. The telephone companies have obtained much statistical data concerning the number and duration of average telephone calls made in particular areas of the United States. From mathematical analyses of these data, trunk lines have been installed in sufficient numbers to insure that the probabilities of establishing calls are within certain tolerances.

Now, when the telephone plant is being used more and more for data transmission from terminal equipment to computers, the statistics of calls has changed dramatically. Instead of calls whose average duration is minutes, these computer calls last for hours. This has had a severe impact on the telephone system. As the number of available trunk lines for calls was reduced, the number of busy signals per call increased, and the entire system capability was being degraded. This was particularly true in the New York City area in 1972. The telephone company has instituted a massive capital expenditure program to increase the number of circuits in its trunk system. Thus the initial effect of using the telephone plant for data communications has been a deleterious one.

7.5. THE TELEPHONE PLANT FOR DATA COMMUNICATIONS

Because it was there and because it was highly developed, the telephone plant was adapted for use with data transmission equipment such as terminals, computers, etc. The telephone plant, being an analog facility designed for voice communications, presented certain problems that had to be surmounted. In this section we look at what some of these problems were, how they came about, and how they were solved. The new construction of digital facilities eliminates many of these problems, so that this section may be considered a historical excursion!

7.5.1. Two-Wire and Four-Wire Circuits

Long-distance facilities, or trunk lines, between different telephone offices are physical four-wire circuits with a pair for each direction, each pair having its

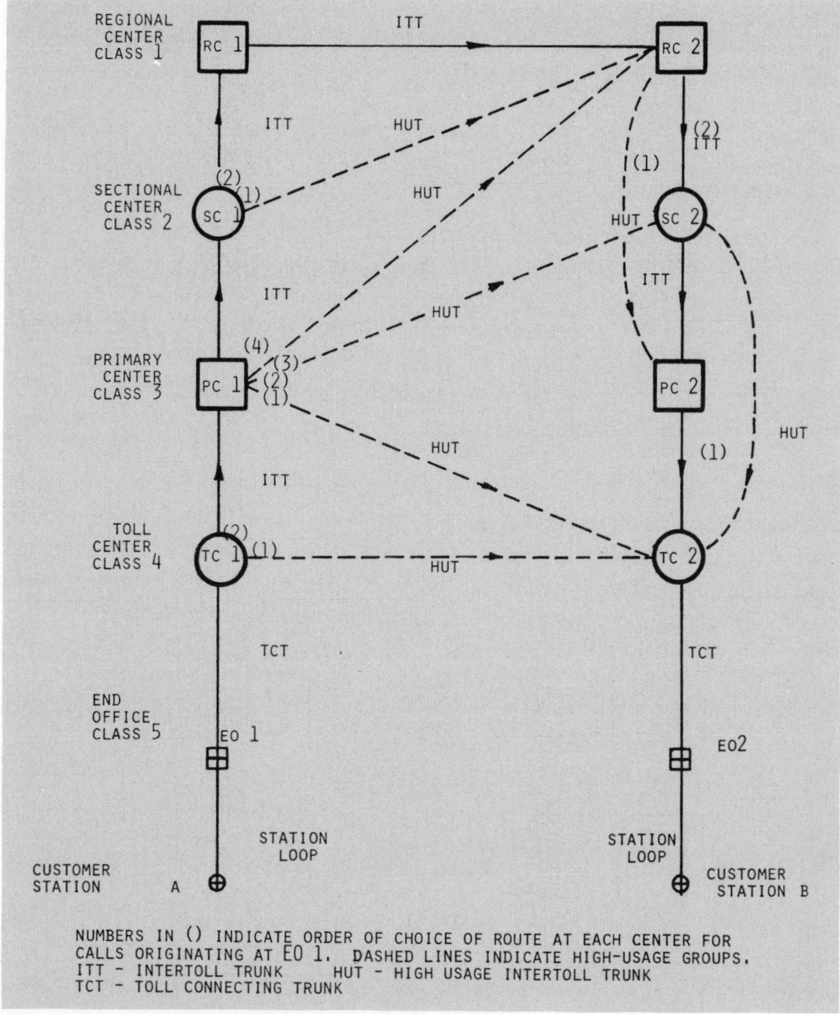

Figure 7.1. The hierarchical switching organization allows many possible circuit paths to be selected in making direct-distance-dialed (DDD) calls.

own set of repeaters. The direction for each pair is (historically) given as E–W (meaning East to West) and W–E (West to East) transmissions in a simplex mode. A telephone conversation can also be carried over two-wire circuits, and for economy, most subscriber loops are two-wire conductors to the exchanges. This minimizes the total number of physical channels required.

It should be pointed out that a four-wire circuit is not a requirement for two-way conversation. It is possible to use two wires by separating the conversations into different frequency ranges for the two directions. Such a channel is called an equivalent four-wire circuit.

7.5.2. Hybrid Circuits

Where the two-wire circuit joins a four-wire trunk, a connecting circuit is needed to transfer the outgoing conversation *to* the appropriate pair of wires and transfer the incoming conversation *from* the appropriate wire pair. This connection is known as a *coil hybrid circuit* with a balancing circuit, and it is shown in Figure 7.2. The balance circuit is based on the principle of the Wheatstone bridge. The Wheatstone bridge is a network circuit used primarily for measurement purposes by balancing resistances in the network branches to bring the voltage to zero.

When conversation is transmitted toward the hybrid circuit from the two-wire line, the signal is divided equally between the incoming and outgoing wire pairs of the four-wire circuit. The part that goes to the incoming pair is attenuated (i.e., reduced in energy) while the other is transmitted. If this circuit were adjusted to match the network perfectly, then no signal would return.

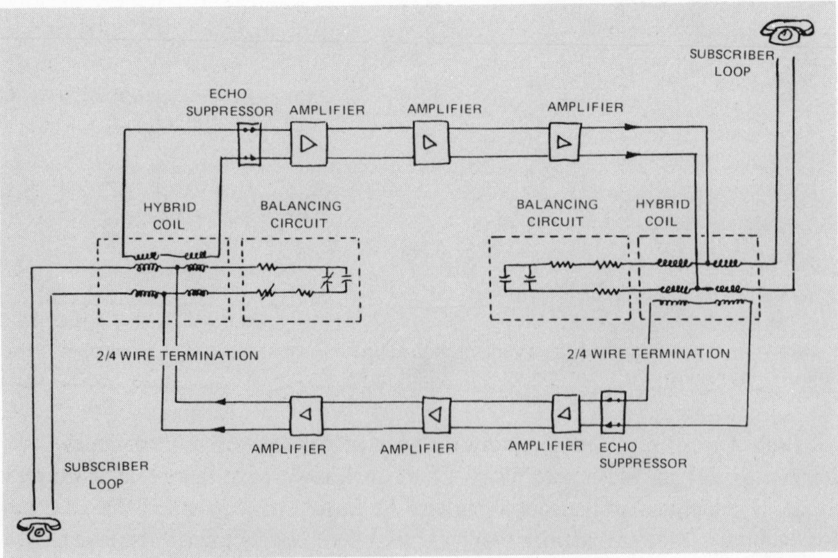

Figure 7.2. On long-distance connections, the four-wire circuits are terminated to two-wire circuits by coil hybrid circuits located in the exchange offices.

7.5.3. Echoes

The impedance of the two-wire line and the network varies with frequency, and since the network (four-wire circuits) and the two-wire lines are not identical, their impedances will vary independently of each other for a given frequency range. Now, when a signal is transmitted on a circuit and meets an impedance mismatch, a portion of the signal is a reflected back toward the source. This reflection is called an *echo*. The common sources of echoes are circuit terminations, line irregularities, and junctions between dissimilar facilities such as in the hybrid circuit.

There are two kinds of echoes that are considered. *Talker echoes* are reflected back toward the receiving station or listener. If the sum of all the gains (of energy levels) exceeds the sum of all the losses at any frequency, the circuit will begin to oscillate or *sing* because of its unstable conditions.[(6)]

Talker echo can seriously affect voice communications. If it occurs with very little delay it tends to increase the *sidetone* in the talker's receiver with the result that the speaker tends to talk at a lower level. If the echo has a substantial delay, such as a few tenths of a second, the human ear separates it from a sidetone, and this has a very disconcerting effect. People will stutter, repeat, or speak in a disconnected manner. For data transmission, talker echo has little effect, because when a set is transmitting in a half-duplex mode its receiver is muted.

Listener echo has little effect in voice communication if the delay is very short because it tends to reinforce the transmitted signal, and the human ear is not selective enough to detect the echo. When the delay time is substantial, listener echo becomes confusing for the listener—as if several people are speaking at once.

For data transmission listener echo seriously affects the receiving equipment because the transmitted signal may echo at the receiving end and again at the transmitting end, thus causing high error rates.

7.5.4. Echo Suppressors

To alleviate the problem of echoes caused by impedance mismatches additional circuitry known as *echo suppressors* was added to the system. The echo suppressor is a device which detects signal levels in the transmitting and receiving paths and compares them to determine how to operate switchable pads that increase signal losses in the other direction. They are installed at a four-wire point in the circuit, as shown in Figure 7.2. In the nonoperating state the pads insert loss in the transmitting path and provide for no loss in the receiving path. This represents the receiving condition.

When the circuit is in a transmitting condition, the signal detected on the transmitting path is stronger than the signal detected on the receiving path. The suppressor removes the pad from the transmit path and puts it on the receive path to maintain the required echo loss. This signal detector is also called a *speech detector*.

Echo suppressors must operate fast enough to prevent clipping of the first syllable in a conversation, but not fast enough to chatter on impulse or static noise. The release time of the pads must be short enough to prevent clipping the first syllable of received signals, but long enough to prevent chatter between syllables, and it must always be longer than any maximum round-trip delay that may be encountered in order to reduce the last echo. In most of the world's telephone systems, echoes with more than 0.045 seconds round-trip delays cannot be tolerated. Thus with voice frequencies traveling at a rough average speed of 100,000 miles/second, a circuit would have to be about 1500 miles long before the round-trip delay reached 0.045 seconds.

Echo suppressors specifically designed for voice have a serious effect on some forms of data transmission. A data system operating in full-duplex, which requires signals to travel in both directions, would not function properly with echo suppressors on the circuit.

7.5.5. Echo Suppressor Disablers

The telephone plant is designed to disable the echo suppressors at tones of certain frequencies (2000–2250 Hz) for at least 400 milliseconds (ms). The echo suppressor stays disabled until there has not been any signal on the line for a period of approximately 50 ms. Thus data equipment when connected to the telephone plant must not leave the line idle (or silent) for 50 ms, or the echo suppressor will have to be disabled again.

The disabling tone is heard as a high-pitched whistle when communications are being established manually over the telephone (or Dataphone®) between a terminal and a computer. When this tone is heard the caller pushes a button marked ''DATA,'' and then the dataset takes over the function of continuously sending tones on the line so that it will not fall silent. The process of disconnecting (or hanging up the telephone) causes the echo suppressor to be enabled again (placed in a receive state).

7.6. DECIBELS

The strengths of electronic signals are typically given in units of *decibels*. The average power of transmission of a sound wave per unit area is called its *intensity*. This power is measured in units such as dynes/cm^2 (dyn/cm^2) or watts/ cm² (W/cm^2). The human ear can detect sound waves whose intensity is as low as 2×10^{-4} dyn/cm² (which corresponds to 10^{-16} W/cm², 10^{-10} ergs, or 3×10^{-24} kWh), and this level is usually referred to as the threshold of hearing.

The modern unit for describing acoustic power is the *decibel* (abbreviated dB), which is defined to be a logarithmic ratio of power levels, as

$$\text{dB} = 10 \log_{10} (P_2/P_1) = 20 \log_{10} (I_2/I_1) = 20 \log_{10} (V_2/V_1) \qquad (7.1)$$

The decibel (commonly used as the standard unit of sound intensity) is a relative measure. If two sound waves have absolute power levels P_1 and P_2 respectively, they are said to differ by some value of decibels. For example, if $P_2 = 2P_1$ then they differ by approximately 3 dB.

To use this method of measuring acoustic intensity requires the choice of a standard level. One standard selected is that of the minimum audibility level of 2×10^{-4} dyn/cm². This value corresponds to zero decibels (0 dB). Loud conversation corresponds to an intensity level of 1 dyn/cm². The decibel level of such conversation is

$$\begin{aligned} \text{dB} &= 20 \log_{10} (I_2/I_1) \\ &= 20 \log_{10} (5 \times 10^3) \\ &= 20 \times 3.699 \\ &= 74 \text{ dB} \end{aligned}$$

Table 7.2 shows some typical dB levels of human hearing.

The human ear is a logarithmic instrument, and thus, if the noise of a piece of machinery sounds twice as great when it is running than when it is quiet, the noise is said to be 2 dB greater than the silence when it is turned off. In fact for noise to sound twice as great, its energy level needs only to be increased $10^{0.2}$, or 1.6 times. Another example is that though the sound energy from street noise may be 10,000 times greater than the sound energy in a room, it does not sound 10,000 times greater. In fact it only sounds 40 times greater, that is, 40 dB.

The advantage of using decibels is that computations involving power losses or gains are arithmetic in dB units. For example, if the power level was reduced

Table 7.2. Typical Decibel Levels of Sounds

0 dB	Threshold of hearing	$I_1 = 2 \times 10^{-4}$ dyn/cm²
30-40 dB	Telephone conversation	—
65 dB	Normal speech at 1 meter	—
74 dB	Loud conversation	$I_2 = 1$ dyn/cm²
100 dB	Street noise	$I_2 = 20$ dyn/cm²
120 dB	Jet-engine noise	—
140 dB	Threshold of pain	$I_2 = 2000$ dyn/cm²

from a ratio of 10,000:1 to a ratio of 100:1, we would have a reduction of 20 dB ($dB_1 = 10 \log_{10} 10{,}000 = 40$; $dB_2 = 10 \log_{10} 100 = 20$; $dB_1 - dB_2 = 40 - 20 = 20$). If a transmission line has a loss of 2 dB/mile, then 25 miles of line would have a 50 dB loss in signal strength.

In telecommunications, all signal-level measurements, noise-level measurements, and transmission and loss levels are given in decibels. There are currently many types of reference levels, resulting in many different kinds of decibel units. Some of these are shown in Table 7.3. The number of different reference levels came about because of the increase in stringent requirements of data transmission circuits. To increase the capacity of transmission systems and keep the overall system load down, modern equipment has reduced the signal level so that it is nearer the noise level.

7.7. COMPANDORS

Signals may be transmitted over voice circuits at low strength—as low as a whisper—or at high strength, as when one shouts into a telephone handset. This wide range of signal strengths must be transmitted over the communications channel intact to the receiver. The entire signal suffers attenuation and must be amplified several times as shown in Figure 7.3. Typically the average signal power level is set such that the signal-to-noise (S/N) ratios of weak signals are low. As attenuation occurs, these signals can fall below the noise level. The

Table 7.3. Decibel Reference Levels

dB	Logarithmic power ratio, $dB = 10 \log_{10} (P_2/P_1)$ or if voltage is used $dB = 20 \log_{10} (V_2/V_1)$.
dBm	Decibels above or below 1 mW (milliwatt) where 0 dBm is 1 mW of power at 1000 Hz in a 600-ohm-resistance impedance.
dBr	Decibels used to refer the signal level at any point in a transmission system to an arbitrary point in the system known as the point-of-zero relative level.
dBw	Decibels above or below 1 W where 0 dBw is 1 W of power at 1000 Hz in a 600-ohm-resistance impedance. It is used extensively in microwave applications.
dBrn	Decibels above a reference noise where the reference noise power of a 1000 Hz tone is 10^{-12} W (or 1 picowatt, pW) or 90 dB below 1 mW (in other words, −90 dBm). This was established by AT&T for measurements of noise interference.
dBa	Decibels for P1A-weighted noise measurements.
dBrnC	Decibels for C-message-weighted noise where 0 dBrnC is −90 dBm.
dBmV	Decibels referring to voltage levels expressed as being above or below 1 mV (millivolt) across 75 ohms resistance. It is used in video transmission.

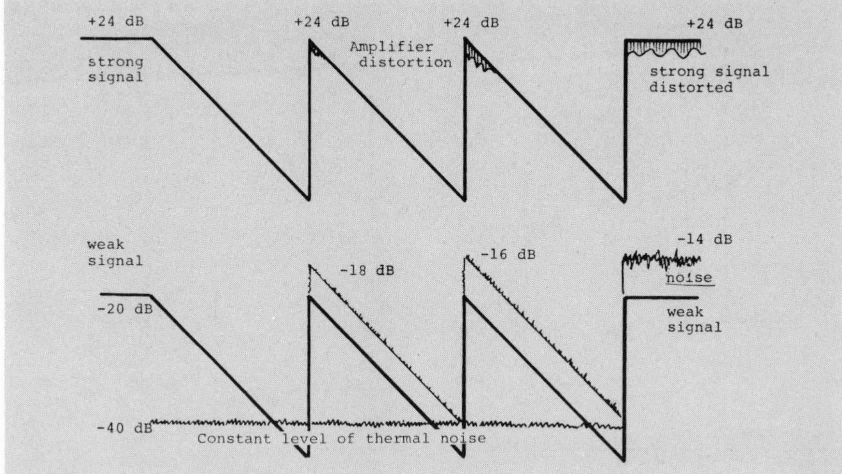

Figure 7.3. Analog signals are periodically amplified to restore attenuation losses. Signals having a wide range of strengths (or volume) suffer distortions at both extremes. The strong signals are distorted by the nonlinearity of the amplifiers. The weak signals could fall below the circuit noise level.

amplification of these weak signals causes the noise to be amplified also, resulting in a distorted signal at the receiver. Remember, this is not a regenerative repeater, but only a circuit amplifier that is installed on the voice circuits.

The strong signals, on the other hand, are also amplified at the repeater. The electronic circuits of the amplifiers do not operate linearly over the full range of the signal, and as a result, the very strong signals are distorted somewhat during the amplification process. This is shown in the upper part of Figure 7.3. To allow satisfactory transmission to take place on voice circuits a device known as a *compandor,* which reduces the *range* of signal strengths transmitted over the channel, is added. A compandor allows for transmission over noisier circuits by providing an effective improvement in the signal-to-noise ratio in a voice circuit by about 25 dB.

A compandor consists of a volume compressor at the transmitting end and a volume expandor at the receiving end. Its function is to give more gain to low-intensity signals, i.e., increase weak signals above the level of noise. This is shown in Figure 7.4. Strong signals, which are less vulnerable to noise, are amplified less or possibly attenuated. This device thus prevents overloading of the transmission equipment. The operation of a typical compandor is shown in Figure 7.5.

The presence of compoandors on circuits used for data transmission introduces nonlinear distortions to the signal because the expandor circuit is not the precise reverse of the compressor. When the circuits are used for voice, these

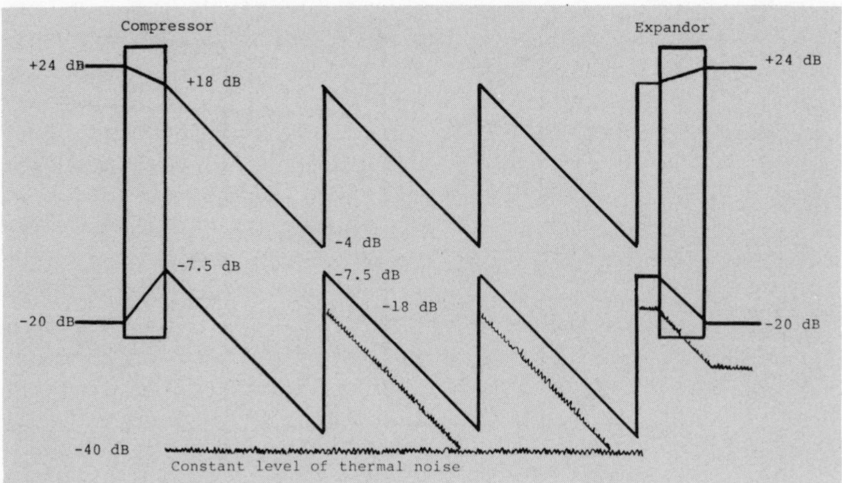

Figure 7.4. A compandor compresses the signal volume range prior to transmission and expands it to original values at the receiver.

distortions are not noticeable; however, they present a serious obstacle to the transmission of data at high rates using, for example, multiple-angle phase-shift keying.

7.8. TELEPHONE SYSTEM SIGNALING

The telephone companies use the same channels that are used for voice communication for the transmission of network or control signals.[7] There are three basic kinds of signals used to provide control capabilities on the telephone plant.

One type is *supervisory signals,* which provide an indication of the status of circuits, trunk lines, and various pieces of equipment. A common type of supervisory signal is the telephone handset on-hook/off-hook indication to the exchange office. When the handset is lifted off its cradle, just prior to making a telephone call, the off-hook signal to the exchange office causes switching equipment to begin looking for an address register in anticipation of a number being dialed. Similarly, at the termination of a telephone conversation, the placing of the telephone handset back on its cradle causes an indication to the switching equipment to break all the circuit paths of the previous call.

The second kind of network signaling is *address signals,* which indicate the particular connections to be made. One example is the signals generated during the dialing process. If the handset is the rotary kind, then dc dial pulses are sent from the subscriber's loop to the exchange office. Touch-tone® telephones transmit multifrequency tones to the exchange office. Interoffice address signals are also used. The multifrequency (MF) signal is a two-out-of-five tone used for interoffice address signaling during a call setup.

The third category consists of the *audible tones* that are transmitted in conjunction with telephone calls. There is the dial tone which is sent from the exchange office to the subscriber indicating that the switching system has found an address register and the person may begin dialing. The busy tone indicates that a call cannot be completed, either because the called party's receiver is in the off-hook status or because all available circuit paths to an exchange office are occupied. These conditions are indicated by differences in the busy tones. The ringing tones are sent to cause the called party's handset to ring and a ring-back tone is sent to the calling party's telephone to indicate that the telephone is ringing. Finally in this category, there is the echo-suppressor disabler tone which was discussed previously.

The effect of network signaling on the use of the telephone plant for data communications is that the available bandwidth for transmission is reduced. Typically these network signals occur in the 2400–2800 Hz frequency range. Unintentional tones sent in these ranges could cause erratic functioning of the telephone switching system. Speech generally does not contain tones of sufficient amplitude in these frequency ranges, so there is not any possibility of its having adverse effects. Data signals, on the other hand, consist of an even distribution of energy over the transmission bandwidth, and therefore the probability of accidentally producing a network signal tone is much greater. Therefore,

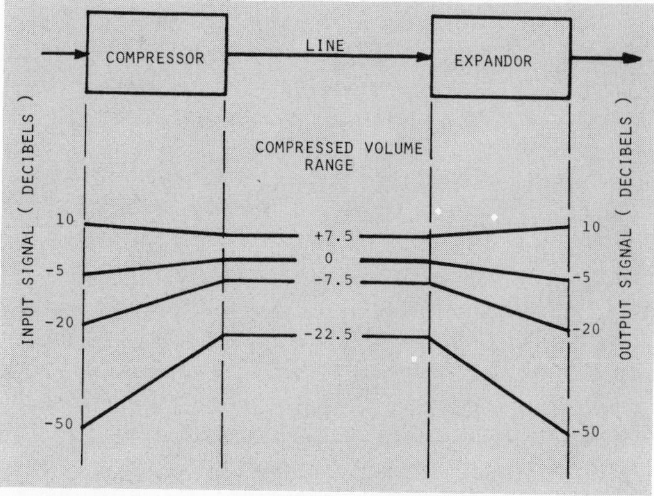

Figure 7.5. The operation of a typical compandor circuit.

to use the switched telephone plant for data, modems have to be designed to use a much reduced bandwidth. Because of this reduced bandwidth modems are not expected to transmit at high data rates.

7.9. SUMMARY

Though the switched telephone plant provided some obstacles to data transmission, these obstacles did not prevent the plant from being used for data transmission. Once they had determined the various effects, data communications engineers designed equipment to eliminate or minimize their interference. In the next chapter all of the different types of channel interferences are presented.

Chapter 8

Transmission Impairments

From the discussion in the previous chapter on the analog telephone plant, it was noted that certain conditions lead to a degradation of the voice channel for data communications usage. In this chapter a summary is presented of the different types of impairments suffered by the communications channels and of the efforts to correct them. At all times it should be kept in mind that the net effect of these distortions is to reduce, or limit, the capacity of the channel by either reducing the available bandwidth or by reducing the ratio of the signal power level to the noise power level. The noise power level includes actual signal distortion.

In voice communications, the human ear and mind effectively neutralize and compensate for distortions present in the audible signal. The information transmission rates are lower in voice communications than in data communications. Thus, even excessive distortions in the received signals do not always impair voice communications, but these distortions are very detrimental to data transfer. These effects become progressively worse as the data rate increases with the signal bandwidth, the number of signal levels (i.e., bits per baud), or combinations of both.

Impairments can be categorized as either random or deterministic. Random impairments, or fortuitous distortions, occur unpredictably; they can be described (i.e., analyzed) using probability functions. On the other hand, deterministic impairments, or systematic distortions, occur because of the types of electronic circuits used in the equipment. That is, the better (usually, more expensive) the circuit, the better the response characteristics of the system will be regarding these kinds of distortions.

8.1. RANDOM IMPAIRMENTS

8.1.1. Gaussian Noise, White Noise, and Thermal Noise

The most common name of this trio is *Gaussian noise,* which is also known as random noise, white noise, or thermal noise. This is the noise level that exists because of the thermal motions of the electrons in the electronic circuits. An example is the background "hum" that one hears upon opening a window overlooking a city on a still evening, or when a radio is turned off-channel (i.e., not tuned to any transmitting station) and the volume is increased. It is known as white noise because it occurs over all frequencies in much the same way that white light is the sum of many spectral components. It is known as thermal noise because it is directly proportional to the system temperature T_s in the relation,

$$N_s = KT_s \tag{8.1}$$

where N_s is the noise power *spectral density* (i.e., the amount of noise over the frequency spectrum) in watts/hertz (W/Hz), and K is Boltzmann's constant (1.38×10^{-23} W/Hz °K). Finally, it is known as random noise or Gaussian noise because its amplitude follows a Gaussian distribution function,

$$P(N) = \frac{1}{r\,(2\pi)^{1/2}} \exp\left[-(N-N_0)^2 / 2r^2\right] \tag{8.2}$$

where $P(N)$ is the probability of the amplitude of the noise power level, and r is the root-mean-square (rms) of the noise voltage. For further discussion, see Reference 1.

While there has been much debate in the literature about the magnitude of the random effect, it has been generally agreed that the noise characteristics of the analog telephone plant can be approximated by the Gaussian distribution function.[(2)] In fact, the N (noise level term) in the Shannon formula

$$C = B \log_2(1 + S/N) \tag{8.3}$$

is derived using a Gaussian distribution function [cf. equation (4.8)].

The Gaussian function provides a means of comparing different modulation techniques. For each modulation case, the probability of error PE, usually stated as bits in error per total bits transmitted, can be expressed in terms of signal levels L, of signal power P_s, and of noise power P_n. As an example, in baseband transmission systems the applicable relations would be

$$\mathrm{PE} = 2\,(L-1)/L\;Q([3P_s/(L^2-1)P_n]^{1/2}) \tag{8.4}$$

where $Q(x)$ is the normal probability integral

$$Q(x) = \frac{1}{(2\pi)^{1/2}} \int_x^{\infty} \exp\left(\frac{-t^2}{2}\right)\, dt \tag{8.5}$$

and the other terms refer to the Nyquist bandwidth, i.e.,

$$C/B = 2\log_2 L \tag{8.6}$$

where C/B is the channel capacity in bits per second per Hz of bandwidth. By selecting values of L_1 and P_s/P_n and using equations (8.4) and (8.6), the values of PE and C/B can be determined and plotted. This has been done by several authors,[3-5] and is shown in Figure 8.1.

8.1.2. Impulse Noise

Another type of random impairment is *impulse noise*, which may also be referred to as line "dropouts" or "line hits." Impulse noises are characterized

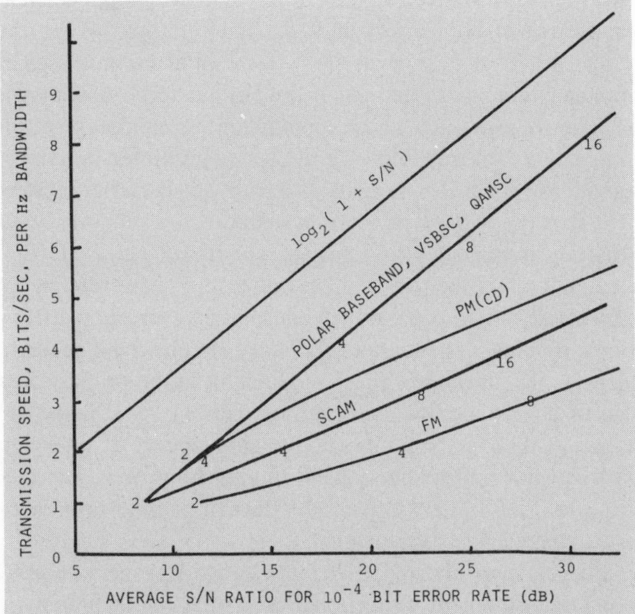

Figure 8.1. Comparison of various modulation methods at different signaling levels under average signal-power limitations. [From W. R. Bennett and J. R. Davey, *Data Transmission* (1965), p. 228, reproduced by permission of McGraw-Hill Book Company.]

by peaks of great amplitude that occur either within or outside the communication system. External impulse noise is caused by atmospheric static, such as from an AM radio during a thunderstorm, or by the static produced when contact relays are operated nearby. Impulse noise may occur when the channel equipment is near some relay switchgear, as it commonly was on the older rotary dial-telephone systems.

Internal impulse noise is caused by poor wiring or by poor contacts, such as a loose connection or a buildup of corrosion on the connections. The term "line dropouts" refers to the absence of a signal, which may be thought of as a signal-cancelling noise. "Line hits" is simply descriptive of the impulse nature of this noise.

The most effective countermeasure to this type of noise is the use of a *grounded shield* where possible.

8.1.3. Phase Jitter[(6–9)]

Phase jitter, sometimes referred to as incidental FM or phase rotations, was of no concern in voice telephone communications. Even though its existence was known, it was not considered a significant measure of telephone channel performance because it had little effect on voice intelligibility. When the telephone plant was adapted for data transmission, phase jitter became a channel performance parameter of concern because it limited the speed of transmission.

Phase jitter is unwanted phase modulation. It can cause errors in a data stream that is being transmitted over a frequency multiplex-derived communications channel, such as the long-haul telephone L-carrier systems. Single-sideband (SSB-AM) is used in these systems; hence, it is necessary to have reference carrier frequencies to translate up in frequency at the (multiplex) transmitter and down at the (demultiplex) receiver. These reference frequencies should be identical at both ends of the channel; however, they differ slightly and this causes the problem. The master oscillatory circuit which generates the reference frequencies has unwanted phase modulation in the primary frequency carrier because of power supply ripple, ground currents, and noisy or "hunting" pilot (frequency) recovery circuits. Phase jitter occurs at rates related to the power line frequency and its harmonics, ringing frequency, and the interaction between the two. Phase jitter is given as values of peak-to-peak deviation of the instantaneous phase angle of the signal.

When the carriers realized that phase jitter was an impairment to data transmission, an equipment correctional program was instituted. It still is an occasional troublesome factor in high-speed transmission over long-haul circuits. Unfortunately, there is no easy method to compensate for, or provide simple circuitry to correct, phase jitter in *existing* systems. The best method for avoiding transmission errors caused by phase jitter is to use multiplex equipment specifically designed for data.

8.1.4. Multiple Path Distortions[10]

These distortions occur because the transmitted signals can take different paths to the receiver that vary in length, and hence, in time. A most prominent kind of multiple path distortion is the *echo* which was discussed in the previous chapter. In general, any circuit that contains impedance irregularities causes echoes, as shown in Figure 8.2a. Such irregularities are likely to occur on a communication channel made up of many different kinds of communications links (or equipment). On the voice channels, hybrid circuits would be the likely sources of impedance mismatches.

Another multiple path effect is known as *multihop*. This is a radiofrequency (RF) phenomenon that occurs when there are radio links in the communications channel. Radio waves in the high-frequency (HF) band, nominally 3–30 MHz, can be reflected off the ionosphere to achieve communications over the horizon. This effect is shown in Figure 8.2b. The reliability of these systems has been estimated at 90%, which is not very good for data communications. The ionosphere is affected by such natural phenomena as sunspots, magnetic storms, sudden cosmic ray or meteor activity, and whether it is day or night.

The third type of multipath distortion occurs with the transmission of microwave signals in the UHF (300–3000 MHz) range beyond line-of-sight, or "over-the-horizon," and is known as *fading*. It is shown in Fig. 8.2c. These microwave systems are called tropospheric scatter circuits because they use the refraction and reflection phenomena in a lower portion, up to 11 km, of the atmosphere called the troposphere. Fading is the partial or total absorption of the energy of the signal by the medium of transmission (in this case, the troposphere). Fading is a phenomenon of the troposphere. Many theories try to explain

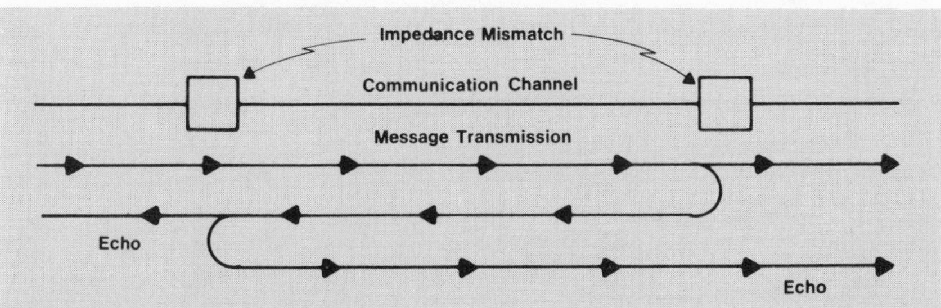

Figure 8.2a. Echoes produced by impedence irregularities such as telephone hybrid circuits that are not balanced.

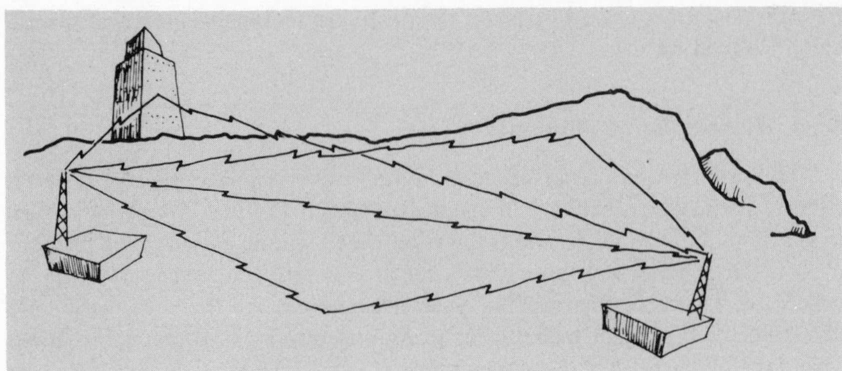

Figure 8.2b. Multihop distortions due to reflections in HF radio circuits cause the signals to overlap by arriving at different times.

it. One suggests that the troposphere consists of stratified layers of air, and that boundaries between layers become partially reflecting surfaces for radio waves. Another theory says atmospheric air disturbances and refractive index irregularities divert radio signals over the horizon.

8.2. DETERMINISTIC IMPAIRMENTS

These distortions result from the characteristics of the steady-state response of the channels. Amplitude-frequency distortion and phase-frequency distortion

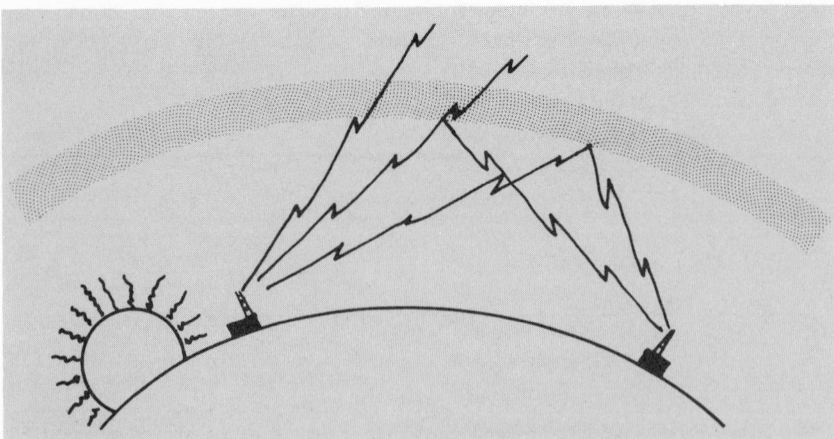

Figure 8.2c. Fading of radio signals occurs with changing altitudes of the ionosphere layers from day to night.

are the two most often referred to, perhaps because effective countermeasures have been designed for these impairments.

8.2.1. Amplitude-Frequency Distortion[11–14]

This impairment is the attenuation of the signal as it varies with frequency over a bandwidth. This is also referred to as frequency response or attenuation distortion. For a voice-band channel over typical cable pairs, the loss variation in decibels is roughly proportional to the square root of the frequency. Detailed data on this effect have been obtained by the telephone companies for the switched voice network[15–17] and are summarized in Figure 8.3.

There are a number of countermeasures used to reduce amplitude-frequency distortion. The telephone companies install loading coils in channel circuits at uniform intervals. This adds a *lumped* inductance to give both a lower and more uniform loss. The characteristics of typical loaded and unloaded cable pairs are shown in Figure 8.4. Note that loading makes the line act as a low-pass filter with an abrupt frequency cutoff.

Another countermeasure to amplitude-frequency distortion available as a carrier service for leased analog voice channels is line conditioning. Because the communication path of a leased channel is invariant with time, electronic circuits

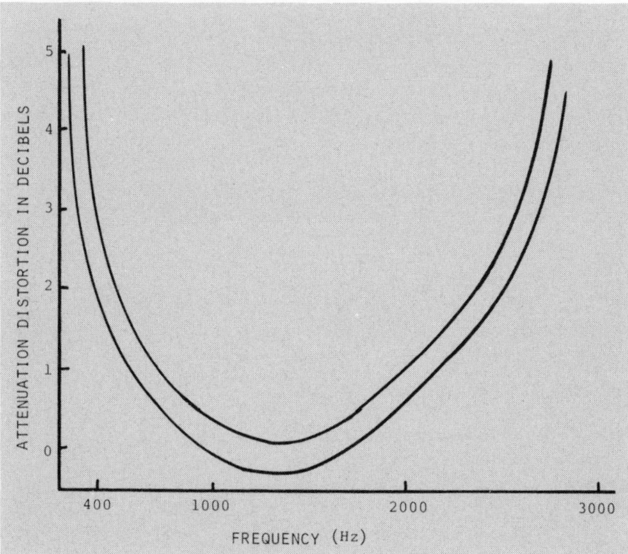

Figure 8.3. Amplitude frequency variation shown as attenuation distortion in dB relative to 1000 Hz. This is also known as frequency response. The data shown are derived from three path lengths: short (up to 175 mi), long (175 to 725 mi), and long (over 725 mi), using the switched network. [Reference 12, p. 15.]

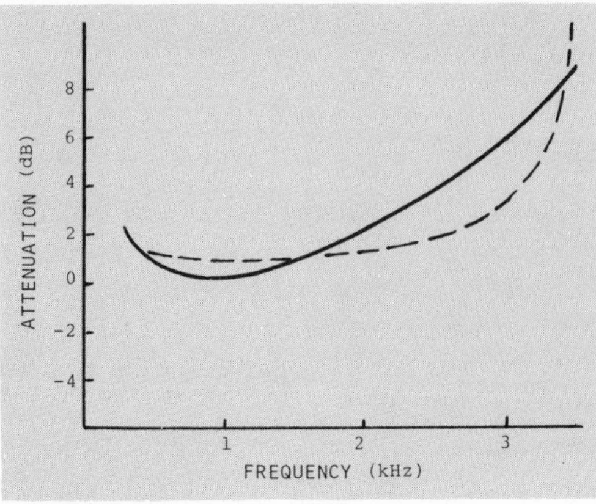

Figure 8.4. The frequency attenuation characteristics of unloaded twisted wire-pair cable, shown as the solid curve, can be improved by "loading" the wire as shown by the dashed curve. Loading is the insertion of series inductance at periodic intervals along the wire pair.

can be added to limit the loss variation to prescribed values over different frequency ranges. Table 8.1 describes the different levels of line conditioning available according to AT&T tariff #260.[18] Figure 8.5 illustrates how conditioning alters the channel. Line conditioning is not available for the public switched network for the simple reason that the circuit path of a connection is not known in advance.

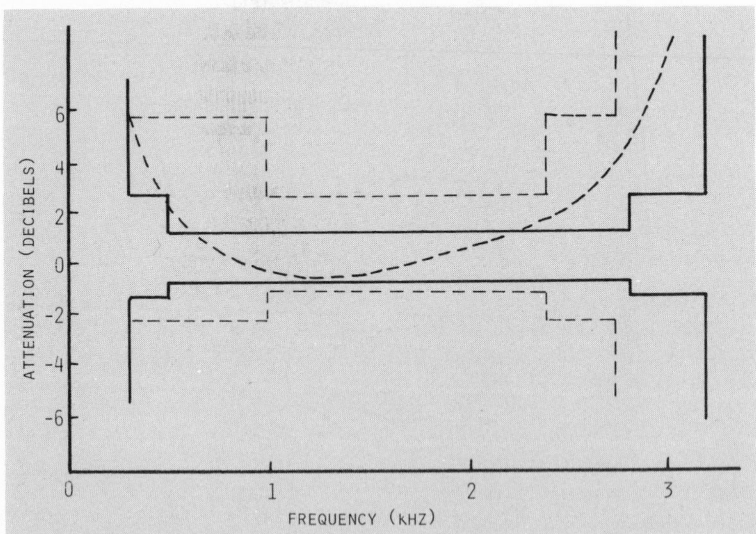

Figure 8.5. Frequency attenuation distortion limits shown as dashed lines for C1 conditioning and as solid lines for C5 conditioning—applicable to an AT&T 3002 type leased private voice channel. The (dashed) curve shows the average frequency attenuation for unconditioned channels.

Table 8.1. Channel Conditioning Arrangements for Private Leased Channels

Private lines leased from the telephone company may be "conditioned" according to tariff specifications to provide better signal response characteristics.

For AT&T leased type 3002 voice channels, conditioning requirements are specified in AT&T Tariff #260 and are shown below.[a]

Envelope delay distortion limits (ms)

Conditioning	Frequency range, Hz	Limit (ms)
C1	1000–2400	1.0
C2	1000–2600	0.5
C2	600–2600	1.5
C2	500–2800	3.0
C3	1000–2600	11
C3	600–2600	0.3
C3	500–2800	0.6
C4	1000–2600	0.3
C4	800–2800	0.5
C4	600–3000	1.5
C4	500–3000	3.0
C5	1000–2600	0.1
C5	600–2600	0.3
C5	500–2800	0.6

Limits of loss deviation[b] (in dB)

Conditioning	Frequency range, Hz	Limits (dB)
C1	1000–2400	−1 +3
C1	300–2700	−2 +6
C2	500–2800	−1 +3
C2	300–3000	−2 +6
C3	500–2800	−0.5 +1.5
C3	300–3000	−0.8 +3
C4	500–3000	−2 +3
C4	300–3200	−2 +6
C5	500–2800	−0.5 +1.5
C5	300–3200	−1 +3

Noise and harmonic distortion limits (in dB)

Signal to	Basic channel	D1 conditioning
C-notched noise	24	28
Second-harmonic distortion	−25	−35
Third-harmonic distortion	−30	−40

[a] The vertical lines indicate the range of frequencies over which the limits [given by the number(s) in the vertical line] apply, e.g., for C1 conditioning, the distortion limit is 1.0 ms from 1000 to 2400 Hz (outside this range of frequencies there is no limit).

[b] With 1000 Hz as the reference frequency.

For the switched network, the countermeasure to amplitude-frequency distortion is known as *equalization*. This consists of electronic circuits installed in the modems at each station to compensate for this impairment in the channel. Three types of such circuits are available: manual, adaptive, and automatic equalization. In modems equipped with adaptive or automatic equalization, the circuit senses the variation in the distortion and automatically adjusts to compensate for changes in the line conditions.

8.2.2. Phase-Frequency Distortion[12–14,18,19]

This type of distortion is the result of deviations from the linear relationship between the phase shift and the frequency. A more common term for this distortion is *envelope delay,* or simply *delay,* which is the derivative of phase with respect to frequency (whose approximate value can be more conveniently represented). This is shown in Figure 8.6

The main sources of phase distortion are loaded cables, carrier channel filters, and echoes from imperfect line terminations (hybrid circuits). Voice communications can tolerate greater amounts of phase distortion than can data communications. Recall that this was also true of phase jitter.

A network in which phase shift is proportional to frequency causes no distortion of a waveform that is made up of harmonically related frequencies. The nth harmonic will have a phase shift n times that of the fundamental frequency. The time displacement of the nth harmonic, however, will be the

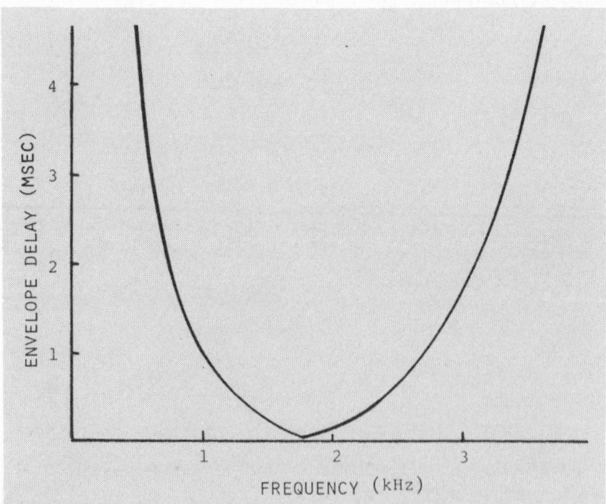

Figure 8.6. Envelope delay distortion for a voice channel defined relative to 1700 Hz illustrates how a signal arrival at a receiver varies with frequency.

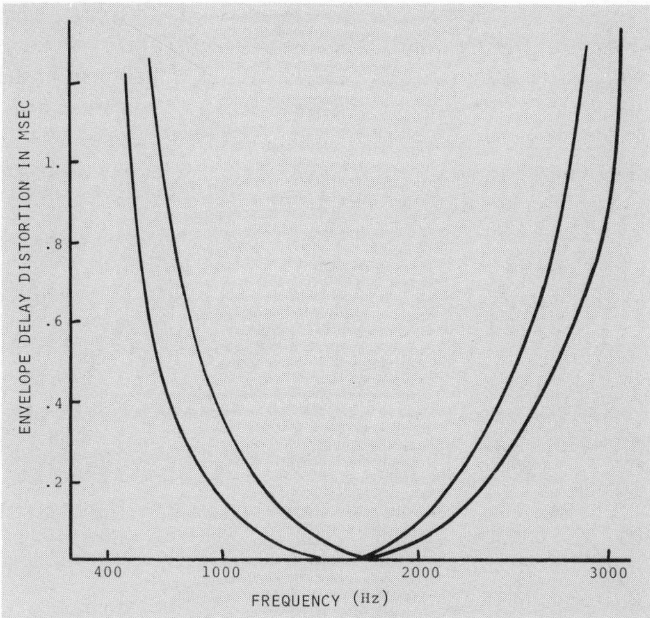

Figure 8.7. Average envelope delay distortion values for voice circuits on the switched network defined relative to 1700 Hz determined for three path lengths. [Reference 12, p. 15.]

same as the fundamental because the period is $1/n$ times the fundamental. All components and the resultant wave itself are delayed by an amount equal to the slope of the phase vs frequency characteristic. The correlation of time delay with the derivative of the phase-frequency characteristic (or envelope delay) is exact only when the system is distortionless, i.e., when the phase shift is proportional to frequency.

Envelope delay is a convenient term to describe the distortion as the departure of the envelope delay from a constant value. This delay is defined relative to a single frequency, rather than being a derivative, and is usually 1700 Hz for a voice channel as shown in Figure 8.7. The delay distortion curve does not directly give the time delay of the signal-frequency components, but instead only the relative slope of the phase characteristic and the relative envelope delay of a very narrowband modulated signal whose spectrum is limited to that immediate region of frequency.

The countermeasures here are linear equalizing networks (e.g., circuits) either as line conditioning for private leased channels or in the modem as equalization. This is similar to attenuation–distortion countermeasures. Figure 8.8 and Table 8.1 show the effects of line conditioning on envelope-delay distortion.

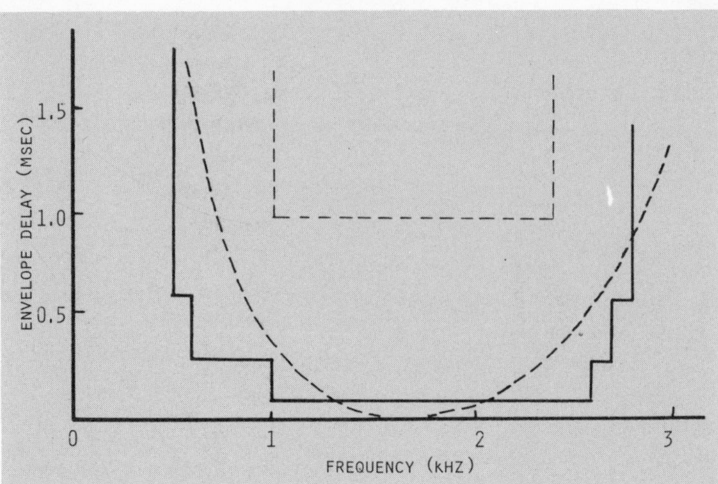

Figure 8.8. Envelope delay distortion limits shown as dashed lines for C1 conditioning and as solid lines for C5 conditioning—applicable to an AT&T 3002 type leased private voice channel. The (dashed) curve shows the average envelope delay for unconditioned channels.

8.2.3. Nonlinear Distortion

Attenuation distortion and envelope-delay distortion are linear effects. They obey the principle of superposition in that responses to individual signal inputs can be added directly to form the composite response. This property of linearity makes the resolution of signal waves into components at different frequencies a potent tool for analysis and measurement. Communications channels are also subject to nonlinear distortion.

Channel nonlinear distortion causes disruption of the harmonic relationships and the creation of spurious frequencies. A type of nonlinearity gives rise to the "Kendall effect," where a moduated carrier signal becomes partially demodulated to a baseband signal. Interference occurs when the baseband overlaps the desired carrier sidebands and cannot be filtered out. This becomes troublesome in facsimile transmissions. (Facsimile transmissions are the sending and receiving of images such as documents or photographs over communications facilities.)

These distortions are caused by saturation effects in magnetic cores, nonlinear electronic circuit characteristics, and crowding or limiting in multichannel modulators and amplifiers such as may be found in frequency-division systems. A particular source of nonlinear distortion occurs in telephone channels having compandors. A compandor consists of a pair of *gain-adjusting circuits* which act to maintain a more favorable signal-to-noise ratio over a communication channel. At the input, the *compressor* (one of the gain-adjusting circuits) reduces the amplitude range of the voice signal which is then transmitted through a noisy channel at a relatively high level without *overloading*. The expandor (the other gain-adjusting circuit) at the output expands the amplitude range to that of the original input. This action is not instantaneous but depends on the envelope of the signal wave over time compared to the duration of a speed syllable. While the variable gain in the two circuits is designed to have equal attack-time characteristics to preserve the original voice waveform, this may not happen because the circuits may not act in a complementary fashion. Such effects impair data signals, although speech reception may not be noticeably affected.

8.2.4. Frequency Offset

Most medium- and long-haul carrier systems are frequency-division-multiplex types and use single sideband suppressed carrier modulation (SSBSC-AM). At the receiving end, the carrier must be reinserted during the demodulation process. Any differences in frequency between the modulating and demodulating carriers causes frequency offset which upsets the harmonic relationships that exist between the signal components.

Most carrier telephone systems employ a frequency lock arrangement which holds any frequency offset to less than one Hertz per *facility section*. This type of impairment may be troublesome on data channels using narrowband frequency modulation. In systems where the demodulating carriers are sometimes derived from, or controlled by, transmitted pilot frequencies, frequency offset rarely is a problem.

8.2.5. Intermodulation Distortion

When a baseband signal, for example, consisting of two frequencies f_1 and f_2 is input to a transmitter device, the output signal will consist of all of the harmonics of f_1 and f_2 *and* cross-product terms. These cross-product terms are tones at frequencies of $f_1 + f_2$, $2f_1 \pm f_2$, $f_1 \pm 2f_2$, etc., which causes intermodulation distortion in the signaling band.

This problem can occur in acoustic coupler devices. Typically these devices are FSK with originate frequencies of F1M = 1070 Hz and F1s = 1270 Hz (for mark and space) and answer frequencies of F2M = 2025 Hz and F2S = 2225 Hz. A cross-product term of F2S − F1M = 2225 − 1070 = 1155 Hz falls in between F1M and F1S. Even though these cross-product terms are of small amplitude compared to the transmission frequencies, care must still be exercised to filter out these unwanted signals.

8.2.6. Quantization Noise

This effect occurs in the demodulation process of a PCM signal. From Chapter 5, the PCM signal created from an analog waveform is encoded according to quantization levels derived from the sampling process. In other words, the analog signal had to be digitized by values carried in a certain number of bits. Now, upon demodulation, a distortion can be introduced up to a maximum of the value of one-half of the quantum step. This distortion is known as quantization noise.

The obvious countermeasure is to increase the number of quantum levels by increasing the number of bits to encode the sample level. This decreases the size of the quantum step and thus reduces quantization noise. The constraint on the number of bits per sample is the amount of available bandwidth for the PCM channel.

Chapter 9

The Common-Carrier Services

9.1. INTRODUCTION

In this chapter the result of a phenomenon that can only occur in a free enterprise society is examined. This is the growth of an industry—the interconnect industry—whose revenues increased from zero to multimillion dollar figures within a decade. Prospects are bright that this trend will continue. Attendent to this remarkable growth was the development of the specialized common carriers and the domestic satellite carriers. These industries grew because of the coincidental occurrence of three favorable factors.

The first factor was the technological developments that were spin-offs of the space age, such as transistorized circuits, circuit miniaturization, etc., along with the implementation of innovative ideas. Secondly, there was a ready market consisting of customers with new applications who were dissatisfied with the available services— in a sense, a vacuum waiting to be filled. Finally, the last factor and catalyst that triggered these industrial growths were decisions by the Federal Communications Commission (FCC) that lowered the barriers to competition. The FCC decisions allowed new companies to bring innovative ideas to the communications marketplace in direct competition with the established common carriers, which resulted in new products and services being offered to customers.

Had this text been written in the 1960s, this chapter would have been very brief because of the limited number of services available. The data communications designer had very few alternatives in the specification of the communication circuits. In the early 1970s this situation changed, perhaps going to the opposite extreme, in that the variety of offerings has increased many times over. The history of this change will be briefly covered.

9.2. THE FEDERAL COMMUNICATIONS COMMISSION

The telecommunications industry is a private enterprise regulated by an agency operating under our tripartite government structure. Congress, enacting the Communications Act of 1934, created the FCC and charged it with regulating all interstate and foreign telegraph, telephone, and broadcast communications. Anything to do with communications, from regulating commercial, amateur, and citizen's band (CB) radio transmission to allocating frequency usage and dealing with communications satellites and their operating companies, comes under the FCC's jurisdiction. Only the aspect of this agency's operations with the telecommunications industry will be considered.

The FCC consists of a seven-member commission (appointed by the President) and a civil service staff organization. The commission is primarily concerned with policy and rule-making and establishing guidelines to be followed. The staff is concerned with the day-to-day implementation of the commission's policies. One way in which the commission formulates regulatory policies is by holding a public inquiry on specific issues. Any individual or organization can present its views to the commission on the issues raised.

The FCC usually becomes involved in the regulation of a private enterprise in one of the following ways: (1) a company files an application to the FCC for a license to establish and operate a communications facility, or (2) a company files an application for a permit to construct a communications link. In essence, the company places itself under the jurisdiction of the FCC. Whenever the company sells communications services to others, it becomes known as a *common carrier*.

9.3. TARIFFS

Companies that are common carriers file tariffs with the regulatory agencies. These tariffs are essentially contracts for the services to be provided to the user and must be made available for viewing by the general public. Separate tariffs are generally filed according to generic categories of service; for example, message toll service, private line services, etc. These tariffs contain descriptions of the services to be provided in considerable detail, and what rates will be charged for these services. It should be noted that in the design of a data communications system, the applicable tariffs should be consulted as the ultimate source of cost information. A listing of such tariffs is given in Table 9.1.

When a tariff is amended for the purpose of implementing a rate change or a change in service, the requested change may be implemented by the common carrier 90 days after the filing date. The regulatory agency may request a 60-day postponement, after which time the new rates or services may be implemented without specific approval. Should the regulatory agency disapprove the tariff amendments at a later date, the changes are nullified. If the disapproved change was a rate increase, the company must reimburse its customers.

When new tariffs (proposing entirely new services) or tariff changes are filed, the FCC typically holds public hearings on the matter and then issues its decisions. If the decisions are controversial (and of late they usually have been), appeals are made to the courts which then issue rulings. The decisions (or rulings) are eventually implemented. All FCC decisions appear as "Docket # (numbers)," and the current literature refers to important decisions by their docket numbers.

For the regulation of intrastate services, the common carriers deal with the particular state's Public Service Commission (PSC), Public Utility Commission (PUC), or some similarly named regulatory body. The procedures described above also hold for the individual states, except that the PSC's rely on public hearings to a greater extent.

9.4. THE REGULATED MONOPOLY

In the telecommunications industry, the common carriers have been in the traditional position of protected, regulated monopolies. The public utility concept was applied in telephony, based on the theory that a monopoly supplier was in the best position to serve the public interest by providing an efficient service at a reasonable price. Prior to the 1960s there was little reason to dispute that theory. AT&T and the Bell System, the largest and virtually sole supplier of telephone services, had evolved analog technology to a degree of perfection unsurpassed anywhere in the world. Telephone message service is so imbedded in this country's way of life that it is taken for granted.

The FCC has broad powers to review rates and tariffs, determine investment and operating practices, and approve new plant installations for the entire carrier communications industry. Historically, the Commission failed to exercise these powers vigorously, and, like many government regulatory agencies, it tended to become dominated by the industry it supposedly regulated. Consequently, maintaining the status quo was high on its list of values to be protected. This situation, however, has been dramatically altered since the early 1970s.

After years of apparent satisfaction with the regulated monopoly as the

Table 9.1. Common-Carrier Services Tariff Directory

Service	FCC Tariff number
Aviation radio telephone	ATT No. 263
Broadband	WU No. 246
Cablegram	See "Telegram"
Conference telephone	ATT No. 263
Datacom	WU No. 257
Dataphone	
Digital Service	See "Private line"
Domestic	ATT No. 260, ATT No. 263 (See "Broadband")
Overseas	See "Datel"
Dataphone-50 (50 kbps switched service)	ATT No. 263
Datel	FC No. 13, ITT No. 48, RCA No. 79, WUI No. 11, WU No. 246
Datrex	ATT No. 260
Experimental purposes	ATT No. 258
Hot line	
Domestic	WU No. 254
Overseas	ITT No. 43, RCA No. 85
INFO-COM	WU No. 252
Leased channel	See "Private line"
Mailgram	WU No. 256, WU No. 260
Maritime mobile radio telephone	ATT No. 263
Packet switched	TELENET No. 1
Picturephone	ATT No. 263
Private line	
Digital	ATT No. 267
Domestic	ATT No. 260, MCI No. 1, SPCC No. 1, WTCI No. 1, WU No. 254
Overseas	ATT No. 260, ITT No. 43, RCA No. 67, RCA No. 58, TRT No. 63, WUI No. 4, WU No. 254

way-of-life of the communication industry, the FCC has done a turnabout and embraced competition as the means of stimulating innovation and efficiency. In its landmark Carterphone decision in 1968 (see Section 9.7 below), the commission broke the carriers' monopoly on the source of terminal equipment and systems to be attached to or interconnected with the telephone network. A second landmark decision (MCI, 1969; see Section 9.8 below) authorized the first specialized private line carrier to enter the market and compete with the Bell System and Western Union. This was followed by the domestic satellite (Domsat) decision (1972), where the Commission reversed itself and invited applications from all interested parties for the establishment of competitive domestic

Table 9.1. (*continued*)

Service	FCC Tariff number
Program service	See "Private line"
Public land mobile radio telephone	ATT No. 263
Rate center listing	ATT No. 255, WU No. 254
Satellite channels	ASC No. 1, WU No. 261, RCA Global No. 1
SICOM	WU No. 251
Special construction	ATT No. 262
TCS (Telex Computer Service)	WU No. 240
Telegram	
Domestic	WU No. 255
Overseas	WU No. 224, WU No. 233, WU No. 236, ITT No. 7, RCA No. 60, TRT No. 60, WUI No. 12
Telephone	
Domestic LD	ATT No. 263
Short period	ATT No. 261
Bridged extensions	ATT No. 259
Overseas	ATT No. 263
Telephoto (Series 4000)	See "Private line"
Television	
Domestic	ATT No. 260
Overseas	Joint No. 2
TELEX	
Domestic	WU No. 240
Overseas	ITT No. 12, RCA No. 52, TR No. 64, WUI No. 5
TELPAK (Series 5000)	See "Private line"
TEL (T) EX	WU No. 240
TWX	WU No. 258
WATS	ATT No. 259
Wideband data	See "Private line" or "DATAPHONE-50"

communications satellites systems. These were the three major decisions that have shaped the course of data communications.

9.5. CONSUMER COMMUNICATIONS REFORM ACT

From 1969 to 1975 these landmark decisions by the FCC opened up the area of leased communications to competition. Immune from competition was the nationwide switched network for voice communications. Now this period produced much court litigation between the established common carriers, principally

AT&T, and the competitive industries, namely, the specialized common carriers and the interconnection equipment manufacturers. Virtually all of the court rulings went against the established common carriers and in effect supported the FCC's pro-competition position.

In 1976 and again in 1977, the telephone industry sponsored the introduction of the "Consumer Telephone Reform Act" in the U.S. Congress. This brief bill, only four pages long, masks many vital and complex issues of national telecommunications policy. But on some matters the intent is crystal clear. The intent of this legislation was to:

1. Bar competition not only in present telephone services but also in any future network communications services that the phone companies may be capable of providing.
2. Transfer jurisdiction over terminals to state regulatory agencies, thus splintering the market.
3. Grant the FCC the power to approve the acquisition of competing carriers by existing carriers in order to guarantee service if competitors fail.
4. Prevent regulatory agencies from declaring that a carrier's rates are too low so long as they cover the carrier's incremental (not full) cost of providing the service.

The introduction of this bill has brought to national attention the question of monopolistic practices in the telecommunications industry and has caused much comment and debate. It is agreed that the Communications Act of 1934 will be revised by Congress, but how that revision will occur is not clear. These issues are of great concern to the designer and the user of data communications systems. Further discussion of these issues can be found in References 1–4.

9.6. THE FCC PUBLIC COMPUTER INQUIRY

By 1966, the FCC was troubled by the increasing communications requirements of computer remote processing applications. The FCC felt that it had to address itself to the regulatory and policy problems created by the increasing interdependence of computer and communications services and facilities. To aid in the formulation policy, the Commission instituted the public computer inquiry in 1966. The response was overwhelming: more than 3000 pages of opinion were submitted, and in 1967 the FCC commissioned the Stanford Research Institute (SRI) to analyze this response. This was accomplished in 1968,[5] and the FCC then allowed for comments on the analyses. It was not until 1971 that the Commission issued its final decision and order.[6] During this lengthy interval, many changes had rendered some of the issues moot. The issues that were covered by the inquiry and the final findings are briefly summarized below.

1. *Regulation of computer services*. The Commission decided in this instance that companies providing data processing services were not subject to regulation regardless of the amount of communications facilities that were used. The question concerned whether or not computer service firms were considered as monopolies or needed industry regulation to best serve the public interest. Because of the existence of a highly competitive situation the commission felt no need to assert regulatory authority.

2. *Protection of privacy*. This issue provided an excellent opportunity for the FCC to study a matter with serious implications in the early years, rather than wait until after-the-fact and then try to correct any inequities. The Commission, however, chose not to take any action on the privacy issue and left such matters to the legislative branch of the government.

3. *Adequacy of common-carrier services and facilities for data transmission*. The response to the commission by the computing community on this issue was overwhelmingly negative. It was alleged that the common carriers were not responsive to the needs of computer technology for communications services, facilities, or equipment, nor were the common carriers inclined to provide such services in the immediate future. In this regard, the common carriers grossly underestimated the market potential in the area of data communications. Subsequent events during the interval of this public inquiry (1966–1971) obviated the need for the commission to make any decisions on this question, although without a doubt, the response to this question certainly influenced other decisions by the commission.

4. *The reasonableness of common-carrier tariff restrictions*. This part of the inquiry addressed itself to the restrictive aspects of the common-carrier tariffs. Specifically, the question was whether or not customer-owned equipment should be attached to the public switched network. This question was also left unanswered because of other decisions by the commission. A second question raised concerning this issue was whether or not customer-owned communications systems should be prohibited from interconnection with the public switched network. Here again, the Commission felt that other decisions made this a moot question. The third aspect of tariff prohibitions concerned the resale or customer sharing of carrier services. At first this issue centered around the bulk private line offerings, known as TELPAK. TELPAK was offered by AT&T as a wideband data-communications service, whose tariff permitted certain classes of customers to share while barring others from doing so. Hence, it is not surprising that TELPAK has been in litigation during most of its history, with the result that the future of this offering is unclear. Of the original four classes, only two classes of service remain: Series 5700 (formerly TELPAK C) and Series 5800 (formerly TELPAK D) with the customers free to permit unlimited sharing. Perhaps sensing the controversy over sharing, AT&T modified its tariffs to permit sharing ("joint use") of its voice- and telegraph-grade private line services.

5. *Common carriers and computer services*. This most important aspect of the FCC inquiry addressed itself to the controversial issues of market entry and industry structure in the communications and computer services areas. With the growth of computer time-sharing technology, common carriers were entering the computer services field with the notion of becoming the information utilities of the future (e.g., Western Union). Furthermore, independent computer service firms were advocating that they be allowed to offer message-switching services to their customers, in addition to data processing or information retrieval services (i.e., "hybrid" systems). The FCC in its 1971 *Final Report and Order* clearly ruled under what circumstances the common carriers may offer data processing services. To wit: The common carriers can provide data-processing services only through affiliates utilizing separate equipment and facilities devoted exclusively to the rendering of data-processing services. Furthermore, the affiliate is prohibited from using the carrier's name, and the carrier is barred from obtaining any data-processing services from the affiliate. Even though these decisions have been appealed, the courts have upheld the main contention; namely, that the separation of communications and data-processing activities is desirable. The second aspect of this question concerned hybrid message-switching systems, that is, those systems which combine both data-processing and communications message switching as a package to the customer. The answer here was not so clear-cut. For instance, the Commission considered deregulation of pure message-switching systems, but concluded that such services are "essentially communications" in nature and "warrant appropriate regulatory treatment as common carrier services under the Act."

Since the FCC had decided that data-processing services would not be regulated, whether communications services were used or not, and that pure message-switching services would continue to be regulated, then how should the "in-between" hybrid system be considered? The commission adopted a guideline which is known as a "primary business test" saying that:

> Where message-switching is offered as an integral part of and as an incidental feature of a package offering that is primarily data processing, there will be total regulatory forebearance with respect to the entire service whether offered by a common carrier or non-common carrier, except to the extent that common carriers offering such a hybrid service will do so through (separate) affiliates. . . . If, on the other hand, the package offering is oriented essentially to satisfy the communications or message switching requirements of the subscriber, and the data processing feature or function is an integral part of, and incidental to message-switching, the entire service will be treated as a communications service for hire, whether offered by a common carrier or a non-common carrier and will be subject to the Communications Act.

Two tests were given to help apply these criteria:

1. Does the service, by virtue of its message-switching capability, have the attributes of the point-to-point services offered by conventional communications carriers, and is it therefore basically a substitute for such services? If so, this suggests that regulation may be applicable.

2. Does the message-switching feature of the service facilitate or relate to the data-processing component, or are the two components essentially independent? In order to avoid regulation, the message-switching feature must not only be secondary in importance when compared with the data-processing aspect of the service, it also must be closely related to it. If the two components are functionally independent, the FCC would regulate the entire service, regardless of the preponderance of the data-processing element.

The major difficulty with the FCC's position was the vagueness of the language. There were too many undefined terms in the ruling. In the late 1970s the position of the FCC was clarified because of the approach taken by two different companies offering the same kind of message-switching services.

One company, Telenet Corp., assumed that it was under FCC jurisdiction from the beginning and filed application with the FCC to operate as a common carrier offering customers a packet-switched service (a form of message-switching service). Approval was duly authorized, tariffs were filed, and the company is operating under regulatory authority.

The other company is Tymshare Inc., which was initially a company offering computer time-sharing services to its customers. With the advent of packet-switching techniques, this company began to offer its customers a packet message-switching service similar to Telenet's. Tymshare, however, initially chose not to be under FCC regulation, but to operate in an open competitive market.

Thus we had two companies offering the same services, one regulated and the other not. The FCC was asked (by Telenet) to put Tymshare under the jurisdiction of the Communications Act and force it to operate as a common carrier for its packet-switched service. Thus the issue was put at the doorstep of the FCC. Tymshare resolved the problem by forming a subsidiary company called Tymnet which petitioned to operate under FCC jurisdiction.

9.7. INTERCONNECTION WITH THE TELEPHONE NETWORK

The interconnection of privately owned terminal devices and communications systems has been prohibited by tariff regulations and by the Federal Communications Commission for many years. If such connections were to be made in an uncontrolled manner they might jeopardize the electrical integrity of the entire telephone network and most certainly would reduce the carrier equipment-rental revenues.

While precedents for foreign attachments have been obtained in the courts, these have typically been treated as singular instances with no general applications. It was not until the Carter Electronics Corp. of Dallas, Texas, brought an antitrust suit against the Bell System in 1966 that the tide of change set in. Southwest Bell threatened to discontinue services to customers who used the Carterphone, an acoustic/induction device used to interconnect the base station of a mobile radio system with the dial telephone network. The antitrust suit was remanded to the FCC because it had primary jurisdiction under the Communications Act of 1934. Historically the FCC had supported the prohibition of foreign attachments in the tariffs. In this instance the arguments were persuasive enough to convince the commission to rule in favor of Carter Electronics. The final decision, in 1968, was a sweeping decision permitting the interconnection of *any* foreign devices (foreign meaning of non-Western Electric manufacture) to the common-carrier communications systems.

The generality of this decision made it a landmark in the history of communications, and it has come to be known as the ''Carterphone decision'' or the ''Interconnection Decision.'' It also served to answer the question of tariff restrictions in the commission's public computer inquiry which had been in progress at the same time.

The carriers responded by seeking FCC reconsideration and judicial review, but they withdrew these motions and revised their interstate tariffs to conform with the FCC decision.

The revised tariffs allowed the attachment of customer-provided devices, such as data modems, to the dial network, and the interconnection of customer-provided communications systems, such as PBX switchboards, to both the dial telephone network and private leased channels. New restrictions, however, were imposed in the revised tariffs:

1. The power and spectral energy distribution of signals entering the switched network from interconnected customer equipment must stay within prescribed limits.

2. A ''protective connecting arrangement'' supplied by the telephone company for a monthly charge is required whenever customer-provided devices or systems are interconnected to the dial telephone network via a direct electrical connection. This coupler, known as the data access arrangement (DAA) or voice access arrangement (VAA), effectively isolates the telphone system from hazardous electrical potentials and ensures that proper signal levels are not exceeded. Telephone company provided attachments, of course, were exempt from the DAA requirements.

3. All network control signaling was to be performed by the telephone

company on the dial network. An exception to this rule became effective in 1971, allowing the attachment of customer-owned tone generating dialing units (but not conventional rotary dials) to the switched network.

These restrictions did not deter companies from using foreign devices in their communications systems, with the result that an industry grew from virtually zero dollars revenue in 1969 to a billion dollar revenue in the 1970s. This is the interconnect industry, which includes suppliers of data modems, various types of private manual and automatic switchboards, communications cost- and utilization-monitoring equipment, communications call-routing equipment, etc.

Competition in the data-communications modem market has caused prices to drop while the throughput of data over dial telephone lines has increased. The telephone companies have responded by offering equipment and services which were alleged to be impossibilities in the 1960s, and at reasonable prices. All of this has definitely benefitted the user.

Many users and suppliers of telephone equipment have strenuously objected to the requirements of carrier-provided DAAs (or VAAs) as being too restrictive. After many years of proceedings, the FCC has decided to permit direct connection of all types of customer-furnished terminal equipment (except PBX switchboards, key telephone systems, and main and coin telephones) to the public telephone network. The equipment must either be certified or it must be connected through registered protective circuitry. This decision was implemented in 1977.

9.8. SPECIALIZED COMMON CARRIERS[7]

In 1963 a small company named Microwave Communications, Inc. (MCI), applied to the FCC for permission to build a microwave relay system between Chicago and St. Louis, a distance of 263 miles. What made this application distinct from other private system applications was that MCI wished to be a common carrier and to offer the public a variety of dedicated private line communications services in direct competition with the Bell System and Western Union.

They argued their case before the Commission, and, in 1969, Microwave Communications, Inc., was finally given approval for construction permits. That they perservered for such a long time is in itself a remarkable feat. The Commission had fully expected that this was a one-time case and that the matter would end with MCI. They were very much surprised upon receiving a flood of over 1900 applications for communications systems from 34 firms proposing to build over 40,000 miles of specialized carrier facilities throughout the country.

This interest was entirely unexpected. A new policy had to be formulated, so the commission instituted a public inquiry on the competition issue. The responses were in favor of competing common carriers, saying that the data-communication needs of the computer community were not being met by the existing common carriers. The Commission issued, in 1970, its specialized common-carrier decision, which is sometimes referred to as Docket #18920. This landmark decision again favored competition in the data communications field. The primary restriction was that the public switched voice-telephone network would remain a protected domain.

Through periods of growth, retrenchment, and mergers the following companies have survived to the 1980s:

MCI Telecommunications Corp. is the parent company for some 18 affiliated companies, the most noteworthy being Microwave Communication, Inc. (the original FCC petitioner), Nebraska Consolidated Communications Corp. (NCCC), and Western Tele-Communications, Inc. (WTCI).

Southern Pacific Communications Co. (SPCC) is a subsidiary of the Southern Pacific Transportation Co. which currently operates the nation's largest private microwave-radio relay system in support of its transportation activities. In 1974, SPCC became the first coast-to-coast specialized common carrier. SPCC acquired the communications facilities of United Video, Inc. giving them a Dallas-St. Louis link. SPCC also acquired the facilities of DATRAN Corporation which allowed them to offer digital transmission services.

United States Transmission Systems (USTS) is a subsidiary of American Cable and Radio Corp., which is a wholly owned subsidiary of International Telephone and Telegraph Corp (ITT). USTS has constructed a microwave facility along the right-of-way of the Transcontinental Gas Pipe Line company from Houston, Texas, to New York and is offering a variety of services.

9.9. VALUE-ADDED CARRIER SERVICES

A value-added carrier takes advantage of large economies of scale realized by the creation of a very large network to fully utilize such expensive resources as transmission lines and message-switching equipment. This network is shared among the carrier's user-subscribers through a tariff charge based mainly on traffic volume. Leasing existing communications facilities, the carrier can obtain as much transmission capacity for each location as is required by the traffic load. Furthermore, this provides the carrier with the flexibility to adapt quickly to geographical demands and subscriber traffic and to provide new types of services as they become available from established common carriers.

The value-added network is different from both present data transmission services and private data networks in that a sophisticated technology known as packet switching is employed for the transfer of messages. The technique of packet switching makes it possible for the value-added carrier, as the operator of the network, to provide any size subscriber with a fast, error-free, response and with low cost-per-transaction data-communications service such as usually found only in private systems.

Value-added networks have their origin in the ARPANET, a nationwide consortium of computers at numerous research centers tied together over a packet-switched network, which is operated in behalf of the government to support research activities of various Federal agencies. In 1973 the FCC approved the concept of value-added networks to be regulated as common carriers and declared an open entry (nonmonopoly) policy permitting potential public network operators to apply for FCC approval. Presently two such organizations are offering value-added carrier services: Telenet Communications Corporation and TYMNET Corporation.

The actual operation of the value-added carriers (VAC) was made possible when AT&T amended its FCC tariff 260 to permit VACs to "resell" the transmission channels they lease from AT&T to value-added network subscribers. Furthermore, AT&T specifically included provisions for lease of Dataphone Digital Service (DDS) lines to VACs for resale in its FCC tariff 267. Other specialized common carriers, as well as satellite carriers, have agreed to provide wideband transmission facilities to the VACs.

The value-added carrier provides a subscriber with data-transfer capability between any two or more dynamically selected user stations, where a user station is defined as a data terminal or host computer. To accomplish this, the value-added carrier leases long-haul wideband channels and invests in computerized interface and switching equipment, high-speed modems, diagnostic facilities, etc., to build a network. The carrier programs the computer interfaces to provide such services as speed conversion, code conversion, error detection, and control for the subscribers as well as to establish and operate monitor centers for the collection of user traffic statistics and billings.

For this service the user pays a tariffed charge based on volume rather than distance. There is a basic charge (approximately $0.50) for a kilopacket, 1,000 packets of up to 1024 bits each, independent of mileage between stations. In addition, there is a monthly charge (and a one-time installation charge) for connecting an access line from the user's station to a port at the value-added carrier's nearest central office. Toll charges for dial-up calls are paid for by the subscriber. The access lines and modems are leased by the carrier and paid for by the subscriber. The carrier assumes operational control and responsibility of the lines and modems, thus relieving the burden of dealing with more than one vendor from the customer.

9.10. CATEGORIES OF SERVICES AND EXAMPLES OF RATES

In this section, some of the different kinds of communications services available for data transmission will be described. These services consist of various communication links put together by the common carriers to provide one or more channels for the subscribers of that service. Currently there are four distinct types of services:

1. Analog services—provision of analog channels.
2. Digital services—provision of digital transmission rates of 2.4, 4.8, 9.6, 56.0 kbps
3. Satellite services—may be either analog or digital channels
4. Value-added services—an end-to-end service for the transfer of messages rather than the provision of channels

The rates for these services have undergone a great number of changes in the mid-1970s, partially because of the introduction of new services and partially because of competitive pressures. The rates given here will only serve as examples and *should not be used* in costing real systems. In all cases, the applicable tariff should always be consulted.

9.10.1 Cost of Carrier Services

There are a number of factors that make up the cost of a communications service. Specifically they consist of:

(1) Interexchange channel charge (IXC). This is typically a cost per airline mile per unit of time. The unit of time can be in months, minutes, or seconds. There are usually minimum time charges.

(2) Station charges. These charges cover the termination of the channel at the customer's premises. For value-added carrier services these charges may be referred to as *port charges*. Several different rates apply depending upon whether the termination is single point, multipoint at the same location, multipoint from the same exchange office, etc.

(3) Channel termination charges. These charges cover carrier equipment costs to terminate an interexchange channel at the exchange office. For example, to multiplex or demultiplex a channel. These charges are also called channel service unit (CSU) or data service unit (DSU) charges when the service is digital.

(4) Data access line (DAL). This is a charge on a per airline mile per unit time (usually a month) to connect the subscriber's station termination at the subscriber's premises to the channel termination at the exchange office. There are several different rate structures depending upon the distance traversed.

(5) Installation charge. This is a one-time charge for installing the service for a subscriber.

9.10.2 Channel Charges

There are several ways in which the interexchange channel charges (IXC) are tariffed. The simplest form is the flat rate per mile per month. The distances are always calculated as airline miles between carrier rate centers using a V-H coordinate* grid. Each rate center is given a unique V-H coordinate number.

Some of the tariffs use a rate step function which is more tedious to work with. The rates per mile decrease with increased distance. That is, the per mile cost of the 10th mile is much greater than the per mile cost of the 100th mile. To illustrate, suppose the tariff for a channel is given as:

Miles	0–15	16–25	26–100	101–1000	1001–
Rate ($/mi-month)	1.80	1.50	1.12	0.66	0.40

Then the calculation for 247 miles would appear as

$$\begin{aligned} \text{IXC} &= 15 \times 1.80 + 10 \times 1.50 + 75 \times 1.12 + 147 \times 0.66 \\ &= \$223.02 \text{ per month} \end{aligned}$$

If one were costing out a network where many of these calculations were required, it would be worthwhile to use a computer. Many consulting organizations do provide such computerized services.

Other forms of the interexchange channel charge are based on time-distance. An example is the direct distance dialing (DDD) service where the applicable rate structure is determined by the time-of-day and the day-of-week of the calling station. In addition there would be one rate for the first minute and another rate for succeeding minutes. Such time-dependent charges are known as message-toll (services) or volume-dependent charges.

9.10.3 Where to Get Rate Information

There are several organizations that publish rates and analyses of tariffs. Frost and Sullivan, Inc., publishes the *World Telecommunications Directory* containing the telecommunications services and tariffs in 45 countries around the world. Another organization, the Center for Communications Management Incorporated (CCMI) in Ramsey, New Jersey, publishes analyses of tariff rates and services.

Datapro, Inc., publishes comparative tariff rates in its periodic reports on

*AT&T designation.

data communications services. Auerbach publishes similar reports. Of course, the place to obtain the correct information is from the carrier's own tariff which should be readily available from the carrier.

9.11. EXAMPLES OF SERVICES FOR ANALOG SYSTEMS

1. *DDD,* or direct long-distance calling, using the public switched network. This service offered by AT&T consists of an IXC charge based on time-of-day and day-of-week and uses a per minute charge with varying distance. Intrastate IXC charges also vary from state to state.

2. *WATS* (wide-area telephone service). This is a dial-up, either inward calling or outward calling, service offered by AT&T for a geographic area to cover a monthly time period. This particular service has undergone a number of revisions and has become more expensive with each change. Initially, for a flat monthly rate, a user had an unlimited number of calls to 6 different bands (or geographic regions) emanating from his state. These bands were, at least in principal, made to contain equal numbers of telephones. This was changed to 5 bands and either a full business days (FBD) or measured time service (MTS). FBD covered up to 240 hours or 14,400 calls in a month and MTS covered up to ten hours or 600 calls in a month. Exceeding either of these limitations resulted in an hourly charge depending upon the type of service. This service was again changed (1977) to provide for three bands in the continental U.S. with band four for Alaska and Hawaii. The rates for inward calls were made different from those for outward calls.

3. *TELEX/TWX*. This is a low-speed switched network service offered by Western Union for the transmission of messages between teleprinter terminals. The rate structure for this service includes IXC mileage charges and varying station charges depending upon the equipment used.

4. *Dataphone 50*. This is a high-speed (50 kbps) switched data service offered by AT&T to subscribers in nine cities of the U.S. Because of its expense and limited availability it was never very popular.

5. *Private leased channels*. These are analog channels offered by the common carriers to subscribers for the transmission of voice, digital data, or video material. It is in these services that competition exists among the specialized common carriers and the established common carriers (Telcos). Table 9.2 shows the different kinds of offerings available by AT&T under tariff #260. From this table only series 1000, 3000, 5000, and 8000 services are applicable to data communications. Within the series 3000 offerings, the 3002 voice channel with a bandwidth from 300 to 3400 Hz is suitable for data transmission.

The tariff for the single-voice channel has undergone numerous changes. In the late 1960s it was known as Schedule 4. This was then changed to type 3002, which is its common reference. Then this service was changed to Hi–Lo, refer-

Table 9.2. A Summary of Private Leased Services Available from AT&T under FCC Tariff #260

Series 1000	Unconditioned channels suitable for dc mark space or binary transmissions up to 150 baud for half-duplex or full-duplex operation on a point-to-point or multipoint basis. The particular offerings are:
	Type 1001 up to 30 baud for remote metering
	Type 1002 up to 55 baud for teleprinter use
	Type 1003 up to 55 baud for radiotelegraph
	Type 1005 up to 75 baud for teleprinters
	Type 1006 up to 150 baud for teleprinters
Series 2000	For voice transmission only.
Series 3000	Voice-grade channels for the transmission of data furnished for half- or full-duplex operations on a point-to-point or multipoint basis:
	Type 3001 for remote metering or supervisory control
	Type 3002 for the transmission of data. Known as Hi-Lo. Conditioning options available
Series 4000	Voice-grade channels for the transmission of telephotograph or facsimile.
Series 5000	Wideband channels for the transmission of data. Formerly known as TELPAK:
	Type 5700 a 240-kHz channel
	Type 5800 a one-MHz channel
Series 6000	Audio program material for AM, FM, and TV.
Series 7000	Video and ETV material.
Series 8000	A 48-kHz channel suitable for data or facsimile transmission:
	Type 8801 a 20-kHz channel for data at 40.8 or 50 kbps
	Type 8803 a 6-voice channel for data at 19.2 kbps or facsimile at 29–44 kHz
Series 10000	Interconnection to customer-provided private communications systems.
Series 11000	Data "pipe" offering in 1972. Not in effect.

ring to having a channel between high-density and low-density rate centers with differing rate structures. This service was again changed to MLS, or MPLS, (multiple private line service) with Class A or Class B rate centers.

It is for the type 3002 channel that conditioning (described in Chapter 8) C1, C2, C4, or D1 is available. The literature refers to this particular type of channel as "PL," "C2," or "C4," "3002-C2," or "private-voice channel". Western Union, MCI, SPCC, and USTS are common carriers that offer private voice channel services similar to AT&T's 3002.

9.12. EXAMPLES OF DIGITAL SERVICES

Digital services are offered by the common carriers for the transmission of digital data at specific rates of 2.4, 4.8, 9.6, and 56.0 kbps. Data Transmission Corporation (DATRAN) pioneered in this field hoping to compete with AT&T, but went bankrupt in 1976. Its facilities were acquired by SPCC, which now offers a similar digital service. AT&T offers Dataphone Digital Service (DDS) to many cities in the U.S. under Tariff #267 and Tariff #260. AT&T was able to offer DDS in response to DATRAN's digital service in a remarkably short period of time by modifying their long-haul analog carrier facilities to carry digital data in the low end of the frequency spectrum [known as data-under-voice (DUV)].

Digital services are extremely good channels, having bit error rates of one in 10^9 to 10^{12} bits, and for this reason they should be used when both end-points are located in cities having such services. For cities not having digital services, an analog link would be required to the nearest digital service city. Because analog circuits have a higher error rate, it is not advisable to mix the services unless economic considerations justify it.

9.13. EXAMPLES OF DOMESTIC SATELLITE OFFERINGS

At present, communication satellite offerings are point-to-point channels between selected cities in the U.S. The following companies are offering satellite services:

- Western Union has two WESTAR satellites and offers a wide range of channels.
- RCA Americom has two SATCOM satellites and also offers a wide range of channels.
- ASC (American Satellite Corp.) has no satellites; it offers services through channels leased from Western Union or RCA Americom.
- AT&T–GTE leases channels from COMSAT's domestic satellites called COMSTAR.

Only certain cities are presently being served. To use satellite channels between cities, terrestrial services must be obtained to the closest city with a satellite antenna.

Chapter 10

Modem Equipment

The modem, which is a contraction of the words modulator–demodulator, is the device that performs the functions of transmitting and receiving the data signals over the communications channel. Modems are used on analog circuits. Occasionally the literature will refer to "digital modems" as loosely describing either the transmission of digital data over analog circuits or the transmission of digital data over digital communication links. In the latter case, the transmitter–receiver is more descriptively referred to as a channel service unit or digital service unit. In other words, modems are not used on digital systems.

The transmitter modulates a carrier frequency by an input baseband signal which may be either a digital or an analog waveform. The receiver accepts the modulated signal and recovers the original baseband signal. The modem, as the implementation of a particular modulation method, can have one or more bits encoded in the modulated signal. That is to say, it is the modulation process that determines the number of signal levels to be transmitted.

10.1. MODEM TERMINOLOGY

The modem is referred to by a number of different names. The carrier companies refer to modems as *data sets*. Note that this term is not to be confused with a computer dataset referring to a secondary storage device. AT&T refers to

Western Electric-manufactured modems as *Dataphones®*. Some confusion arises here also in that the term Dataphone is used to describe several AT&T carrier-provided services for the transmission of digital data. IBM also did not help matters very much when they referred to modems as "line adapters." What makes this term particularly confusing is that devices called line adapters are used in communications peripheral devices to computer systems to adjust and regulate the electrical (voltage and current) levels of the signals. Thus the term line adapter more commonly refers to an interface between a computer port and the data channel. The line adapter may be used whether or not a modem is used.

It should be noted that baseband signals up to 1200 bps can be transmitted over twisted wire pair cables for distances up to 900 meters (about 3000 feet) without using modems.[1] The EIA Standard, however, specifies a maximum distance at 15 meters (about 50 feet).[2,3] If it is desired to transmit at higher bit rates or over slightly longer distances, *limited-distance modems* are available from a number of vendors. This approach provides a data transmission capability for such applications as an in-plant site, a university campus, or a corporate headquarters located in a high-rise office building at a considerable savings in cost compared to common-carrier services. Modems are constructed as either stand-alone devices as shown in Figure 10.1 or as circuit boards that are integrated into terminal devices as shown in Figure 10.2. Modem capabilities have expanded so much that they can be built to perform multiplexing operations.

10.2. MODEM CLASSIFICATION

Modems can be broadly categorized as hard-wired, soft-wired, or limited distance. By hard-wired we mean a modem that is either a stand-alone device or

Figure 10.1. Modem as a stand-alone device. Shown is a Racal/Vadic 3455 modem that operates at 1200 bps full-duplex over the switched network or a two-wire-leased channel. This modem uses the method of quadrature amplitude modulation (QAM) to achieve full-duplex operation on a narrow bandwith voice channel. (Courtesy of Racal-Vadix-Inc.)

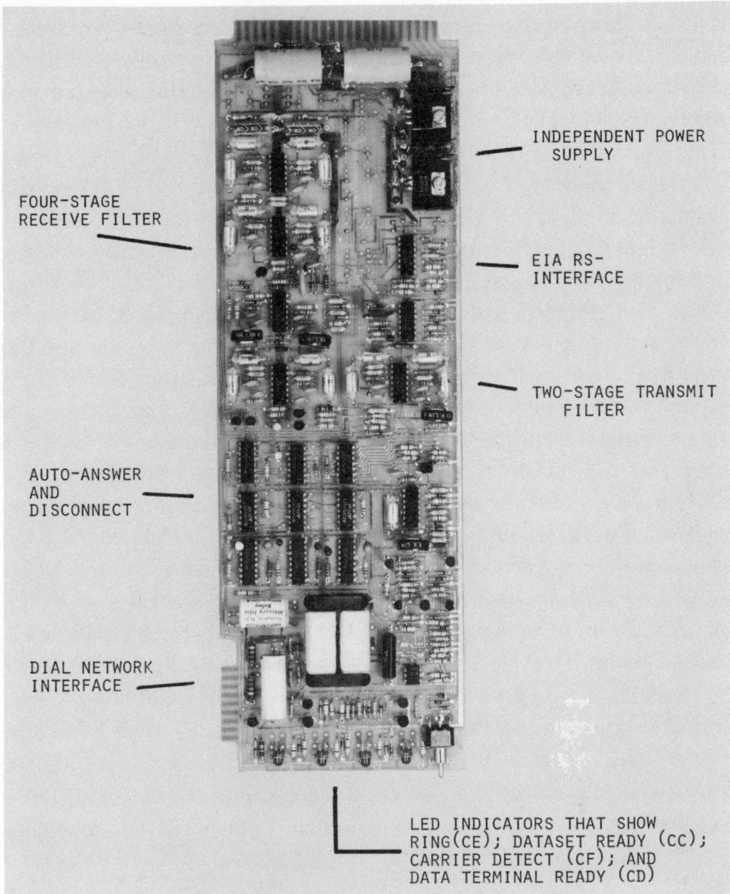

Figure 10.2. Modem as a printed circuit (PC) board is suitable for incorporation into a terminal device or as a rack of modems to computer ports. (Courtesy of Com Data Corp.)

an integrated circuitboard (a part of a terminal) that is connected *permanently* to the communication channel. The modem may be constructed to provide alternate voice or data communications over the channel, or it may provide auxiliary functions such as automatic calling or automatic answering. The term soft-wired refers to acoustic-coupler devices. These are low-speed (up to 600 bps) modems that are attached to the ear-and-mouthpiece of a telephone handset by rubber cups. Acoustic couplers have the advantage of portability. Limited-distance modems, which were previously described, can provide data transmission capability over direct connection wires. The distinction to be made is that direct connection wires do not go through switching or multiplexing equipment as may be found in telephone plant connections.

Modems are also characterized according to the data rates accommodated by the channel: low speed (up to 600 bps), medium speed (600–2400 bps), high speed (up to 10,800 bps) for use on a voice channel whose bandwidth is from 300 to 3400 Hz; and wideband (above 19,200 bps) for use on wideband communication channels.

Low-speed modems almost universally use frequency-shift keying (FSK) as the modulation method (cf. Section 5.7). Figure 10.3 illustrates the frequency allocation for a typical low-speed modem using two frequency tones for the originate mark ("1") and space ("0") and two tones for the answer mark and space. With this arrangement one modem has to be designated the "originate" modem, as shown in Figure 10.4, and the other modem is designated the "answer" modem to receive at the lower frequencies and transmit at the higher frequencies. Low-speed modems are used for keyboard terminal devices such as teleprinters. Acoustic-coupler devices are low-speed modems and have the same frequency spectrum as shown in Figure 10.3. It is possible to have a portable terminal equipped with an acoustic coupler communicate with a hard-wired modem located at the computer port.

Medium-speed voice-band modems are available using a variety of modulation methods. Frequency-shift keying (FSK) can be used at rates up to 1800 bps with the most common being a 1200-bps modem. When the bit rate goes up, the channel bandwidth must increase (cf. Sections 4.6 and 4.7). Figure 10.4 shows the frequency allocation for a 1200-bps modem. Note that only two tones can be transmitted in the bandwidth, while at the lower speed four tones could be transmitted. The arrangement shown in Figure 10.3 allows full-duplex (FDX) operation and the arrangement shown in Figure 10.4 allows only half-duplex (HDX) operation.

Voice-band modems constitute the largest market item and offer the widest

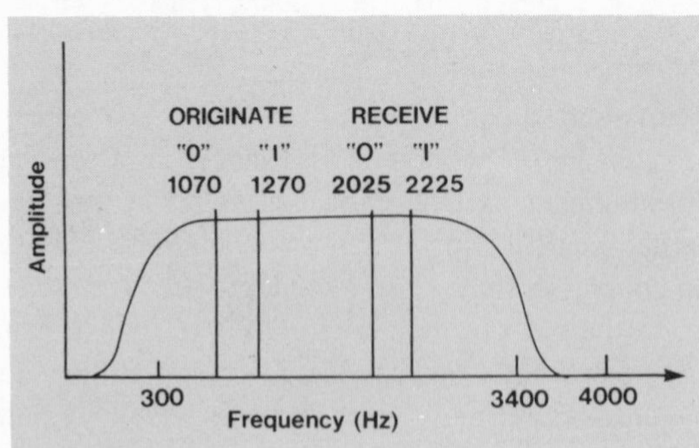

Figure 10.3. The frequency allocation for transmitting tones representing zero and one bits in a full-duplex or half-duplex mode at 300 bps using frequency-shift keying (FSK) as the modulation method.

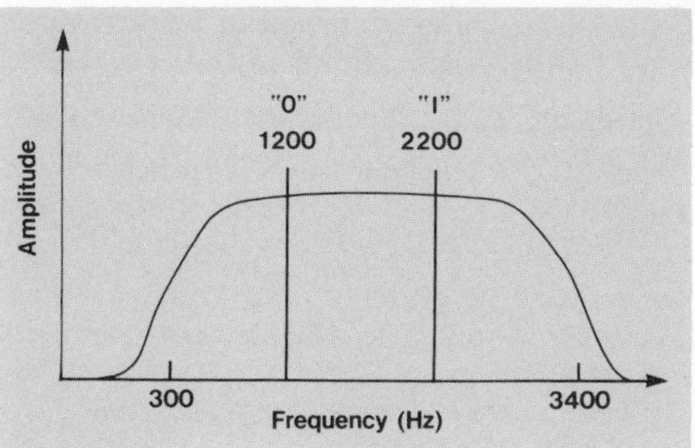

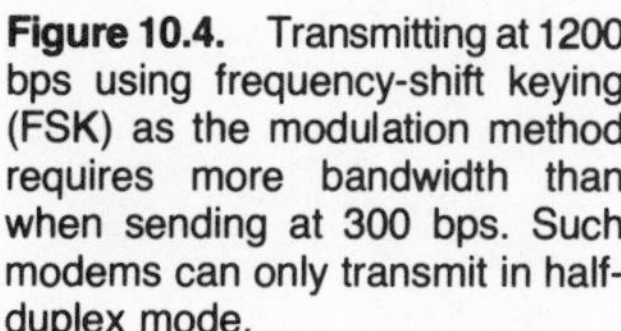
Figure 10.4. Transmitting at 1200 bps using frequency-shift keying (FSK) as the modulation method requires more bandwidth than when sending at 300 bps. Such modems can only transmit in half-duplex mode.

variety of devices. Data rates of up to 10,800 bps are offered in this category of modem. Voice-band modems are designed to operate either on private leased channels or on the switched network. A communication channel on the switched network is subject to distortion due to switching equipment and the operation of echo-suppressor disablers. In addition, the signal characteristics must be such that they do not interfere with the inband supervisory network-control signals. Because of all of these restrictions, data speeds achieved on switched channels are lower than on private leased channels. The characteristics of a private leased channel can be controlled more closely because the channel is connected on a permanent basis (i.e., according to the terms of the lease arrangement). In addition, conditioning may be obtained for leased channels, which improves the response characteristics of the channel, and thus allow higher data rates to be transmitted. Modems are not usually interchangeable between leased channels and switched channels because of different frequency-bandwidth requirements and channel characteristics.

Wideband modems are used for data rates from 19,200 bps on up. The market for wideband modems is small compared to that of voice-channel modems. The common carriers have permitted only carrier-supplied modems to be used on leased wideband channels. For example, the AT&T series 5000 and 8000 channels provide a station-to-station service at specified data rates with their own modems included in the station charges. Thus, at present, wideband modems are used mostly on privately owned communication systems and on point-to-point cables not connected to common-carrier facilities.

10.3. MODEM MODULATION METHODS

There are a number of different modulation methods used in the modems offered today. Table 10.1 lists some of the different types according to data rates. The low-speed modems universally use FSK. In fact FSK is used in modems at

Table 10.1. Different Types of Modem Modulation Methods and Channel Applications as Given by Bell System Modems

Series 100 Binary digital data at low speed, up to 300 bps.			
103A	FSK (F1M = 1070, F1S = 1270, F2M = 2025, F2S = 2225 Hz)		
113A/B	FSK		
Series 200 Binary digital data over voice channels.			
202C	FSK	1200 bps	DDD
		1800 bps	PL(C2)
202D	FSK	1800 bps	PL(C2)
202E	FSK	1200 bps	DDD
		1800 bps	PL(C2)
202R	FSK	1800 bps	PL(C2)
202S	FSK	1200 bps	DDD-asynchronous
202T	FSK	1800 bps	PL(C2)
203A/B/C	VSB	3600 bps	DDD
		7200 bps	PL
208A	8ϕ-PSK	4800 bps	PL
208B	8ϕ-PSK	4800 bps	DDD
209A	QAM	9600 bps	PL(D1)
212A	QAM	1200 bps	FDX (2-wire)
Series 300 Wideband transmission of serial data. Part of wideband service and therefore not available separately.			
301B	PSK	40.8 kbps	
303B	VSB	19.2 kbps	
303C	VSB	50.0 kbps	
303D	VSB	230.4 kbps	
Series 400 Low- and medium-speed parallel digital data transmission.			
403D/E	FSK	10 char/sec	
407E	FSK	10 char/sec (Touchtone)	
Series 500 High-speed parallel digital data.			
Series 600 Voice-band analog and special modulation types.			
Series 700 Wideband-analog and special modulation types.			
Series 800 Auxiliary data units.			

data rates up to 1800 bps. At 2000–4800 bps, four-phase-shift-keying (4ϕ-PSK) is the most popular. Duobinary FM is used at rates of 2000–2400 bps. There are some modems that are vestigial sideband AM (VSB–AM) up to 4800 bps. From 4800–10,800 bps either 4-phase or 8-phase in combination with multilevel AM is used. Quadrature AM (QAM) is used to achieve 9600 bps.

10.4. MODEM INTERFACE SPECIFICATIONS

One of the more significant developments in data transmission has been the adoption of a standard interface between the modem and data terminal commonly known as a 25-pin Cannon, or Cinch, plug. What makes this novel is that by agreement the signals on each of the 25 wires going into the plug have predefined functions. Table 10.2 lists these functions for the 25–pin connector.

This standard interface is known as EIA RS-232C for Electronic Industries Association standard RS-232 version C interface. The similar military designation is MIL-188C for United States Military data communications systems. The European or International standard interface is CCITT V.24, which is similar to RS-232. Compliance with this specification by the modem and data terminal manufacturer should be an essential selection criterion.

Figure 10.5 illustrates some of the different equipment configurations that are possible in a data-communications system. Observe that the RS-232 interface is positioned between the modem and either the terminal or the computer. Each of the wires in the interface carries a specific signal between these devices.

COMPUTER PORT	X	X	X	X	X	X	X	X
LINE ADAPTER		X	X					X
RS-232 INTERFACE	X		X	X	X	X	X	
MODEM	X			X	X	X	X	
LIMITED-DISTANCE MODEM			X					
AUTOMATIC ANSWER UNIT	X			X	X	X		
DATA ACCESS ARRANGEMENT				X				
SUBSCRIBER STATION	X			X	X	X	X	
COMMON CARRIER LINE	X			X	X	X	X	
SUBSCRIBER STATION	X			X	X	X	X	
DATA ACCESS ARRANGEMENT				X				
AUTOMATIC CALLING UNIT				X				
LIMITED-DISTANCE MODEM			X					
MODEM	X			X	X		X	
ACOUSTIC COUPLER						X		
RS-232 INTERFACE	X		X	X	X	X	X	
LINE ADAPTER								X
TERMINAL	X	X	X		X	X	X	
COMPUTER PORT				X				X

Figure 10.5. The possible equipment configurations for analog data transmission systems are shown as they might be arranged in different applications.

Table 10.2. RS-232C Circuit Interface Standards and How They Are Interpreted in Certain Modems

Pin number	Description	EIA RS-232C	CCITT V.24	Modem circuit designations: Bell 113A	Bell 202S/T	Bell 208B	Bell 209A
1.	Protective ground. Electrical frame and ac power ground.	AA	101	AA	AA	AA	AA
2.	Transmitted data. Originating terminal sends via modem.	BA	103	BA	BA	BA	BA
3.	Received data. Originating terminal receives data via modem.	BB	104	BB	BB	BB	BB
4.	Request to send (RTS). Indication to originating terminal modem that the terminal is ready to send.	CA	105	—	CA	CA	CA
5.	Clear to send (CTS). Indication to terminal that modem is ready to send data.	CB	106	CB	CB	CB	CB
6.	Data set ready (DSR). Indication to terminal that modem is not in a test mode and that modem power is ON.	CC	107	CC	CC	CC	CC
7.	Signal ground. Establishes a common reference point between terminal and modem.	AB	102	AB	AB	AB	AB
8.	Received line signal detector (LSD). Indication to terminal that modem is receiving a carrier signal from sending modem.	CF	109	CF	CF	CF	CF
9.	Reserved for test.	—	—	+P	—	T[b]	T[b]
10.	Reserved for test.	—	—	−P	—	T[b]	T[b]
11.	Not assigned.	—	—	—	SCA	—	QM[e]
12.	Secondary received line signal detector. Indication to terminal that its modem is receiving secondary carrier signals from sending modem.	SCF	122	—	SCF	—	—

13. Secondary clear to send. Indication SCB 121 to terminal that its modem is ready to send signals via the secondary channel.	SCB	121	—	—	—	—
14. Secondary transmitted data. Terminal send data via modem over secondary channel.	SCA	118	—	—	—	—
15. Transmitter signal element timing. A signal from modem to sending terminal to provide signal-element timing information.	DB	114	—	—	DB	DB
16. Secondary received data. Received data to originating terminal via modem on secondary channel.	SBB	119	—	—	DCT[c]	DCT[c]
17. Receiver signal element timing. Signal to receiving terminal to provide signal-element timing. Nominally indicates center of each signal element on circuit BB.	DD	115	—	—	DD	DD
18. Not assigned.	—	—	—	—	DCR[d]	DCR[d]
19. Secondary request to send. Indication to modem that originating modem is ready to send via secondary channel.	SCA	120	—	SCA	—	—
20. Data terminal ready (DTR). Indication to modem that terminal is ready to send and receive data.	CD	108.2	CD	CD	CD	—
21. Signal quality detector. Indication from modem that defined error rate exceeded in received data.	CG	110	—	—	—	CG
22. Ring indicator (RI). Signal from modem to terminal that a ringing signal is being received due to an incoming call.	CE	125	CE	CE	CE	—
23. Data signal rate selector. Selects one of two signaling rates in modems having two rates.	CH/CI	111	—	—	—	—
24. Transmit signal element timing. Terminal provides signal element timing to modem.	DA	113	—	—	DA	DA
25. Not assigned.	—	—	CN[a]	—	T[b]	T[b]

[a] Terminal busy. Line to data set made to appear busy.
[b] Reserved for testing.
[c] Divided clock transmitter.
[d] Divided clock receiver.
[e] Equalizer mode—indicates if adaptive equalizer needs retraining.

Figure 10.6 shows the exchange of signals between a terminal and a modem with an automatic answer unit responding to to an originating modem's call. Figure 10.7 shows the exchange of signals between modems during data transfer on a half-duplex channel.

10.5. MODEM TRANSMISSION CHARACTERISTICS

The modem can operate in half-duplex (HDX) or full-duplex (FDX), either synchronously or asynchronously, and in serial-by-bit or parallel-by-bit. Voice-channel modems using the switched telephone network (i.e., either DDD or WATS) for the most part operate as HDX. This is because the telephone plant has consisted of two-wire subscriber loops and four-wire trunks. Two-wire systems, until recently, could only support HDX operation. There are currently

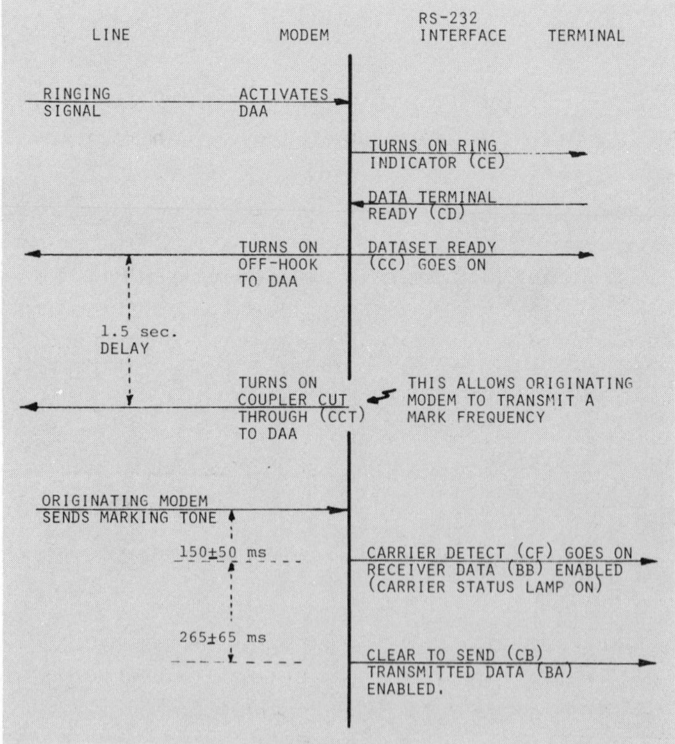

Figure 10.6. Exchange of signals between a terminal and a typical modem with an automatic answer unit and a data access arrangement (DAA).

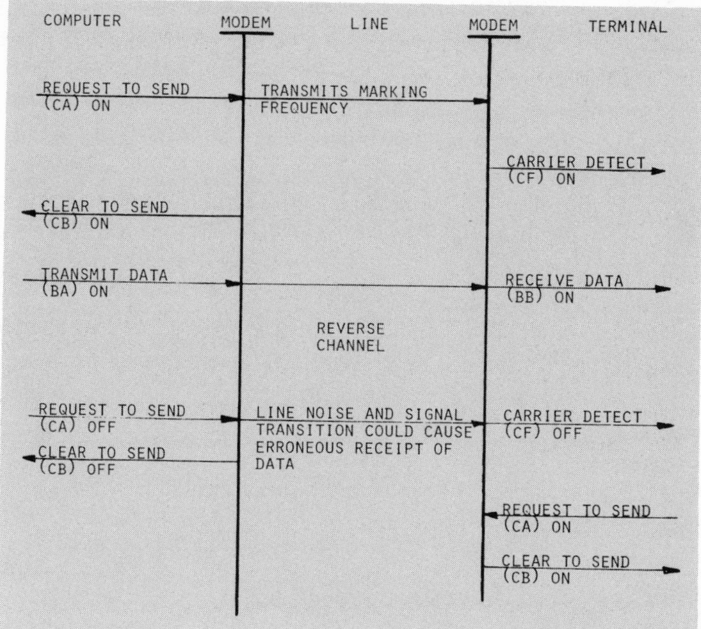

Figure 10.7. Exchange of data signals between modems on a half-duplex (HDX) channel.

several modems available that offer 1200 bps FDX capabilities on two-wire circuits. See Figure 10.1.

The most serious disadvantage of half-duplex operation is the turnaround delay in ARQ systems (automatic request for repeat). Here the receiving terminal must acknowledge the receipt of each error-free block of data or request retransmission of the data block when it contains errors. Thus the HDX communications path must be turned around twice for each data block transmitted: once to send back a reply and the second time to transfer the next data block. The exchange of signals for a turnaround is shown in Figure 10.7 on a half-duplex arrangement. The total turnaround delay T_D in a channel that contains an echo suppressor is

$$T_D = 2(T_{CTS} + T_P + T_M) + T_R + T_{Ack} + T_T$$

In this relation,

T_{CTS} is the delay time in the modem in generating the "clear-to-send" signal in response to the "request-to-send" signal from the data terminal in order to accommodate echo-suppressor turnaround delay. For conventional modems used on the telephone network, this time is about 10–240 milliseconds (ms) and is the most significant contribution to the total turnaround delay.

T_p is the one-way signal propagation (absolute) delay that is dependent on the length of the connective through the network. This delay varies from 2–15 ms for terrestial links and is about 300 ms for satellite links.

T_M is the one-way signal propagation delay through the modem transmitter and receiver circuitry as a pair. This delay can vary from 3–15 ms depending upon the modem design.

T_R is the reaction time of the receiving data-terminal equipment to respond with a "request-to-send" signal to send a reply for the received data block. This delay is usually a few ms, but can be considerably longer depending on the software and the terminal design.

T_{Ack} is the time required for the data terminal to send a reply at the modem bit rate. The reply, usually 4 to 10 characters, is determined by the communication protocol. Each character is from 6 to 11 bits depending upon the communication code and whether the transmission is synchronous or asynchronous.

T_T is the reaction time of the transmitting data terminal to evaluate the reply from the receiving terminal and issue a "request-to-send" signal for the transmission of the next data block. This is usually a few ms and also depends on the terminal design and software capabilities.

Conventional modems operating at 2400 bps would have typical total turnaround times of

$$T_D = 2(100 + 10 + 5) + 3 + 8 + 2 \text{ ms} = 243 \text{ ms}$$

This delay is equivalent to transmitting about 58 ten-bit characters at 2400 bps, and it could cause a substantial reduction in the efficiency of utilization. Most of the delay occurs in the "clear-to-send" signal generation. Some modem manufacturers have reduced this time considerably. In evaluating modem specifications for contemplated HDX operations, this delay should be examined very carefully.

Full-duplex operations avoid this turnaround delay problem, but only at the added expense of a four-wire circuit. This typically costs 10% more per month than a HDX channel when leased from a common carrier. Attendant to the communication cost are the additional costs inherent in the complexity of terminal equipment and software (mainly protocols) required to support FDX operations.

Modems operate either synchronously or asynchronously and either serial-by-bit or parallel-by-bit. A small percentage of modems are parallel-by-bit (which may be thought of as serial-by-character) using multitone FSK modulation and operating at low data rates—approximately 10 characters per second. The majority of the modems are serial-by-bit with the low data rate (up to 1800 bps) being asynchronous and the high data rates (1200–10,800 bps) being synchronous. Modems at data rates from 1200–1800 bps may be either synchronous or asynchronous. Typically when unbuffered keyboard entry devices such as teleprinter terminals are used, the operation is asynchronous because manual input is not continuous. CRT terminal devices, which may be thought of as buffered keyboard entry, can utilize synchronous modems because of the large number of data characters that can be transmitted at one time.

The primary considerations here are costs and channel utilization. As a rule, asynchronous modems are less expensive than synchronous modems. If high data rates warrant it, synchronous modems use channels more efficiently than asynchronous modems. Asynchronous transmission has the built-in inefficiencies of the added start–stop bits.

10.6. MODEM FEATURES

In the consideration of modem specification there are many more options available today than there were before the FCC Interconnect Decision (Docket #18920). Some of these options are highly desirable in terms of increasing transmission efficiencies as well as improving maintenance capabilities in a multivendor situation. The options to consider in modem design are diagnostics, reverse-channel availability, interface specifications, equalization, and compatibility. All of these, of course, are secondary to the evaluation of modem performance.

10.6.1. Diagnostic Options

Most modern modems have some kind of diagnostic capabilities when they are intended for end-user applications as stand-alone devices. These capabilities enable the modem to be conveniently tested on a GO/NO-GO basis. Different modem manufacturers have different approaches to the implementation of this feature. One of the more common approaches is to provide for channel loop-back and a data terminal interface (digital) loop-back switching capability. Some modems are designed so that one modem can switch to one or both of these test modes from the distant end of the line.

The channel loop-back switch enables the digital device connected to the modem to transmit to itself through the modem transmitter and receiver. This is done by disconnecting the modem from the transmission line and connecting the modem transmitter output to the modem receiver input through an appropriate attenuator. The data-terminal equipment's interface loop-back test operates by disconnecting the modem circuitry from the data-terminal equipment and connecting all output signals generated by the data-terminal equipment to the signal inputs of the data-terminal equipment that are usually connected to the modem.

This enables the data terminal to communicate to itself without using the modem circuitry. Both of these features are available for remote loop-back testing using the communication channel. When the data-terminal loop-back test is used remotely, the far-end modem operates as a regenerative repeater.

The modem built-in self-test circuitry must be simple to operate for use by nontechnical personnel. The user should be able to determine if the modem is operating well over the line, and, if the received data has many errors, determine if the modem is defective. This is usually accomplished by using simple pushbutton switches and indicator lamps to show the presence or loss of modulated carrier signals received from distant modems.

A signal-quality indicator on the modem would be very useful to the user–operator. This indicator shows when the received signal quality is sufficient for relatively error-free operation, as well as when the signal quality drops to a level where it is highly probable that the received data contains excessive errors.

An alternative approach is to acquire diagnostic equipment as stand–alone devices in addition to the modem devices. Since 1970 a number of companies have entered this particular market, providing a wide variety of devices that could be readily used by the nontechnical operator. The objective of these diagnostics is to prevent "finger-pointing" between the different suppliers of a data communication system. The common carriers reason that all of this would not be needed (just as it was not available prior to 1970) if they could provide the end-to-end services. Of course, the costs would be appreciably more in such instances.

10.6.2. Reverse Channel

Some modem manufacturers provide a low-speed reverse channel as a method of reducing turnaround delays. The primary channel would operate at 2000–4800 bps data rates and the reverse channel would operate at 5–150 bps. Only ACK/NAK (positive or negative acknowledgement) messages would be sent on this reverse channel, which operates in full-duplex to the primary channel. This greatly reduces the turnaround delays because the modem receive–transmit functions do not have to change until it is desired to alternate the message flow.

10.6.3. Equalization

From Chapter 8 we have seen that the effective countermeasures to frequency-attenuation and envelope-delay distortions are the use of equalization in modem equipment. Remember that the carrier channel can be "conditioned" when used on a lease basis. Modems can be equipped with manual equalization or automatic and adaptive equalization circuits.

Modems equipped with manual equalization have adjusting knobs and an easy-to-read null type of meter. A minimum reading indicates when optimum equalization is obtained. Ease of manually performing the equalization and the amount of equalization possible varies considerably from one manufacturer to another.

Automatic and adaptive equalization are provided by different manufacturers using proprietary methods and add significantly to the cost of modems. Automatic equalization means that the equalization process is automatically initiated and performed. Adaptive equalization continuously adapts the equalization to neutralize any changes in line characteristics that occur during data transmission. A possible method of implementing automatic and adaptive equalization is to use statistical equalizers based on average values of the line characteristics across the bandwidth used by the particular modem.

10.7. COMPATIBILITY

Modems may be compatible with other manufacturer's modems only if they can communicate with each other over a channel. Usually it is not a good idea to mix modem manufacturers on a system. However, significant savings are realizable when modems with fewer options or operational characteristics can be used at some terminal stations. The initial objective of modem manufacturers was to develop Western Electric (WE) modem compatibility to enter that particular market, but as of late, modems have been marketed that are compatible among noncarrier companies.

10.8. SELECTION CRITERIA

As technology progresses and information accumulates, dynamic testing of modems may not be essential before making a definite selection. There was a period of several years, 1970–72, when the interconnect industry was just beginning, during which it was desirable to actually test modems before making a selection. But since those years modem manufacturers have been accumulating data and other information detailing their modem performance capabilities. Thus the problem reduces to what data should be examined in the selection process.

10.8.1. Performance Analysis

The most significant factor in modem performance is the effective net data throughput that can be obtained using the modem. It will suffice to say that these calculations take into account the channel error rates, the block size of data transmitted, and the turnaround delays. Some of the other factors that may be used to provide a comparative evaluation of modem performance are bit error rates, bias distortion for asynchronous modems, and automatic calling and answer tests. More discussion will be found in References 4–7.

A bit error-rate test determines the effective signal-to-noise ratio threshold over a typical transmission line from determinations at different ratios. The results show the approximate distribution of bit errors in terms of number of bit errors in each instance and the time elapsed between consecutive occurrences of bit errors. This information is useful in predicting optimum data block lengths needed to minimize the average number of data block retransmissions.

Bias distortion occurs in asynchronous modems when received data "one" bits are longer than "zero" bits, or conversely. A marking bias exists when "one" bits (marks) are longer than "zero" bits (spaces). The opposite condition is called "spacing-bias." The decision threshold in the receiving modem may not be set at the midpoint between steady-state mark and space conditions. The

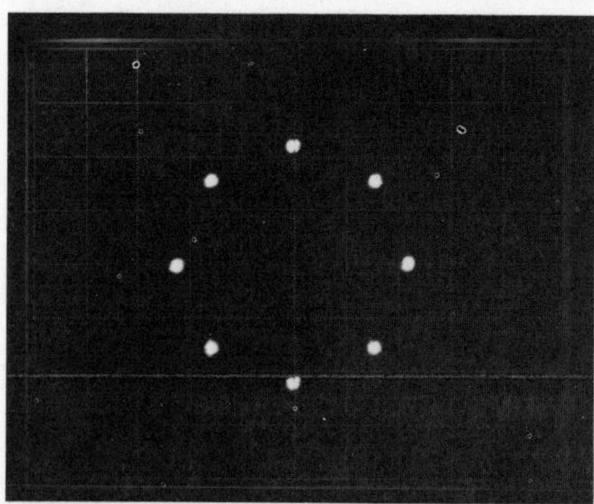

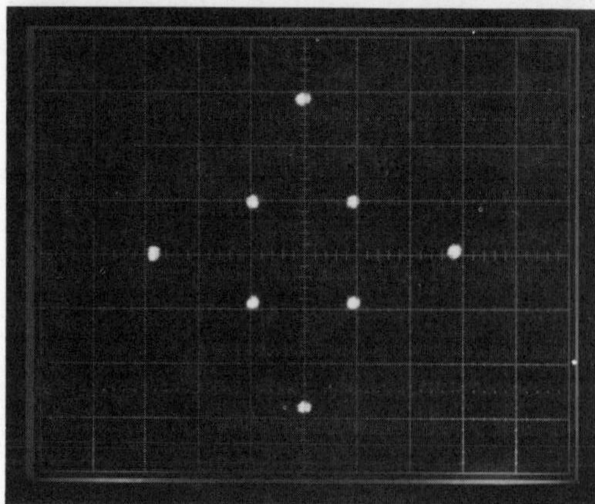

Figure 10.8. Two different signal constellations for an eight-level signal. The circular pattern is for 8-angle phase-shift-keying (PSK) modulation while the other pattern shows a two-amplitude, 8-angle phase-shift-keying modulation. Either pattern is used by the ESE 96/QMCP modem at 7200 bps. (Courtesy of ESE Electronic Systems.)

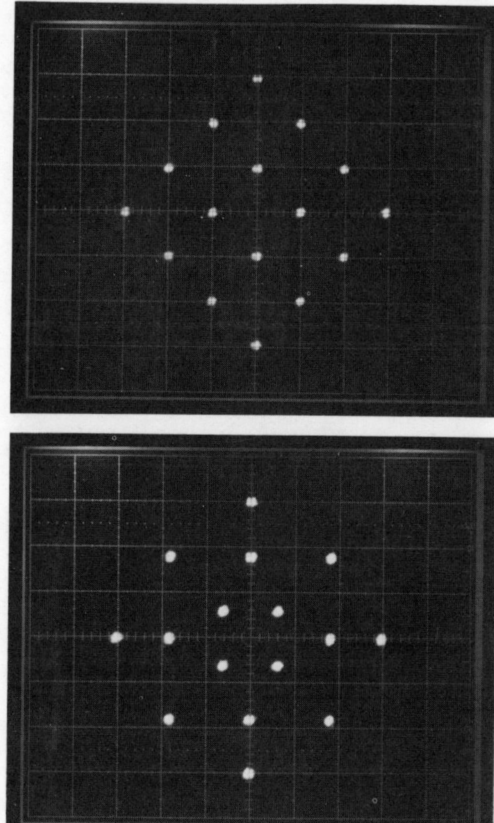

Figure 10.9. Two different signal constellations for a 16-level quadrature amplitude modulated signal used by the ESE 96/QMCP modem when transmitting at 9600 bps. (Courtesy of ESE Electronic Systems.)

asynchronous modem demodulator presents the data to the data terminal without reclocking it into uniform bit lengths, and thus if bias distortion is present, it will not be automatically corrected in the modem. The bias-distortion measurement provides an indication of what margin remains before the receiving asynchronous modem is likely to make bit errors in demodulating the received signal.

Perhaps the best indication of channel performance can be obtained from observing the "signal constellations,"[8,9] or "signal space," or "eye patterns,"[10] displaying the amplitudes and phases of the signal on an oscilloscope. Strictly speaking, the term "eye pattern" refers to a display of signal amplitude versus time on an oscilliscope. The percent of "eye opening" remaining compared to the maximum possible opening gives a good indication of the signal-to-noise ratio margin reserve available before modem performance will deteriorate. A distorted eye pattern with wiggly horizontal lines indicates that attenuation and envelope delay characteristics are not properly equalized.

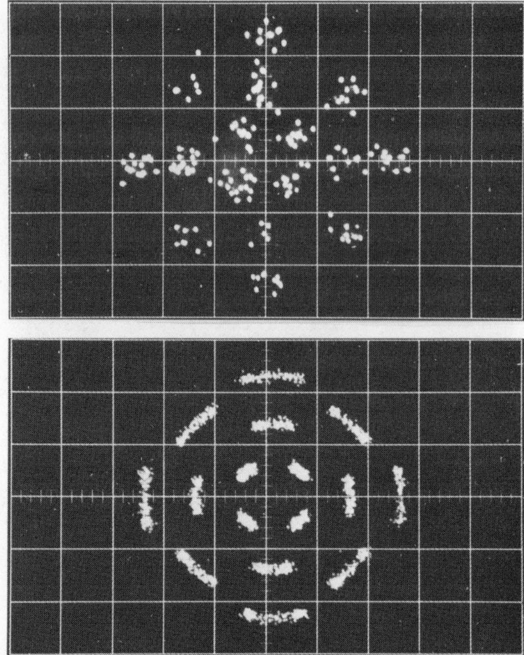

Figure 10.10. Signal constellations as they would appear on a channel with distortion. One shows a dispersion of the signal pattern due to noise while the circular pattern shows a distortion due to phase jitter. The receiver must sample the incoming signal and make a proper decision concerning the bits, which becomes almost impossible when the patterns overlap each other. (Photos are courtesy of Codex Corp., Mansfield, Massachusetts.)

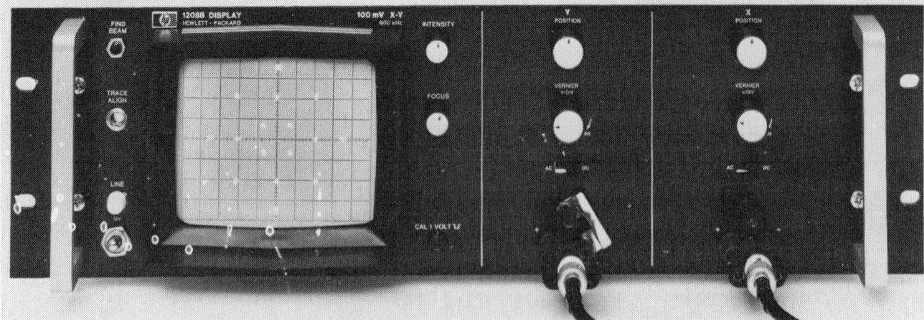

Figure 10.11. An oscilloscope showing a signal constellation as part of the Codex circuit quality monitoring system. Codex refers to signal constellations as "eye patterns". (Courtesy of Codex Corp., Mansfield, Masachusetts.)

Since many of the higher-speed modems use some form of phase modulation, a display of the signal constellation showing both the amplitude and the phases becomes more important. Figures 10.8 and 10.9 show signal constellations for high-speed modems operating on good channels. When the patterns become dispersed as shown in Figure 10.10, noise or phase-jitter distortion is present.

An approach to the multivendor communications system taken by many companies is to build diagnostic capabilities into their systems. Figure 10.11 shows one vendor's approach. It should be noted that unless such devices are built into the modem, more highly skilled personnel would be required to operate more costly equipment.

10.9. AVAILABLE LITERATURE

The ultimate source of information is from the technical specifications available from the modem manufacturers. Comparative data are available in the current literature as modem survey articles as well as in publications such as *DataPro Reports* and *Auerbach Reports*. AT&T presents information about their data sets in technical-specification form having a PUB number. Of course, any additional information should be obtained by writing directly to the manufacturer.

Chapter 11

Terminal Equipment

11.1. BACKGROUND

Terminal equipment refers to devices that use data communications and perform the transformation of data between human readable form and machine usable form. The majority of such devices are keyboard entry with either a platten-printing mechanism or a cathode-ray tube (CRT) display. Prior to 1970 the Teletypewriter® was the predominant terminal with a great deal of attention given to paper-tape operations such as tape preparation, reperforation, reading, and printing (See Figure 2.2). The most common recording medium was paper with impact printing. Any other kind of terminal was considered to be specialized or custom-made equipment.

Since 1970, when the interconnect decision opened up data communications to competitive pressures, new computer applications fostered the growth of the terminal industry to the point that there are hundreds of different kinds of terminals routinely available. Today, terminals cover all the categories from simple terminals to intelligent terminals. Input can be with keyboard-to-optical scanning. Printed output can be obtained by impact printers, ink jet, electrostatic, and even laser devices. Data can be displayed on CRT screens, plasma screens, nixie tubes, LEDs, facsimile, etc. The growth has been such that there is a bewildering array of products to select from. The user is in the fortunate position of having to select devices to fit the application, rather than altering the application to fit the available devices.

The use of terminals shall be examined from two aspects: (1) the terminal as the interface to the user in different applications, and (2) the terminals's role in the data communications network. The user's perception of the system comes, in many cases, from the use of the terminals. The system's efficiency can be enhanced or detracted by the selection of terminal equipment.

11.2. WHAT IS A TERMINAL?

Unfortunately the use of the word terminal in the context of teleprocessing brings to mind many different meanings to different people. The word is applied to anything connected to either side of a communications line and to any device that serves as a man–machine interface regardless of communications.

Common-carrier usage of the word terminal is interchangeable with station or service terminal. Used in this context, terminal means the termination of the interexchange channel of a common-carrier private line service at the customer's premises. Occasionally, this usage is extended to include transmitting and receiving equipment at any location on a premise and connected for private line services. Thus there is the situation where modems, line adapter, and wall jacks (plugs) are referred to as terminals.

In computer terminology, a device may be considered either as a terminal or as a computer peripheral depending upon the length of the channel. A data terminal tied to a computer input–output (I/O) channel is usually referred to as a peripheral device. The computer I/O channel transfers the computer words or characters parallel-by-bit, and therefore requires parallel lines. As the distances increase, parallel wires become uneconomical, and therefore a single pair of wires is used for the transmission of data in a serial-by-bit fashion. The manner in which the data is transferred (i.e., serial or parallel) then determines whether the device is a computer peripheral or a data terminal!

Like everything else, there is the exceptional case of low-speed modems that operate parallel-by-bit using multifrequency tones for transmission.

Another confusion arises when the word "terminal" is used to describe any device that allows someone to directly interact with a computer or data system, regardless of whether the device is on-line or off-line. For example, an interactive graphics terminal that can be a self-contained system having an internal processor capable of being programmed is referred to as a terminal whether or not it is connected to a computer. When internal processing capabilities are available these devices are referred to as intelligent terminals.

11.3. THE NATURE OF THE APPLICATION

The type of computer application clearly dictates the type of terminal device that would be required. For example, there are the following categories of applications where remote terminal devices are considered for *on-line* input and output:

1. data base creation with subsequent updates
2. query-response
3. information displays
4. data collection
5. conversational or interactive
6. transaction update with report generation

Each of these applications should be analyzed for its input and output requirements. Such an analysis for data input might appear as shown in Table 11.1, where the labels (1) to (6) corresponding to the above items are placed to indicate the relative size (small to large) of the number of transactions and the number of characters per transaction that are characteristic of them. The transactions would be documents to be input or separate records (of computer files) to be created or output. These would be the logical records of physical record read/writes of the computer devices.

Now the different categories of devices and their input/output characteristics that could be used as terminals are shown in Table 11.2. By looking at the applications, the kinds of terminal devices that might be suitable could be determined from the two tables.

The data base creation with subsequent updates. This would require initially a high transaction rate with a large number of characters per transaction to input the records as the data base is being created. This would suggest something like OCR equipment, but more realistically the records would be created in an

Table 11.1. Transmission Characteristics of Various Applications[a]

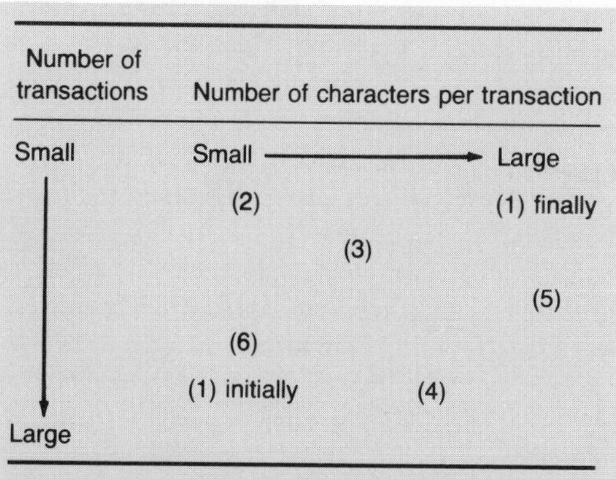

Number of transactions	Number of characters per transaction			
Small	Small →			Large
↓	(2)			(1) finally
		(3)		
				(5)
	(6)			
	(1) initially		(4)	
Large				

[a] The numbers (1) to (6) correspond to those in the list of categories of applications given in the text.

Table 11.2. Transmission Characteristics of Devices

Device		Character rate	
		Input characteristic	Output characteristic
Keyboard	(I)	Low	—
Character printer	(O)	—	Low
Line printer	(O)	—	High
CRT display	(I/O)	Low	High
MICR	(I)	Low	—
OCR	(I)	High	—
Light-pen	(I)	Low	—
Sensors	(I)	High	—
Mark sense	(I)	High	—
COM	(O)	—	High
Plotter	(O)	—	Medium
Facsimile	(I/O)	High	High

off-line manner, such as key-to-tape or key-to-disk, which would then provide a high-input rate to the computer system. The second aspect to this application, the data base update, would suggest few transactions with a large number of characters per transaction. This would suggest equipment such as CRT-keyboard terminals.

The query-response application is characterized by a small number of transactions with a small number of characters per transaction. This is suitable for a keyboard-character printer (e.g., teleprinter) or CRT terminal devices such as shown in Figures 2.2 or 11.1.

The information display is a simplex application where the computer outputs information periodically. Devices such as CRT display units, COM, or even line printers would be suitable depending upon the nature of the information.

The data-collection application is characterized by a large number of transactions with each transaction having a small number of characters. The use of sensors, light pens at point-of-sale (POS) terminals reading Universal Product Codes (UPCs), mark sense, or specialized terminals such as badge readers or inventory label readers, would be appropriate for this application.

The conversational or interactive application is characterized by a medium amount of transactions with a medium number of characters per transaction usually taken over a longer period of time than the other transactions. A keyboard with character printer or CRT display is ideal for this type of application as shown in Figure 11.1. Included are such aspects as program-debugging and computer-assisted instruction (CAI).

The transaction update with report generation is the ''superclerk'' type of application which occurs in the business world, e.g., payroll, inventory, accounts receivable, accounts payable, etc. These are typically characterized as having a large number of transactions with a fairly large number of characters per transaction. Such devices as OCR, mark sense, MICR, and sensors would be applicable for input and line printers applicable for the output.

11.4. THE CHARACTERIZATION OF TERMINAL EQUIPMENT

The primary function of the terminal is to convert human readable characters to and from electrical signal pulses given in the form of a code for the transmission of information. For instance, in keyboard-entry terminals using ASCII code, every keystroke creates a sequence of seven mark–space electrical pulses corresponding to the binary coding pattern for the struck character. Similarly received electrical pulses cause the appropriate character to be printed. These electrical pulses are the baseband signals of the terminal device.

Thus the terminal can be thought of as a code translation device using communication codes. As was noted before, communication codes are designed

Figure 11.1. Interactive applications such as program checking can be made either with a CRT terminal or the teleprinter terminal shown in the background. (Courtesy of AT&T.)

to provide for the control of the information transfer process as well as providing characters for the information transfer. These control characters are for the most part not printable (or not readable) even though they appear on the keys of a terminal keyboard. In data communications systems, the terminal is constructed to respond to these control characters. The degree to which this response is made and the number of control characters involved determines the "intelligence" of the terminal.

For example, the model 33 KSR Teletypewriter® used as a data communications terminal can transmit most of the control characters of the ASCII code, but it responds to very few of them. The control characters to which this terminal does respond are mostly device control characters such as line feed (LF), carriage return (CR), bell (BEL), etc. Communication control characters like inquiry (ENQ) and start-of-text (STX) have no meaning to this device. These devices are considered to be "simple" or "dumb" terminals whose only function is to transmit a character-at-a-time to a communications controller located at a different site. The bottom of Figure 11.2 shows such a terminal configuration, and Figure 11.3 shows the current replacement of the model 33 Teletypewriter.

With the advent of microprocessor technology, more intelligence was added to the terminal and this increased its capabilities considerably. This added intelligence consists of one or more of the following:

Terminal-device address recognition
Buffer storage
Transmission of blocks of characters
Error-detection capability
Automatic response to polling
Automatic request-for-retransmission (ARQ)
Bit- or character-stuffing capability
Protocol implementation
Clustering of several terminal devices
Perform editing
Automatic answering
Data compaction
Back-up storage

As can be inferred from the above list, it practically takes a computer system to support these capabilities. And yet, having processor capability is what is meant by intelligence in a terminal device. The top of Figure 11.2 shows an intelligent terminal configuration. The processor logic and buffer storage is shown as residing in a device control unit (or some similarly named unit) which allows multipoint operation. Additional logic exists in a station control unit which handles all message formatting for particular protocol implementations. Now, in Figure 11.1, the device shown, a keyboard-CRT display, can be a simple terminal with

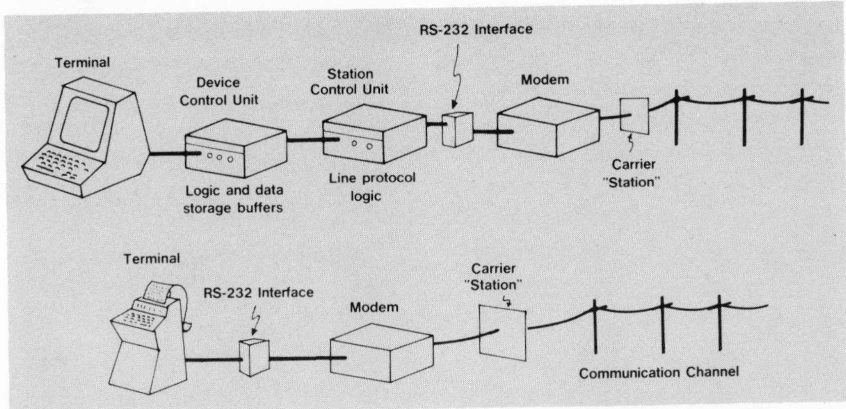

Figure 11.2. Remote terminal configurations can have many degrees of complexity. The top illustrates an intelligent configuration with a station controller and a device controller to handle many terminals. The bottom illustrates a simple terminal configuration.

all the logic in the two control units, or the terminal can be constructed with the circuitry for device and station control housed within the one unit.

11.5. THE SELECTION PROCESS FOR TERMINAL EQUIPMENT

There are presently a sufficient number of different *kinds* of terminals that the designer can be very selective in picking the terminal for the application. The

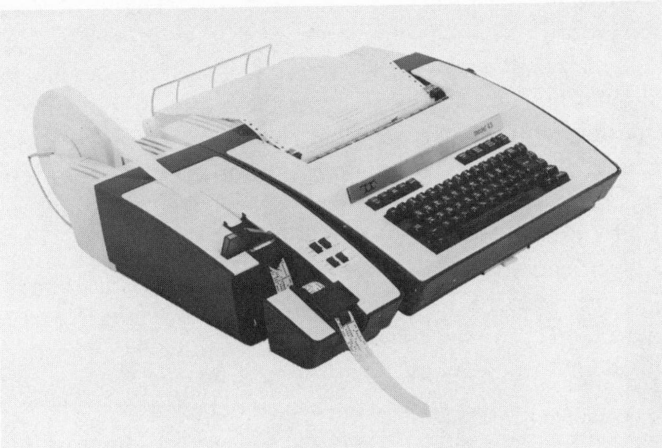

Figure 11.3. The Teletype model 43 ASR is currently offered as a teletypewriter replacement.

question naturally arises as to how should the selection be made? What are the criteria for selection?

The selection of equipment reduces to four operations: data gathering, reduction of specifications, creating a weighting matrix, and analysis of findings. In this approach the data are reduced to a summary, tabular form that is tractable to analysis.

The data-gathering step is the collecting of up-to-data information to form a data base. Equipment information may be obtained from computer periodicals in which summary articles, survey articles, or product spotlight articles appear. The survey type of articles are especially useful in determining the *different* equipment vendors. Equipment information may also be obtained by word-of-mouth, attendance at computer trade-shows, or attendance at computer conferences. The best source of such data, however, is from the vendor or manufacturer of the equipment. It is important to always obtain up-to-date information, for in the highly competitive markets equipment modifications, enhancements, and price fluctuations are not uncommon every few months.

The next step is also part of the data-collection process. As the practitioner in the computer field is well aware, there are numerous ways of describing similar functions. The user must do quite a lot of investigative work before equipment comparisons can be made. The reduction of specifications to commonalities is a necessity if meaningful results are to be obtained from comparing different pieces of equipment. The user must set the definitions and specifications that are meaningful to him and request precisely that information. One way of doing this is to formulate a technical questionnaire, designed to be filled out easily by the equipment manufacturers. Lists of terminal specification items are available that are useful for questionnaire formulation.[1,2]

The next step is to prepare a weighting matrix. This is accomplished by weighting each specification on some arbitrary scale (e.g., one to ten). The type of application greatly influences the weighting factors. For example, how important are cost considerations? (That is, must the minimum cost item be always selected?) Does the application require hard copy output? Multiple copy output? If the importance of some of the equipment features are not known to the user, then the opinions of other users should be collected to determine a weighting factor.[3] All of these weightings are tabulated in a columnar form to produce a matrix. The specifications are listed row-wise in order of decreasing importance. The matrix can be operated on by interchanging columns to collect, in say the upper right-hand corner, all the devices that have the highest weight factors with the most important specifications. Thus, from a field of many possible candidates, a list of a few serious contenders can be obtained.

The final step is the analysis where the user tries to improve his certainty that the selected devices will do the job. Actual equipment demonstrations would be helpful here. Further inquiries to other users might give further insight on device capabilities.

Chapter 12

Designing the System

In this chapter a discussion of how to get down to the business of putting together a data communications system is presented. It is assumed that the particular application has been completely described. This must be done because the data communications system is highly applications dependent. One can only design the general type of system at considerable and unnecessary expense. This is not to say that one should not design systems in a modular way. The design should be general enough to allow for future expansion in equipment or services required. It is imperative that the system designer keep costs in mind at all times.

12.1. IDENTIFY THE PROBLEM

Stated another way, to identify the problem means to know exactly what it is that is to be accomplished. In our environment, the problem is the implementation of a particular computer-oriented application requiring the use of data communications (viz., a teleprocessing application). The problem can be looked upon as consisting of two complementary parts: the functions to be performed, and the objectives to be obtained.

The essential first step is a complete understanding of what objectives are to be attained: What is it that is desired? What is the end product? Unfortunately in the real world of application implementation, the goals often get overlooked or are subverted by the alleged benefits.

The second step of identifying the problem is to understand what it is that the functions —which may be hardware, software, manual procedures, or various combinations of all three of these—are to do in attaining the objective. *How* the functions are to perform their actions is the basis of systems design and analysis. To determine what the functions are to do, the intermediate goals to be achieved must be identified and specified. For example, a function might be a process for the transformation of information whose input would be human-readable documents with output in a machine-useable form. The specification of *how* this is to be accomplished is the basis for the design process described later on.

12.2. COMMUNICATIONS PLANNING IN THE ORGANIZATION

In planning for the automation of some particular application, the questions of organization and, in particular, of where the data communications system belongs in the organization must be resolved. In large corporate organizations the data-communications functions may be contained in a separate communications department, but more often they are a part of the computer department. In the early 1970s, we have seen the emergence of the data-communications specialist as a specific job title; but alas, this only appears to be a short-lived need. For when the system is installed and operating, the services of data-communication specialists become unaffordable luxuries in the corporate overhead budgets. Thus we have evolved to the situation of the communications consultant who goes from job to job, rather than being associated with a single organization. This then points to the approach of using consultants for the communications design and implementation rather than in-house personnel.

12.3. COMMUNICATIONS PLANNING AND INFORMATION NEEDS

In today's technology the emphasis seems to be on the *total* information system analysis and design of an organization. This is in contrast to the specific application design of the early 1970s and prior years. The computer system is now looked on as the mechanism that integrates all of the organization's automation needs and prevents the duplication of effort. Consequently, the identification and centralization of the organization's information is of paramount importance. The distributed computing network design is an apparent contradiction to this philosophy of centralization, as it may use widely dispersed processors with separate data bases. However, "centralization" of information does not necessarily mean geographically centralized; it can mean that information is uniquely located within the organizational structure, which can be geographically dispersed.

In the context of total information systems, the objective of data-communications planning is the achievement of the system's goals. Therefore, information requirements become the *a priori* goals of the data communications system. The primary variable in the data-communications system is the *time-value* of the information, which is the cost to the organization when the information is not available or delayed in reaching the decision-making process. This factor has the single greatest influence on the system design, and yet it most often is overlooked. One reason for this is that until recently there have been few alternatives for communications systems, leaving the designer with the choice of either a less-than-satisfactory system or no system. The designer was concerned with adapting the application objectives. Thus, such considerations as the time-value of information were often overlooked or discarded.

12.4. COMPETITION ALTERS COMMUNICATION DESIGN PERSPECTIVE

With the introduction of competition into the communications field in the early 1970s, the designer of today has a wide variety of communications equipment and services from which to select. This allows for creativity and innovative design while at the same time introducing added levels of complexity in the goal-achievement optimization process.

Underlying all of this technological turmoil are the legalistic aspects (both the court and regulatory agency battles) of which the designer must be keenly aware, as they will undoubtably influence his design selections. While it is true that competition has benefited the user, it is also true that the user, historically, has not made any effort on his own behalf against the attempts to stifle or eliminate the competition.

12.5. JUSTIFICATION AND BENEFITS DERIVED

The determination of the justification for undertaking the application (which is often referred to as the project) is part of the system analysis procedure. The output of the justification determination is the benefits to be derived from doing a particular project. There are two categories of project justification: the cost or expense reductions, and the intangible benefits accrued.

The importance of this discussion is that the justifications selected as the reasons the application should be implemented constitute a bound or limitation on possible implementations. For example, if economy (or reduction of operating cost) is the primary justification for the project, then the approach to implementation would certainly be different than, say, if reducing time delays was the primary justification. In the latter case, expense might not be any consideration, but in the former it is the only consideration.

Teleprocessing applications focus attention on the time-value of information, perhaps more than any other kind of project. This is the determination of the monetary value to be derived by the user from reducing the time of making information available through the use of communication facilities. This is usually part of a cost–benefit analysis which ascertains what benefits are derived for the costs incurred.

12.6. METHODOLOGY OF THE DESIGN

The analysis and design of any complex system is still a process that is "customized" to the particular system being considered. While it is difficult to prescribe the exact analysis procedures for the general system, there are a number of common-sense steps that should be followed. Figure 12.1 illustrates such a process. Advocacy of these procedures is not the issue because they will not be applicable in all instances. Figure 12.1 should be looked on as an aid to organizing the design rather than being the design itself.

The tasks shown in Figure 12.1 for the design of a data communications system reduce to the resolution of the following steps:

Analysis of traffic
Central or host-site operations
Peripheral site operations
The request-for-proposal (RFP)
Evaluation and selection of central site equipment
Evaluation and selection of terminal equipment
Evaluation and selection of modem equipment
Evaluation and selection of communications facilities

Each of these steps is discussed in the following sections.

12.6.1. Analysis of Traffic

This step, which must be accomplished in an early stage of design, provides the key parameters upon which the other design selections will be based. It consists of a determination of the rate of data or information flow between the various points in the system. Typically this rate is stated in units of bits per second although other comparable units, such as characters per second or words per minute, are used. These rates are derived from the time requirements for message transmission.

Both the message contents and the volume of messages need to be defined. These, in turn, are determined from the end-use of the information transferred, i.e., the reports that are generated. It is a good idea to develop a graphical display of the information flow for the organization, and use this as a basis for any traffic calculations. This will portray the various workloads and the geographical distributions of the information requirements throughout the organizational system. This is the telecommunications traffic model in Figure 12.1.

Defining the messages and message volumes gives an indication of the information or data-throughput requirements. Further specification of the nature of these message transactions, such as security and acknowledgment requirements and priority routing, gives some insight into the amount of overhead in the traffic. The total amount of data and information to be transmitted is determined when the communications protocol is selected, because the protocol will add control information to the messages. The amount of redundancy required for error detection and the probable number of retransmissions because of error rates in the communications facilities must be considered. Thus, for purposes of sizing the communications channels, the total number of characters transferred is important. On the other hand, for purposes of sizing processor buffer requirements, the net data throughput (i.e., the amount of information actually transferred) becomes important. How the net data throughput is calculated is discussed in References 1–3 for Chapter 2.

12.6.2. Central and Peripheral Site Operations

How to get a traffic-rate picture was described previously. This is an idea of the raw number of messages that must be exchanged. In this section the way in which the information is to be handled should be characterized in order to determine the final equipment requirements. More specifically, the operations at each site need to be visualized in a time-frame, such as number of messages or transactions per hour, file capacity and number of records to be referenced (updated, added, or deleted) per time interval, frequency of report generations, and data entry-time requirements. In this regard, office layouts with personnel, keyboard entry, and unit record equipment would be helpful.

It must be noted that at this stage of the design the actual equipment is not specified; rather, it is the general functional characteristics of the equipment that are being determined. For example, must computer printout be on multiple-part paper or can some photocopy process using microfilm be employed? Or must the data entry be on a formatted display such as produced by a CRT (cathode-ray-tube) terminal or can a teleprinter device be used? The functional characteriza-

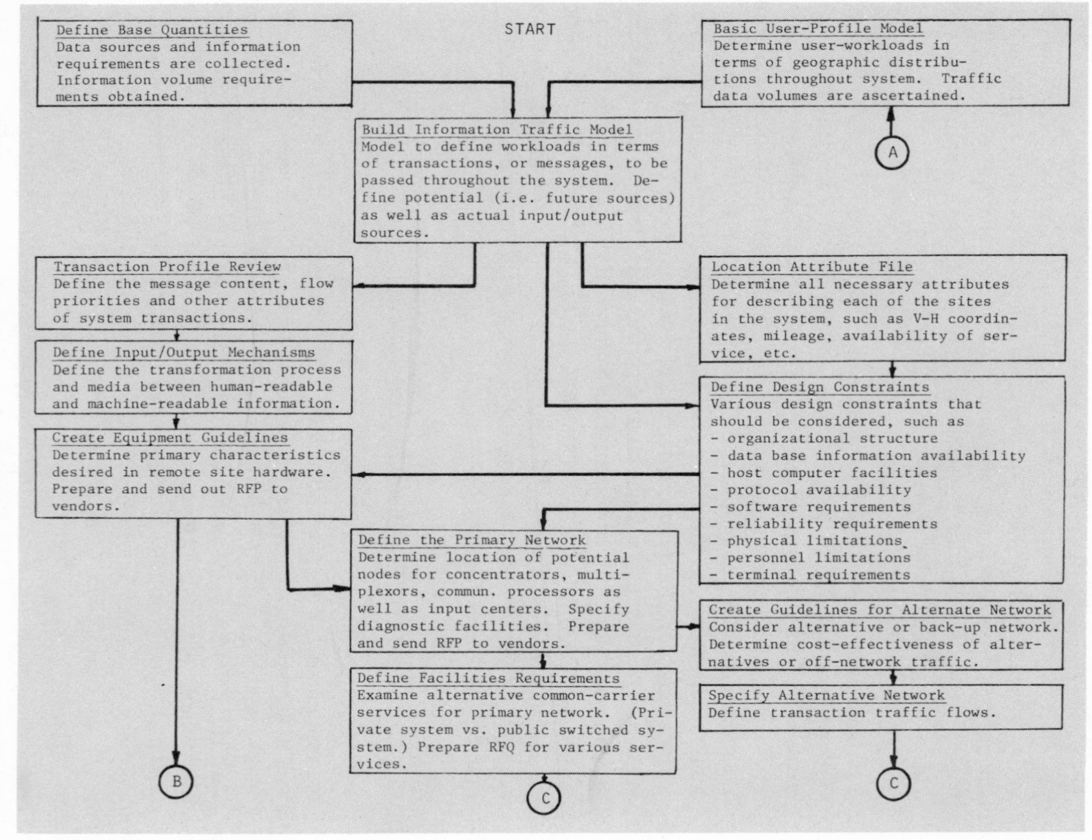
START
Define Base Quantities
Data sources and information requirements are collected. Information volume requirements obtained.
Basic User-Profile Model
Determine user-workloads in terms of geographic distributions throughout system. Traffic data volumes are ascertained.
A
Build Information Traffic Model
Model to define workloads in terms of transactions, or messages, to be passed throughout the system. Define potential (i.e. future sources) as well as actual input/output sources.
Transaction Profile Review
Define the message content, flow priorities and other attributes of system transactions.
Location Attribute File
Determine all necessary attributes for describing each of the sites in the system, such as V-H coordinates, mileage, availability of service, etc.
Define Input/Output Mechanisms
Define the transformation process and media between human-readable and machine-readable information.
Define Design Constraints
Various design constraints that should be considered, such as
- organizational structure
- data base information availability
- host computer facilities
- protocol availability
- software requirements
- reliability requirements
- physical limitations
- personnel limitations
- terminal requirements
Create Equipment Guidelines
Determine primary characteristics desired in remote site hardware. Prepare and send out RFP to vendors.
Define the Primary Network
Determine location of potential nodes for concentrators, multiplexors, commun. processors as well as input centers. Specify diagnostic facilities. Prepare and send RFP to vendors.
Create Guidelines for Alternate Network
Consider alternative or back-up network. Determine cost-effectiveness of alternatives or off-network traffic.
Define Facilities Requirements
Examine alternative common-carrier services for primary network. (Private system vs. public switched system.) Prepare RFQ for various services.
Specify Alternative Network
Define transaction traffic flows.
B
C
C

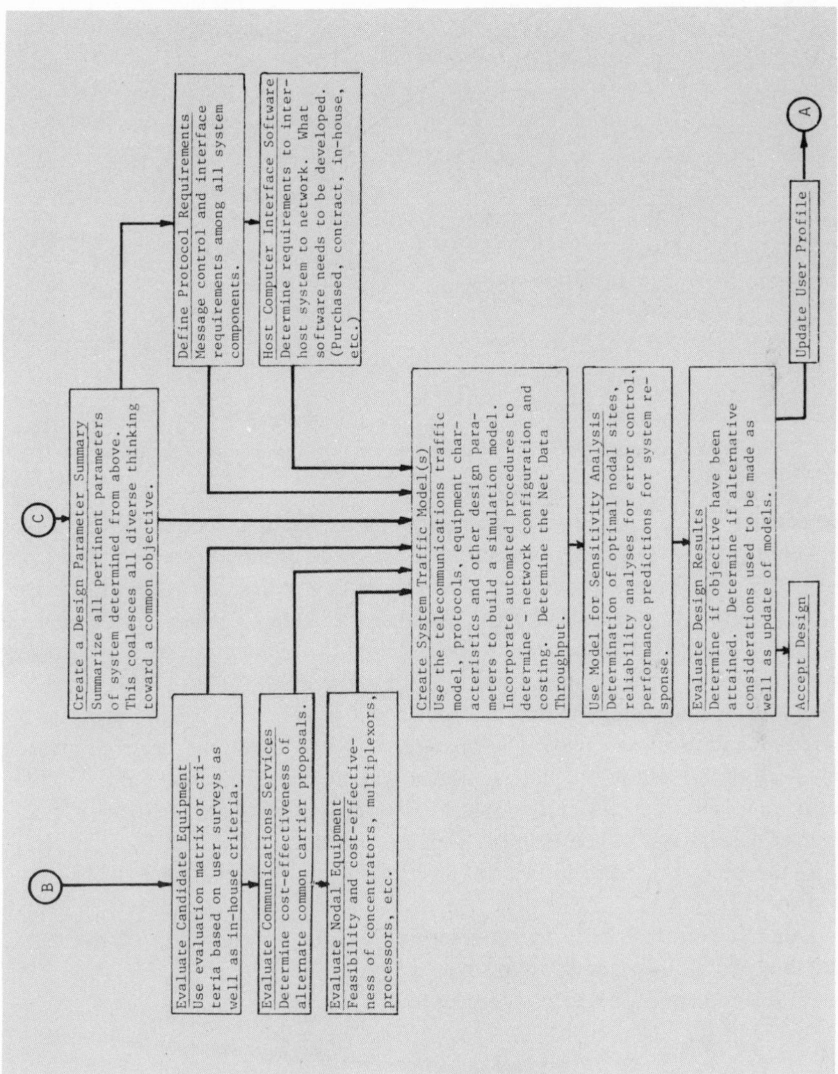

Figure 12.1. Components of a data communications system design.

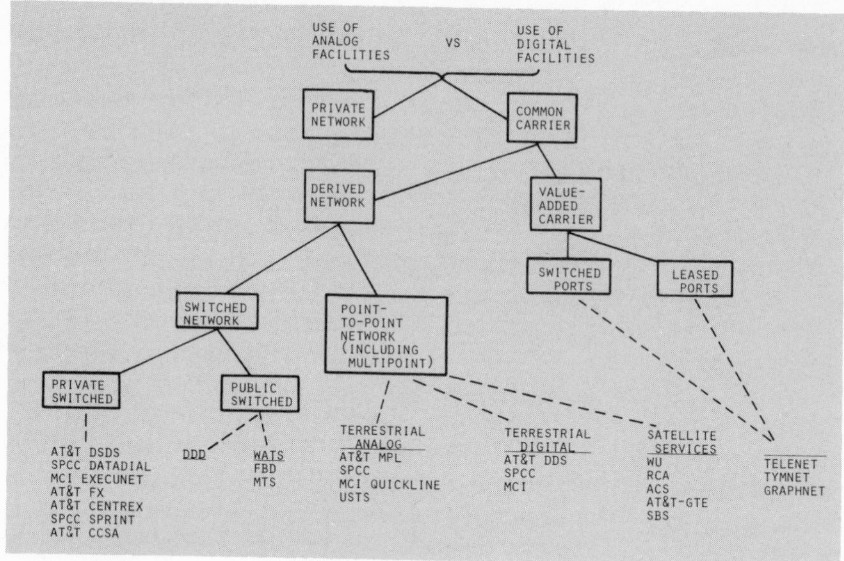

Figure 12.2. A decision tree for the selection of communication facilities.

tions of each site introduce such diverse topics as forms layout or design and office configuration (and interior decoration?) as well as the information flows.

At the central site or host sites where there is a repository of information, more generally known as a data base, the characterizations become more complex when compared to the peripheral sites. Here it is important to determine *how* the information is to be organized and *how* it is to be used. Is the objective of the system to be a data collection and file update? Or is to be enquiry and response, or a combination of the two? The answers to these questions determine the immediacy of the response which is another way of saying the time-value of the information. The response requirements determine the characteristics of the computer system and, when coupled with the communications-traffic analysis, specify the necessary characteristics of a communications processor or front-end processor (FEP).

Other factors that need to be determined from a description of the site operations are summarized as follows:

A. Selection of the access procedure
   1. Polling
      a. Hub- or roll-call polling
      b. Forward address polling
   2. Contention or quiescent
B. Selection of the message protocols
   1. Determination of optimum block size

2. Full-duplex vs. half-duplex operations
3. Use of ARQ vs. FEC methods of error correction

C. Determination of network configuration in terms of information flows.
1. Centralized system
 a. Point-to-point connections
 b. Multipoint connections
2. Distributed network (with multiple-host systems)
 a. Use of message-switching network
  (i) Store-and-forward
  (ii) Packet switching
 b. Use of nodal processors
 c. Use of remote data concentrators

D. Determination of interface standards

12.6.3. The Request-for-Proposal

All of the previous information is summarized by the designer in the form of specifications for equipment to carry out the desired objectives. These specifications form the basis for the request-for-proposal (RFP), which will be sent to the various vendors and suppliers of services. The proposal should be explicit enough to define and describe the operation, but (theoretically) should not be so explicit as to exclude all but one of the vendors from replying.

A question that needs to be addressed in connection with the request for porposal is whether to use a univendor or multivendor system. The choice actually boils down to cost vs. service considerations. If, for example, one selected a large computer manufacturer for the total system, including communications (i.e., end-to-end), then that client would have only one company to deal with for all its service maintenance.* While a multivendor system may provide more headaches servicewise for the user, it usually can result in a lower cost for equipment. Furthermore, competition can introduce innovative ideas to the marketplace more readily than an established, marketing-oriented organization. This approach does put a greater burden on the user to be more involved with the system. Users that do not wish to be so involved obtain either a univendor system or a "turn-key" system at a premium price.

The request-for-proposal (RFP) should address itself to the hardware requirements, possibly the software requirements, and to the communications services requirements. Information should be provided concerning limitations, or bounds (upper and lower), on subsystem equipment capabilities. Redundant or

*But consider the price that would be paid both in operating expenses and in the manipulation of technological innovations by the whims of a monopolistic marketing organization. Carrying it to the extreme of the total elimination of all competition, all services and equipment could be provided by the state. There is much to be said for a multivendor type of system.

back-up support requirements should be specified. The RFP should contain sufficient information to allow the vendor to reply with an intelligent proposal.

12.6.4. Evaluation and Selection of Central and Terminal Site Equipment

Assuming that the user does not opt for a sole-source supplier or for a turn-key system, there would be many choices of hardware to satisfy almost any application. This presents a dilemma to the user as to what criteria should be used to resolve the selection process. Some of the considerations might be:

- cost
- service
- modularity
- convenience of use
- high-mean time between failures
- low-mean time to repair
- experience of other users
- Dun and Bradstreet rating of vendor
- benchmark demonstrations

Different organizations would assign different weights to the items listed above in evaluating the vendor proposals. All that can be really said is that there is not any one best way in the evaluation process. Different situations require different approaches which really boils down to using common sense. The best that textbooks can do is delineate many possibilities or variables to provide a checklist for the user.

Another approach would be to review the periodical literature for the ''this-is-what-we-did'' type of articles on similar situations. The benfits derived would be the avoidance of the pitfalls and mistakes that these articles invariably point out. Ideas could also be obtained at conferences and trade shows where much of the hardware is displayed. Discussions with other conference participants and vendor representatives could be helpful.

12.6.5. Evaluation and Selection of Communication Facilities

The approach taken here is similar to a hierarchical decision structure. The first question is whether to build a private communications system or to use the facilities of common carriers. Private systems are usually justifiable by large organizations geographically disbursed in particular situations. Railroads or utilities that have right-of-ways or land easements are examples. As a rule most organizations use common-carrier facilities, and this is what shall be considered here. Figure 12.2 shows a decision structure.

The next question is whether to use private leased facilities or public switched facilities provided by the common carriers. The two dominant considerations here are the requirements of system integrity and the cost of services. When communications are expected to require large blocks of time, then facilities with stable channel circuits are highly desireable. System integrity involves circuit stability and circuit availability which favors private leased facilities. Private leased facilities are essentially a fixed system with the circuits always having the same routing.

With private leased facilities the question is whether to lease channels or to use value-added networks. The value-added networks are basically a message-switching system with a fast response time. To properly cost out such services, the message traffic must be known to a high degree of accuracy.

If the decision is to lease channels, then the next question is whether to use digital circuits or analog circuits. The tradeoff here is between virtually error-free transmission over digital circuits versus lower-cost analog circuits. With analog circuits modem requirements need to be analyzed along with their costs. This is an area of intense competition between the established common carriers and the specizlized common carriers. The costs of these services vary quite frequently and dramatically. The designer of the communications system should be ever mindful of alternative schemes.

Having gone with private leased facilities through the decision tree, the actual circuit paths have to be determined. This bears directly upon the traffic flows determined in previous parts of the study. If multiplexing equipment can be economically employed, then using multidrop (multipoint) circuits needs to be examined in comparison with point-to-point circuits. The communication system needs to be looked at from a network viewpoint. Should it be a star-type network with centralized control? Or should it be a fully connected network with distributed control? Or should it be a loop network with limited central control? These are management-type decisions that tend to define the philosophy of operation of the organization.

Using public switched facilities is usually justified (1) whenever transmission requirements are low, (2) when remote sites are mobile (or portable), and (3) as back-up to leased facilities. The costs are based on distance and usage, hence the term message-toll services is sometimes used. The decision in this instance is between using DDD (direct distance dialing) and WATS (wide area telephone service). These services were discussed in Section 9.11. The circuits are established every time a transmission is to be made, and therefore they are of variable quality because of different routings through the carrier network.

Chapter 13

Communication Codes and Error Control

13.1. WHAT ARE CODES?

Data and information are transmitted over communications facilities by the use of codes. A code is the representation of symbols used in the data or information. Such symbols are the numeric digits, the letters of the alphabet, and special characters of, say, a typewriter keyboard or the characters used in a graphic display. Collectively these symbols may be referred to as graphic characters, printable characters, etc.

The particular scheme or means used to define the symbol of data or information is called the code. The Morse code, for example, uses "dots" and "dashes" to define the set of characters. Most of the other codes uses groups of bits, which are called "bytes," to define the character sets. When a code uses five bits for each character (such as Baudot), then there are $2^5 = 32$ unique representations available for defining the characters. A seven-bit code has 128 unique representations, an eight-bit code has 256 unique representations, and so forth.

13.2. THE CODING PROCESS

The assignment of different bit patterns to represent particular symbols is the process by which the code is defined. The graphic or printable characters discussed previously are considered as the *information* characters of the code. A code also contains an important set of nonprinting characters that are known as *control* characters.

The control characters provide the means by which (1) devices or equipment can be operated (viz., line-feed, carriage return, etc.); (2) the code can be extended to include characters outside the 2^n constraint (where n is the number of bits of the code); and (3) the control of the transmission can be effected to allow the proper and orderly transfer of messages, information characters, or random bits of data. An example of extending a code would be the use of the control characters ''letters-shift'' or ''figures-shift'' to indicate what succeeding characters are to be used as the five-bit Baudot code. This is analogous to using the upper-case and lower-case keys on a typewriter. These control characters are called *escape* characters—they change the meaning of one or more following characters.

The use of control characters to control the transfer of messages containing information characters is the essence of communications protocol and is covered in Chapter 14. Control of the transfer of messages consisting of random bits, which may have the same pattern as control characters of the code, is known as transparent transmissions. This topic is covered in Section 14.6.

13.3. TYPES OF SYMBOL CODES

There has been a veritable plethora of codes developed for different purposes and various equipment. Descriptions of the history of codes may be found in References 1 and 2. The Morse code is an example of an early form of an asynchronous transmission code which is still widely used today. Since then, codes have been developed for paper-tape and punched-card media. This was followed by codes for internal machine-symbol representation and magnetic surface media. Paralleling these was the development of different kinds of transmission codes. In this section some of these codes will be examined.

13.3.1. Paper-Tape Codes

Paper-tape codes are characterized by punching a hole in the paper tape for a 1 bit and no hole for a 0 bit. Each bit in a character is punched in a channel, which runs lengthwise along the type; thus a Baudot code requiring five bits per character would be punched on a five-channel paper tape as shown in Figure 13.1.

The Baudot code contains symbols for letters-shift and figures-shift corresponding to lower-case and upper-case keys on a typewriter. These characters are examples of escape characters. They change the meaning of subsequent characters. Table 13.1 shows the bit patterns for the Baudot code. Note that the lower

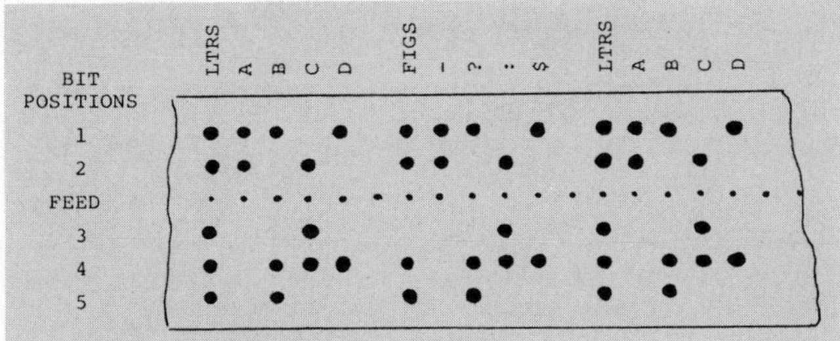

Figure 13.1. The Baudot code is a five-bit code that is used on the older terminals. It is shown punched on five-channel paper tape. The characters, letter-shift (LTRS), and figures-shift (FIGS) change the meanings of subsequent characters.

case is the same, but variations in symbol definitions for the upper-case mode give rise to different forms of the Baudot code. Table 13.1 also illustrates the effect of the letter-shift and the figures-shift character. This code was used in communications between early models of Teletypewriter machines.

13.3.2. Punched Card Codes

The codes for punched cards are directly related to the equipment used to punch and read the cards, using as few holes as possible to represent the characters. The Hollerith 80-column, the Sperry-Rand 90-column, and the IBM 96-column are some examples of the different codes used on punched cards. The Hollerith code is the most widely used for punched cards. Each character is represented by one to three holes in twelve possible positions (ten numeric and the *X* or *Y* fields).

13.3.3. Internal Machine and Magnetic Media Codes

Computers were initially constructed to store and manipulate binary representations of real numbers. As the applications progressed from the scientific to the commercial areas, the need arose for the storage and manipulation of character data. This progressed rather haphazardly with each manufacturer going a different route for defining the codes. Table 13.2 shows the character codes for the Univac 1108 computer, the Control Data Corp. 3200 Series computers, and the Burroughs Common Language Code for the B-5700 computer. Note how vastly different these codes are from each other.

Many of the first and second generation computers used six bits for character representation, known as binary-coded decimal (BCD). One notable deviation was the IBM-650 computer which used the biquinary code. The RCA 301 computer used the excess-three code. The third generation computers introduced octal and hexadecimal representations along with an extension of the character

Table 13.1. Bit Patterns for the Baudot Code in Asynchronous Format[a]

Function	Pulses							Character obtained with	
	st.	1	2	3	4	5	stop	LS	FS
Letters shift (LS)		■	■	■	■	■	■		
Figures shift (FS)		■	■		■	■	■		
		■	■				■	A	-
		■	■			■	■	B	?
			■	■	■		■	C	:
		■			■		■	D	$
		■					■	E	3
		■		■	■		■	F	!
			■		■	■	■	G	&
				■		■	■	H	#
			■	■			■	I	8
		■	■		■		■	J	'
		■	■	■	■		■	K	(
		■	■			■	■	L	)
				■	■	■	■	M	.
				■	■		■	N	,
					■	■	■	O	9
			■	■		■	■	P	Ø
		■	■	■		■	■	Q	1
			■		■		■	R	4
		■						S	Bell
						■	■	T	5
		■	■	■			■	U	7
			■	■	■	■	■	V	;
		■	■			■	■	W	2
		■		■	■	■	■	X	/
		■		■		■	■	Y	6
		■				■	■	Z	"
Line Feed			■				■		
Carriage return					■		■		
Space bar				■			■		

[a] The set of characters obtained with the figures shift mode is used by the U.S. government in AUTODIN and represents but one of many variations used.

Table 13.2. Six-Bit Internal Codes of Several Computer Manufacturers for Representations of Characters[a]

Octal value	Binary value	Univac 1108 (Fieldata)	Control Data 3200	Burroughs common language
00	000000	≥	0	0
01	000001	[	1	1
02	000010	]	2	2
03	000011	#	3	3
04	000100	≤	4	4
05	000101		5	5
06	000110	A	6	6
07	000111	B	7	7
10	001000	C	8	8
11	001001	D	9	9
12	001010	E	±	#
13	001011	F	=	@
14	001100	G	″	?
15	001101	H	:	:
16	001110	I	;	>
17	001111	J	?	≥
20	010000	K	+	+
21	010001	L	A	A
22	010010	M	B	B
23	010011	N	C	C
24	010100	O	D	D
25	010101	P	E	E
26	010110	Q	F	F
27	010111	R	G	G
30	011000	S	H	H
31	011001	T	I	I
32	011010	U	LTRS	.
33	011011	V	.	[
34	011100	W	)	&
35	011101	X	'	(
36	011110	Y	@	<
37	011111	Z	!	-
40	100000	)	-	×
41	100001	-	J	J
42	100010	+	K	K
43	100011	<	L	L
44	100100	=	M	M
45	100101	>	N	N
46	100110	&	O	O

(continued)

[a] Note how the collating sequences would vary.

Table 13.2. ***(continued)***

Octal value	Binary value	Univac 1108 (Fieldata)	Control Data 3200	Burroughs common language
47	100111	$	P	P
50	101000	*	Q	Q
51	101001	(	R	R
52	101010	%	°	°
53	101011	:	$	*
54	101100	?	*	-
55	101101	!	#	)
56	101110	,	%	;
57	101111	\	FIGS	$
60	110000	0		
61	110001	1	/	/
62	110010	2	S	S
63	110011	3	T	T
64	110100	4	U	U
65	110101	5	V	V
66	110110	6	W	W
67	110111	7	X	X
70	111000	8	Y	Y
71	111001	9	Z	Z
72	111010	'	&	,
73	111011	;	,	%
74	111100	/	(	≠
75	111101	.	Tab	=
76	111110	⌑	BS	]
77	111111	stop	CR	"

set. Presently the two major codes that are used universally are the Extended Binary Coded Decimal Interchange Code (EBCDIC) and the American Standard Code for Information Interchange (ASCII). The EBCDIC code shown in Figure 13.2 is an eight-bit code allowing for the definition of up to 256 different symbols.

The ASCII code shown in Figure 13.3 is a seven-bit code allowing for the definition of up to 128 different symbols. Because most current computers use hexadecimal internally, ASCII is extended to eight bits as a code for a particular machine by using the eighth bit to indicate character parity. Figure 13.3 illustrates the former as Univac 70/7 computer code.

Magnetic media usually follow the internal machine code or the paper-tape code format. On magnetic tape, for example, the magnetized spots required to represent the code symbols are referred to as tracks with seven-track or nine-track tape being the most common.

0123 ← → 4567

HEX →		0	1	2	3	4	5	6	7	8	9	A	B	C	D	E	F
↓		0000	0001	0010	0011	0100	0101	0110	0111	1000	1001	1010	1011	1100	1101	1110	1111
0	0000	NUL	SOH	STX	ETX	PF	HT	LC	DEL			SMM	VT	FF	CR	SO	SI
1	0001	DLE	DC1	DC2	DC3	RES	NL	BS	IL	CAN	EM	CC	CU1	FS	GS	RS	US
2	0010	DS	SOS	FS		BYP	LF	EOB	PRE			SM	CU2		ENQ	ACK	BEL
3	0011			SYN		PN	RS	UC	EOT				CU3	DC4	NAK		SUB
4	0100	SPACE										¢	.	<	(	+	|
5	0101	&										!	$	*	)	;	¬
6	0110	−	/									∧	,	%	_	>	?
7	0111											:	#	@	'	=	"
8	1000		a	b	c	d	e	f	g	h	i						
9	1001		j	k	l	m	n	o	p	q	r						
A	1010			s	t	u	v	w	x	y	z						
B	1011																
C	1100		A	B	C	D	E	F	G	H	I						
D	1101		J	K	L	M	N	O	P	Q	R						
E	1110			S	T	U	V	W	X	Y	Z						
F	1111	0	1	2	3	4	5	6	7	8	9						¤

Bit Positions: 0 1 2 3 4 5 6 7

Significance: 2^7 2^6 2^5 2^4 2^3 2^2 2^1 2^0

Figure 13.2. The Extended Binary Coded Decimal Interchange Code (EBCDIC) is used as the internal code of many current computers.

b_7 b_6 b_5 →					0 0 0	0 0 1	0 1 0	0 1 1	1 0 0	1 0 1	1 1 0	1 1 1
Bits: b_4 ↓	b_3 ↓	b_2 ↓	b_1 ↓	Column → Row ↓	0	1	2	3	4	5	6	7
0	0	0	0	0	NUL	DLE	SP	0	@	P	`	p
0	0	0	1	1	SOH	DC1	!	1	A	Q	a	q
0	0	1	0	2	STX	DC2	"	2	B	R	b	r
0	0	1	1	3	ETX	DC3	#	3	C	S	c	s
0	1	0	0	4	EOT	DC4	$	4	D	T	d	t
0	1	0	1	5	ENQ	NAK	%	5	E	U	e	u
0	1	1	0	6	ACK	SYN	&	6	F	V	f	v
0	1	1	1	7	BEL	ETB	'	7	G	W	g	w
1	0	0	0	8	BS	CAN	(	8	H	X	h	x
1	0	0	1	9	HT	EM	)	9	I	Y	i	y
1	0	1	0	10	LF	SUB	*	:	J	Z	j	z
1	0	1	1	11	VT	ESC	+	;	K	[	k	{
1	1	0	0	12	FF	FS	,	<	L	\	l	¦
1	1	0	1	13	CR	GS	−	=	M	]	m	}
1	1	1	0	14	SO	RS	.	>	N	^	n	~
1	1	1	1	15	SI	US	/	?	O	_	o	DEL

Figure 13.3. The American Standard Code for Information Interchange (ANSCII), which is a seven-bit code, is shown for order of bits in a character as $b_7b_6b_5b_4b_3b_2b_1$.

13.3.4. Transmission Codes

In transmission codes the idea is to provide assistance in error detection aside from parity considerations, and also to provide control functions. Some examples of transmission codes are the Fieldata code, shown in Table 13.3, used for military data transmission; the eight-bit BCD code shown in Figure 13.4 for

Table 13.3. Fieldata Code

	Standard code	Paper tape code	Data character
	8765 4321		
Sequence of bits in serial transmission	0100 0000	1100 0000	Master space
	1100 0001	0100 0001	Upper case
	1100 0010	0100 0010	Lower case
	0100 0011	1100 0011	Line feed
	1100 0100	0100 0100	Carriage return
	0100 0101	1100 0101	Space
	0100 0110	1100 0110	A
	1100 0111	0100 0111	B
	1100 1000	0100 1000	C
	0100 1001	1100 1001	D
	0100 1010	1100 1010	E
	1100 1011	0100 1011	F
	0100 11C0	1100 1100	G
	1100 1101	0100 1101	H
	1100 1110	0100 1110	I
	0100 1111	1100 1111	J
	1101 0000	0101 0000	K
	0101 0001	1101 0001	L
	0101 0010	1101 0010	M
	1101 0011	0101 0011	N
	0101 0100	1101 0100	O
	1101 0101	0101 0101	P
	1101 0110	0101 0110	Q
	0101 0111	1101 0111	R
	0101 1000	1101 1000	S
	1101 1001	0101 1001	T
	1101 1010	0101 1010	U
	0101 1011	1101 1011	V
	1101 1100	0101 1100	W
	0101 1101	1101 1101	X
	0101 1110	1101 1110	Y
	1101 1111	0101 1111	Z
	1110 0000	1010 0000	)
	0110 0001	0010 0001	–

the IBM 1050 series equipment; the Teletype data interchange code shown in Figure 13.5; and the coding in a 4-of-8 code to transmit data encoded in a six-bit BCD shown in Figure 13.6. The latter code is an example of an N-out-of-M class of codes which requires all characters to be encoded using M bits which must contain exactly N one bits. The van Duuren ARQ system uses a 3-out-of-7 code on radio-telegraph circuits.[3] This code allows $7!/(4!3!) = 35$ different symbols

Table 13.3. (*continued*)

Standard code	Paper tape code	Data character
0110 0010	0010 0010	+
1110 0011	1010 0011	<
0110 0100	0010 0100	=
1110 0101	1010 0101	>
1110 0110	1010 0110	-
0110 0111	0010 0111	S
0110 1000	0010 1000	(*)
1110 1001	1010 1001	(
1110 1010	1010 1010	"
0110 1011	0010 1011	:
1110 1100	1010 1100	?
0110 1101	0010 1101	!
0110 1110	0010 1110	.
1110 1111	1010 1111	⊕ (stop)
0111 0000	0011 0000	0
1111 0001	1011 0001	1
1111 0010	1011 0010	2
0111 0011	0011 0011	3
1111 0100	1011 0100	4
0111 0101	0011 0101	5
0111 0110	0011 0110	6
1111 0111	1011 0111	7
1111 1000	1011 1000	8
0111 1001	0011 1001	9
0111 1010	0011 1010	,
1111 1011	1011 1011	;
0111 1100	0011 1100	/
1111 1101	1011 1101	.
1111 1110	1011 1110	= Special
0111 1111	0011 1111	Idle
0001 1010	1001 1010	WRU
1011 1111	1111 1111	Delete

Parity bit
Control bit
Data bits

WRU, Delete: These are control characters because the seventh bit of the standard code is O. (The sixth and seventh bits of the tape code are the same.)

DATA CHARACTERS:

Normal shift

Character	S	B	A	8	4	2	1	Parity
1	0	0	0	0	0	0	1	0
2	0	0	0	0	0	1	0	0
3	0	0	0	0	0	1	1	1
4	0	0	0	0	1	0	0	0
5	0	0	0	0	1	0	1	1
6	0	0	0	0	1	1	0	1
7	0	0	0	0	1	1	1	0
8	0	0	0	1	0	0	0	0
9	0	0	0	1	0	0	1	1
0	0	0	0	1	0	1	0	1
a	–	1	1	0	0	0	1	0
b	0	1	1	0	0	1	0	0
c	0	1	1	0	0	1	1	1
d	0	1	1	0	1	0	0	0
e	0	1	1	0	1	0	1	1
f	0	1	1	0	1	1	0	1
g	0	1	1	0	1	1	1	0
h	0	1	1	1	0	0	0	0
i	0	1	1	1	0	0	1	1
j	0	1	0	0	0	0	1	1
k	0	1	0	0	0	1	0	1
l	0	1	0	0	0	1	1	0
m	0	1	0	0	1	0	0	1
n	0	1	0	0	1	0	1	0
o	0	1	0	0	1	1	0	0
p	0	1	0	0	1	1	1	1
q	0	1	0	1	0	0	0	1
r	0	1	0	1	0	0	1	0
s	0	0	1	0	0	1	0	1
t	0	0	1	0	0	1	1	0
u	0	0	1	0	1	0	0	1
v	0	0	1	0	1	0	1	0
w	0	0	1	0	1	1	0	0
x	0	0	1	0	1	1	1	1
y	0	0	1	1	0	0	0	1
z	0	0	1	1	0	0	1	0
.	0	1	1	1	0	1	1	0
$	0	1	0	1	0	1	1	1
,	0	0	1	1	0	1	1	1
/	0	0	1	0	0	0	1	1
'	0	0	0	1	0	1	1	0
&	0	1	1	0	0	0	0	1
–	0	1	0	0	0	0	0	0
@	0	0	1	0	0	0	0	0

Upper shift

Character:	S	B	A	8	4	2	1	Parity
=	1	0	0	0	0	0	1	
c	1	0	0	0	0	1	0	1
;	1	0	0	0	0	1	1	1
:	1	0	0	0	1	0	0	0
°C	1	0	0	0	1	0	1	1
'	1	0	0	0	1	1	0	0
–	1	0	0	0	1	1	1	0
+	1	0	0	1	0	0	0	1
(	1	0	0	1	0	0	1	0
)	1	0	0	1	0	1	0	0
A	1	1	1	0	0	0	1	1
B	1	1	1	0	0	1	0	1
C	1	1	1	0	0	1	1	0
D	1	1	1	0	1	0	0	1
E	1	1	1	0	1	0	1	0
F	1	1	1	0	1	1	0	0
G	1	1	1	0	1	1	1	1
H	1	1	1	1	0	0	0	1
I	1	1	1	1	0	0	1	0
J	1	1	0	0	0	0	1	0
K	1	1	0	0	0	1	0	0
L	1	1	0	0	0	1	1	1
M	1	1	0	0	1	0	0	0
N	1	1	0	0	1	0	1	1
O	1	1	0	0	1	1	0	1
P	1	1	0	0	1	1	1	0
Q	1	1	0	1	0	0	0	0
R	1	1	0	1	0	0	1	1
S	1	0	1	0	0	1	0	0
T	1	0	1	0	0	1	1	1
U	1	0	1	0	1	0	0	0
V	1	0	1	0	1	0	1	1
W	1	0	1	0	1	1	0	1
X	1	0	1	0	1	1	1	0
Y	1	0	1	1	0	0	0	0
Z	1	0	1	1	0	0	1	1
.	1	1	1	1	0	1	1	1
!	1	1	0	1	0	1	1	0
,	1	0	1	1	0	1	1	0
?	1	0	1	0	0	0	1	0
±	1	0	0	1	0	1	1	1
+	1	1	1	0	0	0	0	0
–	1	1	0	0	0	0	0	1
*	1	0	1	0	0	0	0	1

CONTROL CHARACTERS

(Either shift)
(Either setting of S bit)

Backspace			1	0	1	1	1	0	
End of transfer			0	0	1	1	1	1	
Delete			1	1	1	1	1	1	
Down shift			1	1	1	1	1	0	
Carriage return			1	0	1	1	0	1	
Prefix			0	1	1	1	1	1	
Idle			1	0	1	1	1	1	
Reader stop			0	0	1	1	0	1	
Space			0	0	0	0	0	0	
End of block			0	1	1	1	1	0	
Up shift			0	0	1	1	1	0	
Line feed			0	1	1	1	0	1	
Tab			1	1	1	1	0	1	
Restore			1	0	1	1	0	0	
Bypass			0	1	1	1	0	0	
End of heading			0	0	1	0	1	1	
Punch on			0	0	1	1	0	0	
Punch off			1	1	1	1	0	0	

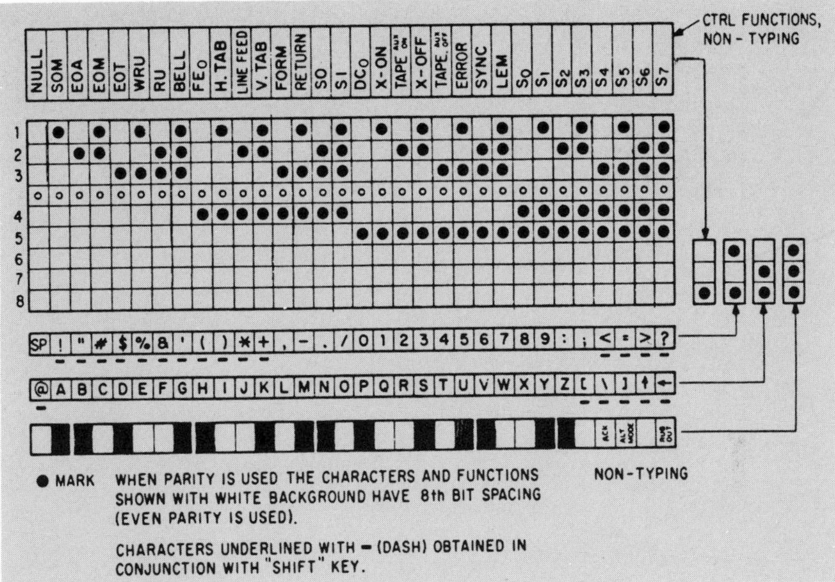

Figure 13.5. The Data Interchange Code is a version of ASCII that was used on some of the early teletype terminals.

to be defined. Every character must have exactly 3 one bits and 4 zero bits or it is in error. The touch-tone system shown in Figure 13.7 and which uses multifrequency tones is an example of an N-of-M code. In this case there are 1-of-4 by 1-of-4 or 16 different possible symbols. Only 12 are actually defined.

The dominant transmission code today is the seven-bit ASCII, followed closely by the eight-bit EBCDIC code. What this brief discussion of the different kinds of codes points out is that the code translation function discussed in Section 2.2.2 is essential to the data communications subsystem. It is hoped that the trend toward diverse codes has been successfully checked by defining the ASCII and EBCDIC codes as standard for use by all manufacturers.

13.4. ERROR CONTROL

The main objective of a data communications system is to send messages over a noisy channel without having undetected errors. That is, every error

Figure 13.4. Transmission for the early IBM 1050 Series terminals used an eight-bit binary coded decimal (BCD) code.

	BCD CODE							4-OF-8 CODE							
CHARACTER	C	B	A	8	4	2	1	1	2	4	8	R	O	X	N
Space	1								1	1	1		1		
0	1			1		1			1		1	1			1
1							1	1					1	1	1
2						1			1				1	1	1
3	1					1	1	1	1			1			1
4					1					1			1	1	1
5	1				1		1	1		1		1			1
6	1				1	1			1	1		1			1
7					1	1	1	1	1	1		1			
8				1							1		1	1	1
9	1			1			1	1			1	1			1
A		1	1				1	1				1	1	1	
B		1	1			1			1			1	1	1	
C	1	1	1			1	1	1	1				1	1	
D		1	1		1					1		1	1	1	
E	1	1	1		1		1	1		1			1	1	
F	1	1	1		1	1			1	1			1	1	
G		1	1		1	1	1	1	1	1					1
H		1	1	1							1	1	1	1	
I	1	1	1	1			1	1			1		1	1	
J	1	1					1	1				1		1	1
K	1	1				1			1			1		1	1
L		1				1	1	1	1					1	1
M	1	1			1						1	1		1	1
N		1			1		1	1			1			1	1
O		1			1	1			1	1				1	1
P	1	1			1	1	1	1	1	1				1	
Q	1	1		1							1	1		1	1
R		1		1			1	1			1			1	1
S	1		1			1			1			1	1		1
T			1			1	1	1	1				1		1
U	1		1		1					1		1	1		1
V			1		1		1	1		1			1		1
W			1		1	1			1	1			1		1
X	1		1		1	1	1	1	1	1			1		
Y	1		1	1							1	1	1		1
Z			1	1			1	1			1		1		1
/	1		1				1	1				1	1		1
#				1		1	1	1	1		1	1			
.		1	1	1		1	1	1	1		1				1
$	1	1		1		1	1	1	1		1			1	
&	1	1	1						1	1	1				1
%			1	1	1					1	1		1		1
—				1					1	1	1			1	
RM			1	1		1			1		1		1		1
SM			1	1	1	1	1	1		1	1		1		
WS	1		1	1	1		1		1		1	1		1	
?		1	1	1	1	1			1	1		1	1		
IDLE								1			1	1	1		
ENQ/NAK								1			1	1		1	
SOR/ACK1								1	1			1		1	
SOR/ACK2								1	1			1	1		
EOF									1		1	1		1	

Figure 13.6. A special fixed count was the four-of-eight code adapted to transmit data coded in a six-bit BCD code.

occurring during the transmission process must be detected. Using the construction of the communications code alone is not sufficient for this purpose. A *redundancy* must be added to the message that does not add to the information content but that does provide the capability of detecting errors.

Adding redundancy to messages raises questions about transmission effi-

	FREQUENCY (HERTZ)			
	697	770	852	941
1209	1	4	7	*
1336	2	5	8	0
1477	3	6	9	#
1633	n/a	n/a	n/a	n/a
	TOUCH-TONE CHARACTER			

Figure 13.7. Touch-tone codes use pairs of frequencies to transmit the characters on the telephone instrument.

ciency. Sending messages with 100% redundancy results in a transmission efficiency of 50%. In other words, it would cost twice as much to send such messages. The question is How to send messages with the minimum amount of redundancy to give the smallest probability of undetected errors and be within reasonable manufacturing and operating costs? As will be described below, there are several schemes used for error detection.

Once an error has been detected in the receiver, one of two methods are used to correct the error. The first method is to have the message containing the error retransmitted. This procedure for error correction is called either the *ARQ* (automatic request for repeat) method or the *ACK/NAK* (positive acknowledgement/negative acknowledgement) method. Typically, in this scheme every transmitted message must be acknowledged by the receiver.

The second method involves having enough redundancy built into the message so that the receiver can correct any detected errors. Systems using these techniques are called forward error correcting (FEC) systems. The messages are treated as long strings of bits with redundancy bits inserted in particular positions to allow the receiver to detect errors and to locate those bits in error.

The majority of the data communications systems presently use ARQ except where the time-value of information is high enough to justify the expense of the additional complexity required in FEC systems. However, with the current trend of cheaper microprocessor components, it is foreseeable that the cost of FEC systems could be competitive with ARQ systems.

13.4.1. Character Error Detection and Correction

The transmission of asynchronous characters over a communications channel requires some error-control mechanism. Almost universally such systems use a single bit, known as a *parity* bit, for the detection of errors. The parity bit is 1 (odd parity) or 0 (even parity) when the number of "one" bits in the character is odd or even, respectively.

Typically where simple keyboard terminals are used, the method of error correction is one of program response. At the terminal end, a human operator would cause the message containing the characters in error to be retransmitted in some manner. At the computer end, a program would initiate the retransmission.

13.4.2. Message Error Detection and Correction

A message is said to consist of a group of characters transmitted as a block. The block is framed by suitable control characters as defined by a communications protocol (cf. Chapter 14) to indicate the start and end of the text. The text contains the information of the message. Errors in the message can be detected by either checking the format or by using a code-check process.

Checking the message format involves determining the proper beginning and ending of each element such as word, frame, and field as well as such things as sign, size or range of values, numeric vs. alphabetic, etc. These checks are programming in nature and highly dependent upon the particular application. Thus, they are difficult to describe in general terms.

Coding checks, on the other hand, involve the addition of redundancy to the message by performing logical operations at both the transmitter and at the receiver. The two major classes of codes are *block codes* or *convolution* codes.

13.4.2.1. Block Codes

As block codes, messages are considered to be of some fixed number of information bits with a number of redundant bits added by some logical process. Another way of saying this is that messages of k information bits are transformed into blocks of n bits with the addition of $n-k$ redundant bits. There are many kinds of transformations that are possible.

The block structure is well suited for ARQ systems. The two main types of block codes are *constant-ratio codes* and *parity-check codes*. The constant-ratio codes use a block structure in which the ratio of 1's to 0's is a constant; in other words, an N-of-M code. These codes have $M!/[N!(M-N)!]$ possible symbols. Errors are detected by counting the number of 1's received. An odd number of bits in error will be detected, but an even number will be undetected. Because of this and its low transmission efficiency, constant-ratio codes have limited applications.

The majority of block codes used for error control are parity-check codes. These codes are n-bit blocks that are formed by mathematically relating a sequence of k information bits to $n-k$ parity bits. Two important types of parity-check codes are cyclic codes and geometric codes.

13.4.2.2. Geometric Codes

Consider the simplest type of parity, that of adding one bit to k information bits to make the total number of 1's odd (or sometimes even). This coding

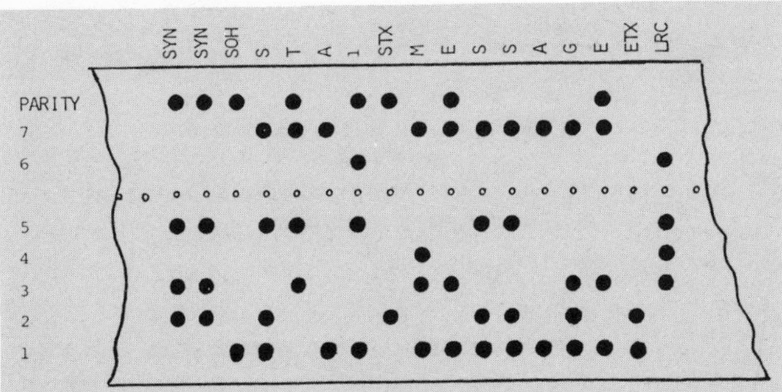

Figure 13.8. The VRC/LRC method for error detection requires the longitudinal redundancy check (LRC) character to be formed as even parity on all of the bits of each character of a message block.

scheme will detect all single-bit and odd-numbers-of-bits errors, but it will not detect an even-number-of-bits error. Geometric codes attack this deficiency by extending parity to more than one dimension. If a message were to consist of a block of characters, each character containing, say, seven bits (viz., ASCII code), then the geometric code would involve adding one parity bit to each character and one parity bit to each level of bits for all the characters in the block. This is illustrated in Figure 13.8. The parity bit on each character is called *VRC* for vertical redundancy check. The character formed by the parity bit at each bit level is called *LRC*, for longitudinal redundancy check. This particular kind of geometric code is called the VRC/LRC method, and it is used in many transmission systems—especially when the ASCII code is employed.

The problem with VRC/LRC systems is that certain patterns of even numbers of bits in error are not detectable. This is shown in Figure 13.9. If N ASCII characters are to be transmitted by this method, the efficiency is $7N/(8N + 8)$. When $N = 1$ the efficiency is 7/16 and asymptotically approaches 7/8 as N becomes large. This code is more apt to detect errors for small values of N than large N because there are fewer ways for undetectable bit patterns to form, as shown in Figure 13.9. The price to pay is the high degree of redundancy in such cases.

13.4.2.3. Cyclic Codes

An important class of parity check codes are the cyclic codes, or polynomial codes. These codes are attractive for two reasons. First, the encoding and determination of the parity values of a cyclic code can be easily implemented using simple shift registers with feedback connections. Secondly, it is possible to find various simple and efficient decoding methods using algebraic techniques.

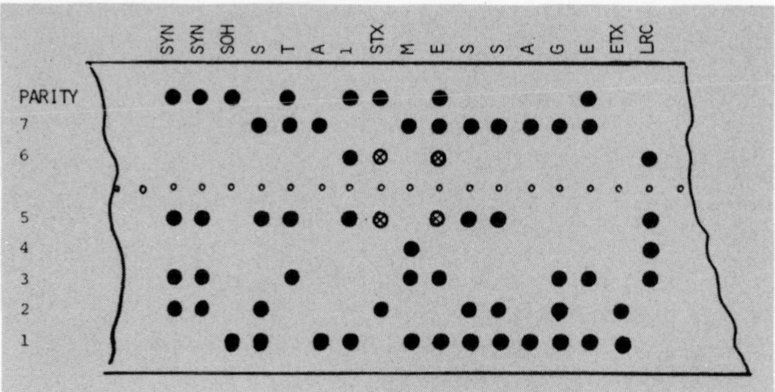

Figure 13.9. The VRC/LRC error-detection method fails when bit errors occur so as not to change the parity values in the transmission. This is indicated by ⊗.

The following example is used to illustrate how cyclic codes work. Suppose a message is to be transmitted consisting of the following bits:

1101 0011 0111

The basic approach is to represent the strings of bits as polynomials in x with the bits as the coefficients. Thus the message polynomial $M(x)$ is

$$\begin{aligned} M(x) &= 1101\ 0011\ 0111 \\ &= 1x^{11} + 1x^{10} + 0x^9 + 1x^8 + 0x^7 + 0x^6 + 1x^5 + 1x^4 + 0x^3 + 1x^2 + 1x \\ &\quad + 1 \\ &= x^{11} + x^{10} + x^8 + x^5 + x^4 + x^2 + x + 1 \end{aligned}$$

Now the message polynomial $M(x)$ is to be operated on by a generator polynomial $P(x)$ of lower degree p in the following manner:

$$\frac{M(x)\, x^p}{P(x)} = Q(x) + \frac{R(x)}{P(x)}$$

$M(x)x_p$ adds p zeros in the lower-order positions without changing the coefficients of the high-order bits of $M(x)$. The division by $P(x)$ is performed using modulo-2 (or exclusive OR) arithmetic with no carries. Thus

$$\begin{array}{ll} 0 + 0 = 0 & 0 \cdot 0 = 0 \\ 0 + 1 = 1 & 0 \cdot 1 = 0 \\ 1 + 0 = 1 & 1 \cdot 0 = 0 \\ 1 + 1 = 0 & 1 \cdot 1 = 1 \end{array}$$

The generator polynomial $P(x)$ is selected according to certain criteria specified below. For this example

$$P(x) = (x + 1)(x^4 + x + 1) = x^5 + x^4 + x^2 + 1 = 110101$$

This division is performed to yield a quotient $Q(x)$ which is discarded and a remainder $R(x)$ which is appended to the message $M(x)x^P$ to give the transmitted message

$$T(x) = M(x)\,x^P + R(x)$$

Modulo-2 arithmetic is always used. To illustrate by the example:

$$M(x)x^p = 1101\ 0011\ 0111\ 00000 \text{ (p=5 from above)}$$

```
                             100 0010 10101      = Q(x)
P(x) = 110 101      | 1101 0011 0111 00000      = M(x)x^p
                      1101 01
                      -------
                          111 011
                          110 101
                          -------
                            1 1101 0
                            1 1010 1
                            --------
                                111 100
                                110 101
                                -------
                                  1 00100
                                  1 10101
                                  -------
                                    10001      = R(x)
```

The transmitted message $T(x)$ is

$$T(x) = 1101\ 0011\ 0111\ 10001$$

At the receiver, the received message is operated on by the *same* generator polynomial $P(x)$, and if there were not any errors in transmission, the resulting remainder should be zero:

$$\frac{T(x)}{P(x)} = \frac{M(x)x^p + R(x)}{P(x)} = Q'(x) + \text{zero remainder}$$

Now if the communication channel is noisy enough to cause errors, the pattern of errors could be represented by a polynomial $E(x)$ similar to $T(x)$, and $T(x) + E(x)$ would be the received message containing errors. At the receiver,

$$\frac{T(x) + E(x)}{P(x)} = \frac{T(x)}{P(x)} + \frac{E(x)}{P(x)}$$

If $E(x)/P(x)$ generates a nonzero remainder then an error is detected. For this example, suppose

$$
\begin{aligned}
E(x) &= 0000\ 1111\ 1000\ 00000 \\
T(x) &= 1101\ 0011\ 0111\ 10001 \\
\hline
T(x)+E(x) &= 1101\ 1100\ 1111\ 10001
\end{aligned}
$$

```
                      100 0111 00111        = Q'(x)
P(x) = 110 101  | 1101 1100 1111 10001      = T(x) + E(x)
                  1101 01
                       1000 11
                       1101 01
                        101 101
                        110 101
                         11 0001
                         11 0101
                             100 100
                             110 101
                              10 0010
                              11 0101
                               1 01111
                               1 10101
                                 11010      = R(x)
```

Since $R(x)$ is not zero, an error is detected.

The remainder $R(x)$ created by this process and appended to the message is known as the CRC (cyclic redundancy check) character. Several simple circuits are shown in Figure 13.10 that perform the division operations. Devices such as the Motorola Universal Polynomial Generator, shown in Figure 13.11, are commercially available with a choice of generator polynomials.

The form of the generator polynomial is crucial to this method. In general, a proper generator polynomial will detect all burst errors whose bit length is less than the number of bits in the generator polynomial. In the above example, all bursts of four bits or less are detectable. A burst error refers to a group of incorrect bits within one message block. The length of a burst error is the number of bits in a group having at least the first and last bits in error.[1] More detailed descriptions of the characteristics of the generator polynomial may be found in References 2–5.

In summary, cyclic codes are relatively more powerful in the detection capability than any other type of code for a given level of redundancy.

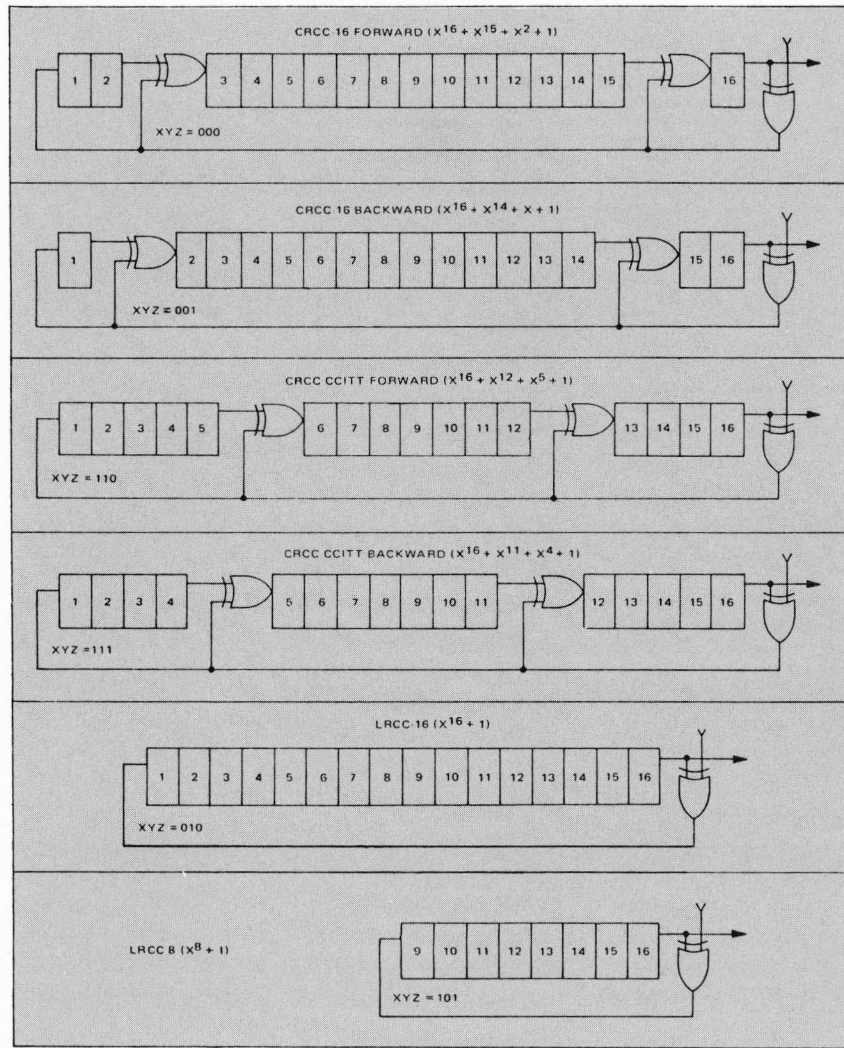

Figure 13.10. Circuits that perform the cyclic redundancy check (CRC) operation consist of bit-shift registers and an exclusive OR adder. (Courtesy of Motorola Corp.)

13.4.2.4. Convolutional Codes

Convolutional codes differ from the block codes discussed in the previous sections. These codes offer the best practical method for forward error correcting (FEC) systems with coding efficiencies (ratio of information bits to total informa-

UNIVERSAL POLYNOMIAL GENERATOR (UPG)

The MC8503 Universal Polynomial Generator (UPG) is used in serial digital data handing systems for error detection and correction. The serial data stream is divided by a selected polynomial and the division remainder is transmitted at the end of the data stream as a Cyclic Redundancy Check Character (CRCC). When the data is received the same calculation is performed. If there were no errors in transmission, the new remainder will be zero.

The MC8503 offers four of the more common polynominals for error detection techniques including a read forward and reverse on the CRCC-16 and CRCC-CCITT polynomial functions. These polynomials can be generated by changing the binary select codes as shown in Figure 1.

- Four Unique Polynomial Codes in One Package
- Compatible with TTL
  Maximum Fan-Out = 1 TTL Load
- Data Rate = 5 MHz Typical
- Total Power Dissipation = 400 mW Typical
- +5.0-Volt Operation

Typical Applications Include:

- Floppy Discs
- Cassettes
- Data Communications

BIPOLAR LSI

UNIVERSAL POLYNOMIAL GENERATOR

PLASTIC PACKAGE
CASE 646

FIGURE 1 – AVAILABLE POLYNOMIALS

CODE SELECT			POLYNOMIAL	
X	Y	Z		
0	0	0	CRCC-16 (Fwd)	$x^{16} + x^{15} + x^2 + 1$
0	0	1	CRCC-16 (Bkwd)	$x^{16} + x^{14} + x + 1$
1	1	0	CRCC-CCITT (Fwd)	$x^{16} + x^{12} + x^5 + 1$
1	1	1	CRCC-CCITT (Bkwd)	$x^{16} + x^{11} + x^4 + 1$
0	1	0	LRCC-16	$x^{16} + 1$
1	0	1	LRCC-8	$x^8 + 1$

Figure 13.11. The cyclic redundancy check (CRC) is available commercially as a LSI chip. (Courtesy of Motorola Corp.)

tion and parity bits) of 50–75 percent. These codes would be used in high-data rate applications above voice-grade speeds.

Convolutional codes do not have a fixed block structure, but provide a continuous bit stream of interleaved information and parity bits encoded by shift registers and logic circuits according to a fixed set of rules. For further details on convolutional codes, see References 4 and 5.

13.4.3. Error Correction

Like convolutional codes, the topic of error-correcting codes leads into great complexities. The *concept* of coding for error correction can be demonstrated for a very simple case. Table 13.4 illustrates how a Hamming code can be used to detect one bit in error and determine which bit it is.

The scheme can be set up using m parity bits with message lengths of n bits where $n = 2^m - 1$. This allows k information bits where $k = n - m$. Parity bits are inserted into the message at bits positions 2^{j-1}, where $j = 1, 2, \ldots, m$. An mx$(2^m - 1)$ coding and decoding matrix is created. By treating the message-bit string as a vector, a vector-matrix multiplication yields equations to determine

Table 13.4. Example of the Hamming Code Error Correction Method

1. Message length = 7 bits
   Information bits = 4 bits = 1100
   Parity = 3 bits = P_1, P_2, P_3 whose value is to be determined

2. The encoding process is as follows:

$$[P_1\ P_2\ 1\ P_3\ 1\ 0\ 0]\begin{bmatrix}0&0&1\\0&1&0\\0&1&1\\1&0&0\\1&0&1\\1&1&0\\1&1&1\end{bmatrix} = \begin{cases}P_1+0+1+0+1+0+0=0\\0+P_2+1+0+0+0+0=0\\0+0+0+P_3+1+0+0=0\end{cases}$$

   Using exclusive OR arithmetic, the three equations obtained yield

$$P_1 = 0 \qquad P_2 = 1 \qquad P_3 = 1$$

3. The transmitted message is 0 1 1 1 1 0 0.

4. Suppose an error occurs in the fifth bit (from the left) causing the received message to be 0 1 1 1 0 0 0.

5. The decoding process is as follows:

$$[0\ 1\ 1\ 1\ 0\ 0\ 0]\begin{bmatrix}0&0&1\\0&1&0\\0&1&1\\1&0&0\\1&0&1\\1&1&0\\1&1&1\end{bmatrix} = \begin{cases}0\ 0\ 1\ 0\ 0\ 0\ 0=1\\0\ 1\ 1\ 0\ 0\ 0\ 0=0\\0\ 0\ 0\ 1\ 0\ 0\ 0=1\end{cases}$$

   The three sums obtained are written as a binary number; here it is 101_2 which is the binary value for 5 and therefore the fifth bit is in error.

the values of the parity bits in the encoding procedure and the value of the erroneous bit in the decoding process. Table 13.4 illustrates this for $m = 3$, $k = 4$, and $n = 7$. Further material on this complex topic may be found in References 6–9.

Chapter 14

Communication Control Procedures

14.1. BACKGROUND

The topics of this chapter have received scant attention prior to the 1970s. This was due primarily to the lack of options in constructing a communications network and to the lack of intelligent terminal devices for whatever networks were constructed. The early 1970s saw the introduction to the marketplace of logic capabilities in the form of mini- and microprocessors with a reduction of the costs of the circuit components. These events resulted in the development of minicomputers and intelligent terminals, that is, terminals that practically have a computer processor built into them.

It naturally followed that these intelligent terminals were incorporated into communications networks and systems. Since every terminal site had the potential for initiating and conducting information transfer to every other terminal site, including the computer systems, it became quite obvious that some rules had to be established to prevent the information transfer of a communications system from degenerating into a chaotic babble. This was not unlike using *Robert's Rules of Order* for the conduct of a meeting.

This evolved to the formalization of communication control procedures as sets of rules (or procedures) governing the interactions between communicators. In present-day terminology, these procedures are referred to by various terms such as "protocols," "handshaking," "line control," "line discipline," and "data link controls." The early protocols were referred to by the term "handshaking," but recently handshaking has evolved to specifically refer to the call establishment (viz., dialing the telephone) part of the overall protocol.[1]

By analogy to natural language communication, the nature of protocols can be, perhaps, more readily ascertained.[2] Data messages (sentences) are exchanged alternately between machines (people) which (who) are communicating (talking). The messages (sentences) are composed of strings of characters (words) arranged according to definite syntax (grammatical rules). The characters (words), in turn, are constructed from strings of bits (letters). Protocols (rules of etiquette) govern the way (manner) in which messages are exchanged (conversation takes place).

14.2. PROTOCOLS: NEEDS, FUNCTIONS, AND ACTIVITIES

The specific conditions present in a data communications system that necessitate the implementation of a protocol can be readily identified as follows:

1. The *stations are far apart* and interaction takes place using communications facilities.
2. The *communications facility is shared* for use by both control and data flow. The data stream is interspersed with control information, whose sole function is to insure the correctness of the transfer. Hence, it must somehow be distinguishable from the data.
3. The *communications facilities are serial* in nature because it is not economically feasible to provide more than one channel for parallel communications transfer.
4. The stations may be two, as in *point-to-point* connections, or they may be many, as in a *multipoint* system. This latter condition requires some mechanism for allowing a variable number of stations to be present on a system and to communicate with each other in an orderly manner.
5. The *communications facilities are not error-free,* and, therefore, provision must be made to allow transmission to proceed even when errors are inevitable. This is perhaps the most important reason for having communication protocols, for if the facilities were error-free the rules of protocol would reduce to contention situations, such as described in (4) above, and would simplify considerably.
6. The communication links may be *present at all times,* as in a leased line system, or they may be *temporary* as in a switched system. Different kinds of protocols are required to account for the way a connection might be established.

Because the above conditions are inherently present in a communication system, the functions performed by protocols can be summarized as follows:

1. To establish and terminate a connection.
2. To assure message integrity during the passage of data between two stations.
3. To provide for the orderly interleaving of control and data information with a mechanism to distinguish between them.

If one were to design a protocol, the performance of the above functions should be the primary objective. Other considerations that enter into the design specifics include such things as:

1. The determination of station identity(ies) and status, such as ready-condition.
2. The control of the actual message transfers.
3. The procedure for inviting a station to send a message, that is, the polling function.
4. The mechanism for arbitration among stations contending for the use of a communications facility when only one can use it at any instant of time.
5. The provision for recovery of the affected transmission in the event of detection of errors.
6. The mechanisms for the addition of redundant information for the detection and correction of errors.
7. The procedures for transmitting data with a random format without misinterpretation as control information.
8. The allowance for synchronization and code differences among a wide variety of communication devices.

Protocols should at least consider, if not incorporate, each of the above items in their design. Note, that for the moment only point-to-point and multipoint situations are considered in this discussion of protocol systems. Protocols for computer networks shall be considered later.

14.3. COMMUNICATIONS SYSTEM ORGANIZATION

Communications protocols are designed according to the organization and application of the data communications system. Within each organization type, the protocol must define the master–slave relationships and how such relationships occur. The different kinds of organizations are:

1. *The nonswitched point-to-point.* This is the tie-line or the private leased line. The master station may be specifically designated and all other stations on the line become the slave stations. The master station directs the flow of messages to and from the slave stations. Such systems can be referred to as star-type networks.

2. *The nonswitched multipoint*. This is also known as a multidrop system. The communications channel is shared among several stations. Every station can "hear" all of the transmissions to every other station. The protocol must specify a master station that "polls," or invites, the slave (or in this case the stations are referred to as tributary) stations for message transfer. This type of system can also be a contention type where the master station is the one that "seizes" control of the communication facility. The master station is a temporary master in this case.

3. *The switched point-to-point*. This is the dialed call. The protocol must be concerned with the method of channel establishment, or how the connection is made, using automatic calling units (ACUs) and other such devices. Of equal concern, the protocol must differentiate between orderly terminations and abrupt disconnections.

4. *The switched multipoint*. This is the dialed conference call or a dialed multipoint configuration. For the duration of the connection this system is treated just like a multipoint in (2) above. Again, particular attention must be paid to the connection and the termination procedures.

5. *Loop systems*. This is a particular type of multipoint configuration in which a complete circuit (loop) is formed. This configuration tends to use less transmission path than star-type systems, with the data traveling from station to station. Thus, in this type of organization, a higher degree of intelligence is required at each station for passing on messages to other stations.

14.4. POLLING SCHEMES

The communications protocol defines a master–slave relationship for point-to-point configurations and a master–tributary relationship for multipoint configurations. Typically, a master station initiates its transmission and "invites" the slave stations to send their messages. In a multipoint system, the master station *polls* the tributary stations, asking of each whether it has anything to transmit. In some of the literature a master station in a polled environment is designated a control station, and the terms master and slave are used to indicate which station is transmitting and which station is receiving in a half-duplex mode. On full-duplex systems, stations act as master and slave concurrently.

Several types of polling methods are used. The most common is the *roll-call* where the master station polls each of its tributary stations, in turn, in a repetitive cycle. This method is easy to implement and control. A second method is the *hub-polling* or *forward-polling* system where each station, upon being polled, polls the next succeeding station. The configuration appears similar to a spoked-wheel. The primary advantage of this kind of system is in reducing message transfer times when the distances are great.

A different method of multipoint control is the *quiescent* system. In these systems, a station transmits only when it has a message to send. Each station then "contends" for the communication channel. The protocol must include schemes for tie-breaking simultaneous contentions among two or more stations. A major disadvantage of this kind of system is that a station could be disabled without other stations knowing it. In the quiescent systems, the master status is not located in a single station, but is instead transitory in that any station contending for the communication channel also contends for master status.

14.5. COMMUNICATIONS DIRECTIONALITY

Another consideration for protocol definition is the directionality of the communications in the system (see Table 2.6). Practically all communication links are capable of full-duplex (FDX) transmission. The only restriction is the availability of the required frequency bandwidth to sustain FDX. The traditional deterrent to having FDX systems was the capability of the terminal hardware devices and of the software. More recently, however, most of the hardware devices have been constructed to allow full-duplex transmission. Thus, the problem today is the lack of adequate software in the computer and terminal systems to support FDX.

14.6. TRANSPARENCY IN COMMUNICATIONS PROTOCOLS

Protocols may operate in either a bit mode or a character mode. The control functions are defined either by particular control characters or by particular bit patterns being received and acted upon. For example, a character may indicate the start-of-text (STX) while another character may indicate end-of-text (ETX), and so forth. A particular bit pattern "01111110" may indicate the start of a message.

A problem arises whenever it is desired to transmit a message consisting entirely of random bits. The transmission of a digitized photograph would serve as an example, where each dot of the photograph is coded for color, shade, etc., into a group of bits. In such cases it is entirely possible that the sequences of bits would exactly duplicate the bits of protocol control characters, thus inadvertently causing control functions to be performed in the midst of a message transmission. For example, one sequence of bits could disconnect the channel!

The technique for solving this problem is known as *transparency* or transmitting in the *transparent mode*. Protocols that are character oriented (i.e., requiring transmissions to be in bits grouped as though they were characters) use an escape character [viz., data-link escape (DLE)] to indicate transparent transmissions. A very particular combination such as DLE-STX would be used to indicate the start of a transparent text message, and the character pair DLE-ETX would indicate the end of the transparent mode.

Whenever a group of transmitted bits have the same pattern as, say, DLE-ETX, then the message mode would be terminated. To prevent this the transmitter scans each character prior to transmission, and if a bit pattern is the same as the DLE character, the transmitter inserts or "stuffs" another DLE character immediately after that bit pattern into the message stream. This technique is called *character stuffing*. For example, if the message stream consisted of the bits whose patterns replicated the characters

A DLE X 7 DLE DLE ETX Z

and was to be sent in transparent mode, then the transmitter would send the following:

DLE STX A DLE <u>DLE</u> X 7 DLE <u>DLE</u> DLE <u>DLE</u> ETX Z DLE ETX

The underlined characters are stuffed into the message stream. The receiver must look at the incoming message stream two characters at a time. If the first received character is a DLE then (1) if the second is a DLE also, it is deleted or (2) if the second is an ETX then it properly ends the transparent mode. If a DLE has been deleted, then no matter what the third character is, no control function is performed.

Systems that operate in a bit mode typically have only one control character, called the *flag,* and which has the bit pattern "01111110." On these systems for every five consecutive "one" bits of data a "zero" bit is stuffed into the stream. The receiver examines the incoming stream and deletes this inserted bit after encountering five consecutive "one"bits. This technique is known as *bit stuffing*. It is usually built into the hardware as a receiver function.

14.7. METHODS OF PROTOCOL REPRESENTATION

In discussions of the implementation of time-dependent functions, the visualization of such mechanisms is probably the most serious deterrent to their understanding. And because they are time varying, depiction of the interacting processes becomes a very difficult task.

Several mechanisms for the graphical representation of protocols have been proposed in the literature. The most common are the time-line graph, the ANSI graph, and the state transition graph. Another type is the flow chart, which is similar to the system analysis logical flow charts. These representations have been referred to as communication-control graphs.

Figure 14.1 shows the organization of a time-line diagram. The station-to-station communication appears as a horizontal heading, and the activities of the

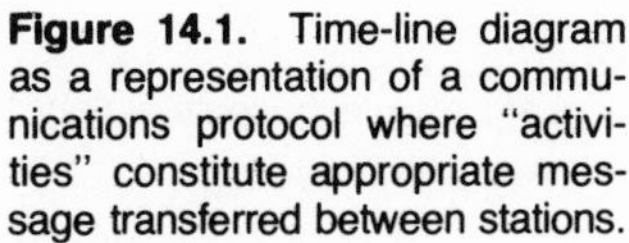

Figure 14.1. Time-line diagram as a representation of a communications protocol where "activities" constitute appropriate message transferred between stations.

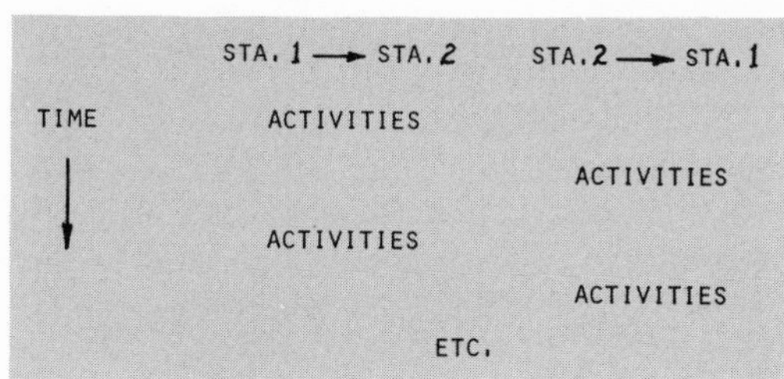

protocol appear in a time progression which is implied down the vertical axis. This type of representation is suitable for depicting all the characters of a message transfer. For multipoint systems more stations could be included along the horizontal heading.

Figure 14.2 shows the ANSI (American National Standards Institute) representation of the activities of a protocol. This representation is more compact than a time-line graph as it shows iterative transactions between stations. The stations are not readily identified on this type of representation and can only be followed by line turnaround indications. Consequently, this representation is appropriate for half-duplex (HDX) systems and would be difficult to use in depicting full-duplex systems.

Figure 14.3 shows the activities of a protocol on a state–transition graph. This differs from the ANSI representation in that the various states that the system can be in are shown as nodes, and the activities cause transitions in the system from one state to another. This approach is more theoretical than the previous two, and other than incorporating a matrix representation of this information, at present there is little advantage in using this approach.

14.8. PROTOCOL PHASES

A protocol consists of three parts: a channel-establishment phase, a message-transfer phase, and a channel-termination phase. Within each phase, the activities of the involved stations must be specified with regard to every possible circumstance that may arise.

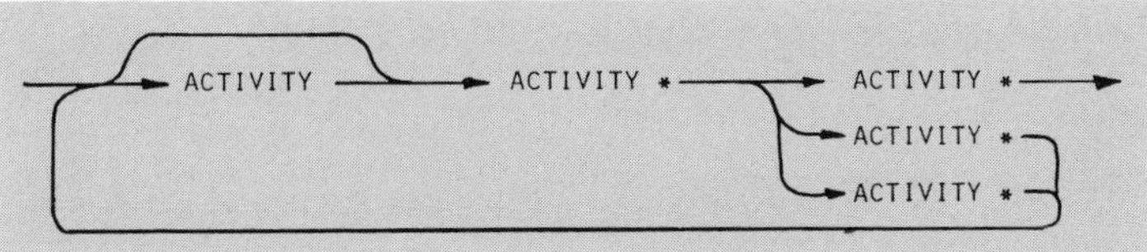

Figure 14.2. ANSI representation (X3.2.8) for a communications protocol. Iterative flows between activities stations not specifically indicated; * indicates line turnaround.

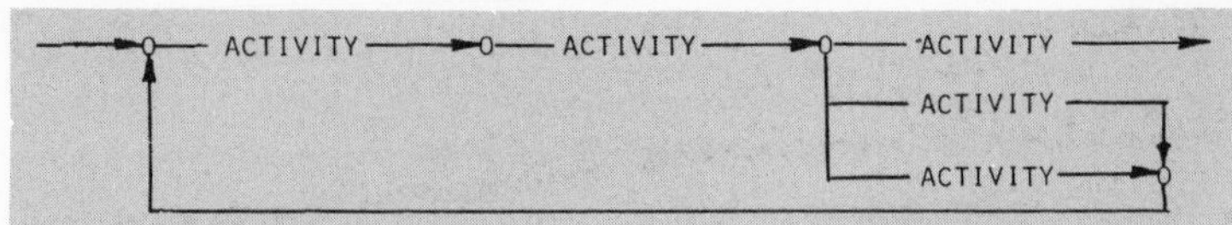

Figure 14.3. State transition graph used for a communication protocol representation. Transitions from state to state are shown.

The channel-establishment phase describes the procedure by which a channel is made ready for communication, in other words, how a connection is established. This is what is commonly referred to as *handshaking*. The message-transfer phase describes how the information flow is to take place and what error detection and correction procedure is to be used. The channel-termination phase describes an orderly termination process for releasing the communications channel.

14.9. TELEPHONE CONVERSATION PROTOCOL

A telephone conversation between human shows clearly how a protocol works. The protocol describes all of the activities involved, although most of them are done unconsciously. Figure 14.4 shows a telephone conversation protocol in the form of a time-line diagram. Looking at Figure 14.4, one might be surprised at how much is included as part of the protocol.

For this protocol, the activities of the exchange office need to be described, in addition to those of the calling and the called stations, because of certain signals emanating from that office which influence the activities of the calling and called stations. Note that if the emphasis of the protocol were on the telphone plant, then the activities of each exchange office in the call's path would have to be specified. This entails delineating all of the switching options as shown in Figure 7.1.

The channel-establishment phase ends with the addressor identification. During the message-transfer phase, we unconsciously use an ACK/NAK (acronym for positive acknowledgment/negative acknowledgement) where the ACK message is either a "yes" or a grunt like "ugh-huh" and the NAK message being something like "what was that?" or "say it again." In general, the protocol should describe the actions to be taken for every "what if . . ." case.

14.10 MODEM CONNECTIONS

The channel-establishment phase of the protocol is often referred to as "handshaking." For modem devices the channel establishment protocol is the most important because the devices are transparent to information transfer. Figure 14.5 shows the procedure for the exchange of signals during the channel-establishment phase. The interface circuits refer to the pin designations of the RS-232 standard interface specification (see Table 10.2).

An important use for Figure 14.5 is the determination of timings when the modems can be made ready to receive or transmit data. It is these delays that determine line turnaround times.

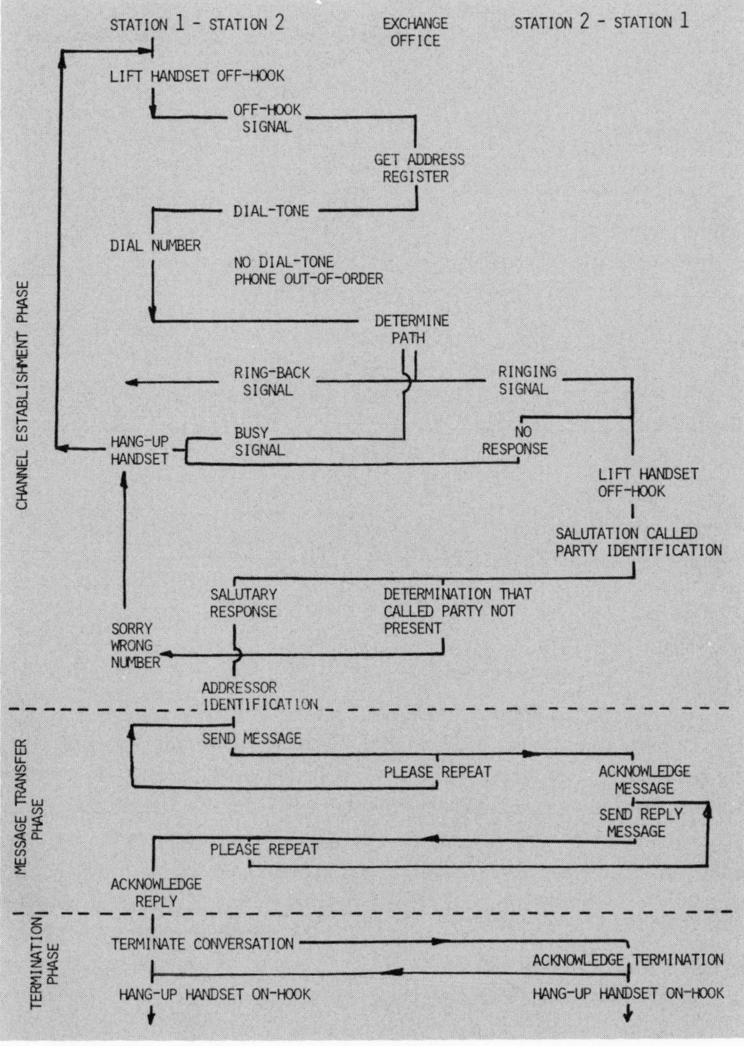

Figure 14.4. Time-line diagram of a telephone conversation protocol.

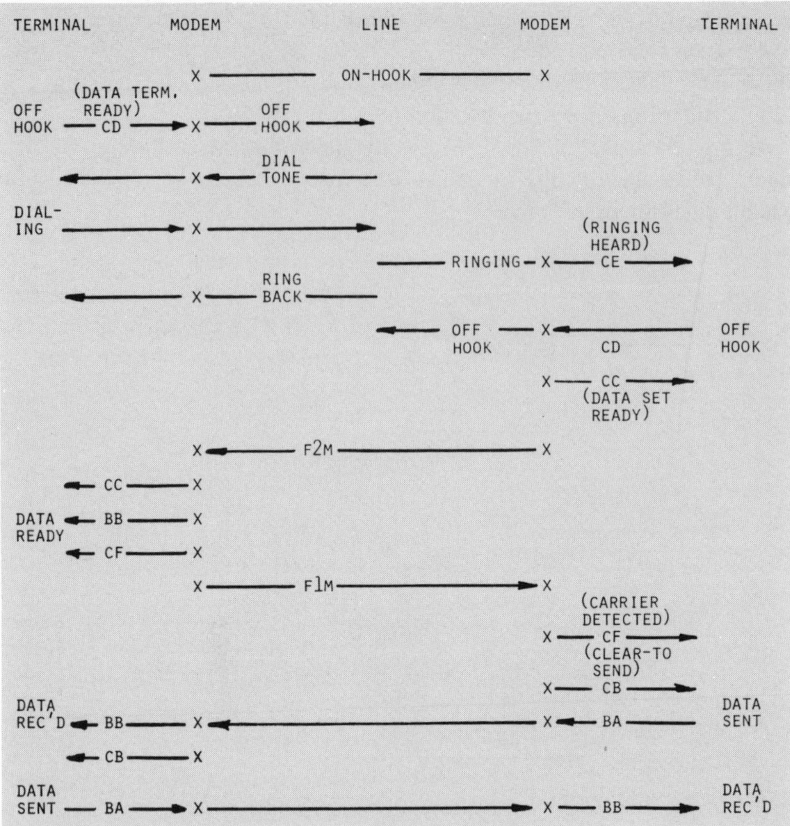

Figure 14.5. Exchange of signals over channel and interfaces during modem "handshaking" operation.

14.11. COMPUTER PROTOCOLS

When communications take place between inanimate objects, such as machines, elements of the communication code must be used to control the transmission of information. These elements, or control characters, must be recognized as such by the devices to cause specific actions to take place. For example, receipt of an end-of-transmission (EOT) character might cause a device to disconnect (i.e., hang up) a dialed call. Another control character might cause a device to convert from the receive state to the transmit state, and so forth.

In the data communications system, these actions may be taken automatically by the modem or terminal as a hard-wired mechanism. Some (or all) of the control functions may be programmed in the terminals or computer processors.

Figure 14.6 shows a simplified point-to-point protocol with the important control characters explained. It should be noted that the characters in Figure 14.6 are replaced by one or more equivalent characters from the actual code used (such as ASCII or EBCDIC).

14.12. BINARY SYNCHRONOUS COMMUNICATIONS (BSC)

One of the early well-described protocols was the IBM Binary Synchronous Communications (BSC) procedures as described by Eisenbis.[3]. BSC is a protocol that is primarily oriented toward devices and systems using 8-bit characters, either EBCDIC or ASCII. BSC is designed for half-duplex operation only. The essential features of this protocol are:

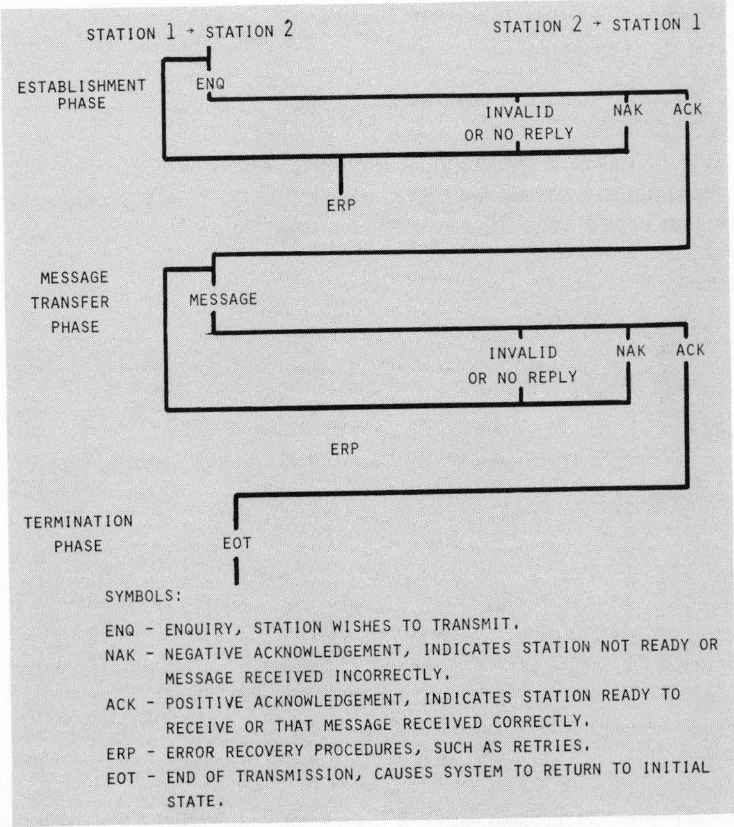

Figure 14.6. Time-line diagram for the exchange of messages on a point-to-point basis.

a. Messages must be blocked for synchronous transmission.

b. Each block has a block-check character (BCC) appended to it. This may be an 8-bit longitudinal redundancy check (LRC) character when ASCII code is used, or a 16-bit cyclical redundancy check (CRC) character when EBCDIC code is used.

c. The ARQ method of error detection is used with an odd–even acknowledgement message system (i.e., ACK0 is sent in reply to even-numbered messages, while ACK1 is sent in reply to odd-numbered messages, where ACK0 and ACK1 are made up as combinations of code characters).

d. The protocol emphasizes equipment synchronization with the requirement of sending synchronization (SYN) characters after every line turnaround and within a specified time period.

e. The protocol provides for transparent transmission.

f. The protocol may be used on point-to-point or multipoint systems and requires the specification of a master station. Figure 14.7 illustrates the use of BSC on a two-station point-to-point system.

14.13. FULL-DUPLEX DATA-LINK CONTROL

As was indicated earlier, the full-duplex capability of channels and most terminal equipment was not realizable because of inadequate software. A number of protocols have developed as a first step toward full-duplex transmission, such

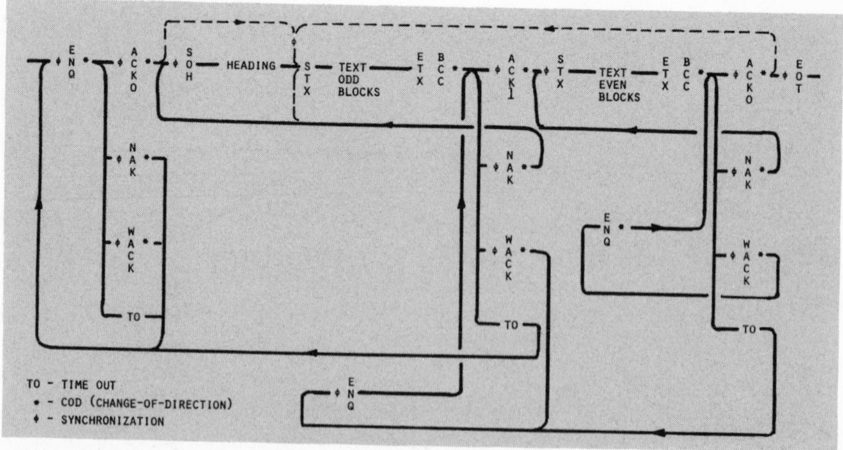

Figure 14.7. An ANSI representation of a two-way alternate (HDX) nonswitched point-to-point contention system using binary synchronous communications (BSC) protocol.

as:

1. Synchronous data-link control (SDLC) developed by IBM.
2. High-level data-link control (HDLC) developed by ISO (International Standards Organization).
3. Digital data-communications message procedures (DDCMP) developed by Digital Equipment Corporation.
4. Burroughs data-link control (BDLC) developed by Burroughs.

The list continues to grow as more manufacturers enter the expanding market of computer communications networks.

14.13.1. Synchronous Data-Link Control (SDLC)

As an example of these types of protocols, we shall briefly describe the IBM synchronous data-link control (SDLC) protocol.[4] All messages are sent as frames, that is, delimited by a flag character which is the unique control character. The system is transparent to all communication codes and is bit-oriented. All SDLC frames have a standard format:

Flag	Address	Control	Text	Check sequence	Flag
8 bits	8 bits	8 bits	Variable	16 bits	8 bits

SDLC employs a two-sequence frame-numbering scheme, 0 through 7. Each buffered station sends a number, or count, sequence to identify the frame that is being transmitted, and within that frame, the count sequence of the next frame it expects to receive from the other station. The send and receive counts are independent of each other, thus permitting unbalanced load transmission in either direction. SDLC uses the ARQ method of go-back-n-frames. A station can have as many as seven frames outstanding; that is, not acknowledged at any instant.

The control field in the SDLC frame indicates that the frame either (1) contains information to be transferred, (2) contains supervisory commands, or (3) is in a nonsequenced format. Figure 14.8 shows the control-field organization for SDLC. Bit number five in the control field is used by the primary station to poll (invite) a secondary station to initiate transmission when it has a value of 1. The secondary station responding to a poll sets bit five to 1 indicating the final frame has been transmitted. In all other instances this bit is set to zero. Figure 14.9 shows a sequence of information frames transmitted in a full-duplex mode. For each station that sends sequence count N_s indicates the number of the current frame being transmitted. The value in the receive sequence count N_R indicates that frame $N_R - 1$ was received with no detected errors and that frame N_R is the next expected frame. The transmitting station, in turn, can clear its buffers of all frames up to $N_R - 1$. In the figure, note that the second station's frames take

CONTROL FIELD

BITS	1	2	3	4	5	6	7	8	MEANING OF VALUES
	0								INFORMATION TRANSFER FORMAT
			N_S						SEND SEQUENCE COUNT
				1					IN COMMAND MODE MEANS POLL IN RESPONSE MODE MEANS FINAL FRAME
							N_R		RECEIVE SEQUENCE COUNT
	1	0							SUPERVISORY COMMAND FORMAT
			0	0					RECEIVE READY (RR)
			0	1					REJECT (R)
			1	0					RECEIVED NOT READY (RNR)
			1	1					(RESERVED)
					SAME AS ABOVE				
	1	1							NONSEQUENCED FORMAT
			M	M		M	M	M	MODIFIER FUNCTION BITS

Figure 14.8. The values of the bits in the control field of an SDLC frame define the type of frame.

longer to send (because of more information) than station one's. In these cases the receive sequence count update allows for multiframe acknowledgments.

14.13.2. DDCMP Protocol

Another approach to full-duplex data link control was taken by Digital Equipment Corporation in the development of their digital data communications message protocol (DDCMP).[5] This protocol requires three control characters to distinguish among data, control, and bootstrap messages. The ASCII characters SOH (start-of-header), ENQ (enquiry), and DLE (data link escape) are used respectively. The DDCMP data message format appears as:

S Y N	S Y N	S O H	COUNT 14 BITS	FLAG 2 BITS	RESPONSE 8 BITS	SEQUENCE 8 BITS	ADDRESS 8 BITS	C R C	INFORMATION ANY NO. OF 8-BIT CHAR.	C R C

The essential difference between this protocol and the other protocols is that the COUNT field contains the number of characters in the information field of the message. The implication of this is that a buffer of sufficient capacity is required to assemble and hold the message in order to determine the number of characters to be transmitted. The number of characters in the information field can be of variable length up to 16,383 bytes. The message number (modulo 256) is placed in the SEQUENCE field by the transmitting station. The RESPONSE field contains

```
                    sta 1 → sta 2        sta 2 → sta 1

                          f
sending frame 2
received frame 3        I,2,4              f
looking for frame 4                                   sending frame 5
                                         I,5,2        received frame 1
                          f  →                        looking for frame 2
sending frame 3
received frame 4        I,3,5            ← f
looking for frame 5
                                                      sending frame 6
                          f  →           I,6,3        received frame 2
                                                      looking for frame 3
sending frame 4
received frame 5        I,4,6
looking for frame 6
                          f  →
sending frame 5                          ← f
received frame 5        I,5,6
looking for frame 6
                          f  →                        sending frame 7
sending frame 6                          I,7,5        received frame 4
received frame 6        I,6,7                         looking for frame 5
looking for frame 7
                          f  →
sending frame 7
received frame 6        I,7,7
looking for frame 7
                          f  →
                                         ← f
                                                      sending frame 0
                                         I,0,0        received frame 7
                                                      looking for frame 0
```

Figure 14.9. Full-duplex transmission of information frames using SDLC show the values of the acknowledged messages in the send and receive sequence counts in the control fields.

the sequence number of the last received message that did not have any detected errors. DDCMP does not require an acknowledgment message for all messages. The implication is that there can be up to 255 unacknowledged messages outstanding at any time.

The heading and the information are individually checked for errors using the polynomial method (which is described fully in Chapter 13). The error-detection redundancy is in the 16-bit CRC (cyclic redundancy check) field.

14.13.3. DDCMP Control Messages

There are five types of DDCMP control messages as shown in Figure 14.10, all of which begin with the ENQ character. The *acknowledge message* (ACK) is used to acknowledge messages correctly received in the event there are not any data messages to be sent. Conversely, the *negative acknowledge message* (NAK) is an indication to the transmitting station that an error was detected in the (RESPONSE+1) message, and that a retransmission was required. Both of these

	COUNT (8)	FIELD (6)	FLAG	RESPONSE	SEQUENCE	ADDRESS	CYCLIC REDUN-DANCY
BITS	14		2	8	8	8	
ACKNOWLEDGMENT	ACK	FILL	(F)	RESPONSE	FILL	(A)	CRC
NEGATIVE ACKNOWLEDGMENT	NAK		(F)	RESPONSE	FILL	(A)	CRC
REPLY	REP	FILL	(F)	FILL	SEQUENCE	(A)	CRC
START	STRT	FILL	(F)	FILL	FILL	(A)	CRC
START ACKNOWLEDGE	STAK	FILL	(F)	FILL	FILL	(A)	CRC

RESPONSE: CONTAINS THE SEQUENCE NUMBER OF THE LAST GOOD MESSAGE RECEIVED.
SEQUENCE: CONTAINS THE SEQUENCE NUMBER OF THE LAST MESSAGE TRANSMITTED.
FILL : CONTAINS ZERO BITS USED AS FILLER.
(A) : CONTAINS THE DESTINATION ADDRESS.
(F) : CONTAINS THE FLAG BITS USED FOR LINK CONTROL.

Figure 14.10. Control message formats for DDCMP protocol.

messages are used in half-duplex transmissions. If the transmitter has not heard from the receiver within a predetermined period of time and unacknowledged messages are accumulating, a *reply message* (REP) is sent to the receiver. The response to this message must be either an ACK or NAK message.

The process of initiating a message exchange begins with a start message (STRT) being sent by a station seeking to transmit to another station. The sequence field contains the number of the next message to be transmitted. The receiving station then replies with a *start acknowledgment message* (STAK). It acknowledges the message number to be received and also indicates what number will be assigned to the next data message sent by the receiver station.

A special type of protocol message is the *maintenance message* which begins with the DLE character. This message is used to load a program into a remote computer. Its format is the same as a data message except that no acknowledgment is required and the sequence number always starts at zero. The maintenance message is provided for the convenience of updating programs in remote computers that are part of a network constructed for such purposes as message switching, supervisory control, etc.

14.14. SUMMARY OF PROTOCOLS

Table 14.1 presents in summary form the characteristics of different protocols, given in rough chronological order of their development. Further material may be found in References 6–16.

Table 14.1. General Summary of Protocol Systems[a]

	GDP	STR	83B	ASCII	BSC	SDLC	ADCCP	HDLC	BDLC	BOLD	CDCCP	DDCMP	UDLC
Number of control characters	5	6	0	10	16	1	1	1	1	1	1	3	1
Number of code characters	53	64	58	128	256	bit	bit	bit	bit	bit	bit	128	bit
Code name	BCD	trancode	Baudot	ASCII	EBCDIC	any	any	any	any	any	any	ASCII	any
FDX	no	yes	no	yes	no	yes	yes	yes	yes	yes	yes	yes	yes
Data transparency[b]	no	no	no	CS	CS	BS	BS	BS	BS	BS	BS	CT	BS
Asynchronous operatior	yes	no	yes	yes	no	no	no						
Synchronous operation	no	yes	no	yes	yes	yes	yes	yes	yes	yes	yes	yes	yes
Point-to-point	yes	yes	yes	yes	yes	yes	yes	yes	yes	yes	yes	yes	yes
Multipoint	no	no	yes	yes	yes	yes	yes	yes	yes	yes	yes	yes	yes
ARQ	no	yes	no	yes	yes	yes	yes	yes	yes	yes	yes	yes	yes
Error detection[c]	V	V	0	V	C16	CIT	C16	CIT	C16	C16	C16	C16	C16

[a] GPD = (general purpose discipline) early IBM protocol. STR = (synchronous transmit-receive) an IBM protocol. 83B = AT&T selective calling system. SDLC = synchronous data link control) protocol implemented in IBM's system network architecture (SNA). ADCCP = (advanced data communications control protocol) established by American National Standards Institute (ANSI) and initially defined in X3.28-1967 Standard. HDLC = (high-level data link control) protocol formulated by the International Standards Organization (ISO) and published in standard ISO 3309. X.25 = proposed by the CCITT and adopted by the ISO is a standard for international data communications using packet switched networks and HDLC as the link protocol. BDLC = (Burroughs data link control) a protocol for use with Burroughs computer equipment. BOLD = (bit-oriented data link control) a protocol for use with NCR equipment and is a subset of ADCCP. CDCCP = (Control Data communications control program) a protocol for use with Control Data Corp. (CDC) equipment. DDCMP = (digital data communications message protocol) a protocol implemented for Digital Equipment Corp. (DEC) products within their digital network architecture (DNA). UDLC = (Univac data link control) a protocol developed by Sperry Rand's Univac Division.

[b] CS—character stuffing; BS—bit stuffing; CT—count.

[c] V—VRC/LRC; C16—CRC-16; CIT—CRC-CCITT.

PROBLEMS

1. What are the primary objectives of any protocol?
2. Explain how ARQ is accomplished by data link control?
3. What are the different phases of a data communications protocol? Explain what each phase accomplishes.
4. What is meant by the following terms:
   a. polling systems
   b. contention system
   c. point-to-point
   d. multipoint or multidrop
   e. switched
5. What is meant by "transparent" data communications? How is it accomplished in character-oriented protocols? In bit-oriented protocols?
6. Many keyboard devices use 7-level ASCII in a synchronous transmission (by adding 1 parity, 1 start, and 2 stop bits) as eleven-bit characters. The carriage return on a typical terminal (a model 33 KSR) takes 195 ms. Can the sequence of characters CR LF % T A S K be transmitted to the terminal using 110 bps communications lines without losing any of the printing characters? Justify your conclusions. The line feed (LF) operation can take place during the carriage return (CR).
7. Can the line rate be increased to 330 bps and not lose any print characters of the above sequence? What steps can be taken to insure that characters are not lost because of the speed of transmission? Assume that the terminal device is not changed.
8. Synchronous operations with asynchronous modems usually mean that the clock for bit synchronization is sensitive to long strings of zeroes or long strings of ones. Describe how the transmission of such long strings can be prevented from occurring either by the protocol or by signal encoding.

Chapter 15

Future Developments

Having mastered the basics of data communications covered in the preceding chapters, the reader should now be able to continue on his own. With each passing month exciting new developments are described in the periodical literature and in the press. Items previously passed over should now catch the reader's eye and invite detailed perusal. In addition, knowledgeable questions can be presented to the different vendors in order to ascertain the cost–benefits of the equipment or services desired.

There will be many new issues and developments surfacing in the 1980s in the telecommunications field as well as in the computer field. These include all areas from hardware innovations to software implementations to regulatory decisions. The system designer and the system implementor, as well as management, should be keenly aware of the impact these developments have on their teleprocessing applications.

15.1. SOFTWARE DEVELOPMENTS

The major area of advancement in the 1980s will be in software development. In the 1970s hardware technology has far outstripped the software capabilities. The first area will be in full-duplex operations. The communication channel, the modem devices, and the terminal units all presently have the capability for full-duplex operation. Communication protocols are being designed to implement full-duplex operations. What remains is to develop teleprocessing applications to operate in a full-duplex mode. This involves mastering the concepts of synchronous processes. With the rapid development of operating systems for multiprocessor computer systems, there should be a quick transition to using similar techniques in applications programs.

The second area for software development is in computer communication networks. There is much progress in this area already, but various software houses as well as the computer manufacturers will begin to offer software packages for such networks. The difficulty to overcome is to successfully link the protocol for the network to an application program using the network.

The third area for software development is in distributed processing systems. This is where a multiprocessor computer system is looked upon as having its processors separated geographically. Each job (or program) has various tasks that are performed on the different processors. The operating systems on each processor have to successfully interact with the various job tasks under conditions of concurrent task executions as well as sequential task executions. This area certainly presents a formidable challenge to the art of programming.

15.2. HARDWARE DEVELOPMENTS

The trend is clearly towards digital systems. Presently everything up to the analog modems is being built for digital capability. The only thing remaining analog is the channel transmitter and receiver portion of the modem. For the developmental and manufacturing expense involved, it appears that quadrature amplitude modulation (QAM) is the best that can be achieved in terms of capacity at favorable signal-to-noise ratios.

The alternative then, is the development of digital transmission systems.[1] The 1980s will see great refinements in the use of fiber optic transmission systems using modulated coherent light waves to transmit digital signals. The large available bandwidths will be exploited to achieve huge transmission rates, measured in gigabits per second. Except for multiplexing, there are at present very few applications that would require such high bit rates. But then, if technology showed that it could be done, someone would develop an application that would make use of the technology!

The trend toward digital systems is being pushed along by the rapid development of *codec* (for coder–decoder) techniques, and vice versa. Voice messages in digital form can be stored-and-forwarded in computer systems. Digital transmissions require regenerative repeaters instead of amplifiers with an attendant reduction of noise levels. In fact, the control of noise makes these devices attractive for the high-fidelity music markets.[2]

Hardware technology is already looking at VLSI (very large-scale integrated) circuits with further miniaturization. The effect of this will be to provide more powerful computer processor logic in smaller modules to control the operations of many different devices found in the home and in the office. Terminals will be developed with forward-error-correcting (FEC) capability. This will increase the transmission efficiency. Digital systems have lower error rates which, along with FEC, will require no message retransmission. VLSI hardware will enable compact terminals to be constructed that will implement sophisticated protocols and be highly portable.

15.3. REGULATORY ACTIONS

Historically, the Federal Communications Commission has acted to protect the monopoly common carriers from competition. This was drastically changed with several landmark decisions of the early 1970s which allowed competition in all areas of the telecommunications industry. The net result has been that the federal and state courts have been involved in practically every decision made by the FCC.

This culminated in action by the U.S. Congress to rewrite the Communications Act of 1934. The Consumer Communications Reform Act (CCRA) of 1978 was the initial effort. The final outcome, however, will be the Communications Act of 198? which it is hoped will address the problems of competition and subsidization in the telecommunications industry.

There are a number of judicial actions that will have to be eventually resolved. These will definitely provide interesting reading in the news media. Foremost is the U.S. Government antitrust suit against AT&T, where divestiture of Western Electric from AT&T is one of the main actions sought. This rivals the U.S. Government's antitrust suit against IBM for longevity and interest. Another case is the court injunction against allowing SBS (Satellite Business Systems) to operate as a communication-satellite common carrier where the issue appears to be whether or not a competitive impact study was performed before the FCC gave its approval to SBS.[3]

With the Consent Decree of 1956 and the FCC Computer Inquiry I and Computer Inquiry II, will the traditional common carriers be able to offer data processing services in competition with computer vendors? Specifically, AT&T is planning an offering known as Advanced Communications Services (ACS) which involves store-and-forward message switching as well as network capabilities to its subscribers. This service is similar to Telenet's packet-switching service. Telenet became a susidiary of GT&E (General Telephone & Electronic Corp.) in 1979. With AT&T's expected entry into the value-added network market, this will definitely put competitive pressure on SBS, which also can be regarded as a value-added network. Congressional legislation could dramatically alter this potential showdown between IBM and AT&T.[4,5]

Because of unfavorable count rulings against tariff restrictions on the resale of leased communication channels, the wideband channels series 5700 (formerly Telpak C) and series 5800 (Telpak D) were withdrawn as offerings to net subscribers. This leaves series 8000 as the only leased wideband channels available for data communications usage. With a maximum of 10,800 bps rate on voice circuits, the need for greater capacity will certainly result in some new wideband offering for analog transmission. Dataphone Digital Service® is available at 56,000 bps, but it is not widely available.

15.4. CONCLUSIONS AND SUMMARY

All of the aforementioned issues have potential economic impact upon the user of communications facilities. In teleprocessing applications, communication costs will be the largest factor to consider in implementation. Software development costs could possibly exceed the communications cost. Equipment costs, in terms of processing capability, are declining. Thus, with tariffs rapidly changing, the teleprocessing system designer and the operations manager of the implemented system should always be aware of the primary system costs and, even more importantly, the cost of alternative approaches. The days of the sole equipment or services supplier are gone.

REVIEW QUESTIONS

1. Describe an application for which the system response time must be almost instantaneous and where this is the *most* important consideration in the system design. State the reasons for your selections.
2. Describe an application (with suitable literature references) where the use of a terminal with a "light pen" would be the *most* important consideration. State the reasons for your selection.
3. Describe an application (with suitable literature references) where the use of a receive-only (RO) terminal would be the *most* important consideration. State the reasons that determine this case.
4. What is a "graphics terminal?" Describe the salient characteristics that differentiate this type of terminal from others.
5. Discuss the advantages and disadvantages of incorporating interim responses and echoplexing in a terminal-communications system. Explain what each means.
6. In data communications, three levels of synchronization are required: at the bit level, at the character level, and at the message level. Describe how each is accomplished.

7. In a nationwide data communications network consisting of high-speed (56 kbps) synchronous communications line, describe two different methods of maintaining synchronization throughout the entire system.

8. What are the differences or distinctions between the terms "base-band," "bandwidth," and "voice channel?"

9. What are the advantages of using higher frequencies for transmission over using lower frequencies? For example, why is it more desirable to transmit in the GigaHertz range than the kiloHertz range?

10. The T1-carrier system transmits digital signals at 1,544,000 bps. What is the maximum rate of transmitting digital data (i.e., computer generated) over the T1-carrier? Why is there a difference?

11. A baseband signal of 0 to 5 kHz amplitude modulates a 2.37 MHz carrier (double side band). What is the spectrum of the transmitted signal?

12. What is the meaning of the term RS-232C? What is the international equivalent of RS-232C?

13. What is an acoustic coupler? Where is it used? What are the advantages and disadvantages of using an acoustic coupler?

14. Describe an application (with suitable literature references) where a keyboard (printer optional) terminal using an acoustic coupler would be the *most* important consideration in the design of the system. Explain why you made this selection.

15. What is the DAA? Where and why is it required? What are the conditions where the DAA is not required? (at least two examples)

16. What is adaptive equalization? Where is it used? For what purpose is it used?

17. Discuss in a qualitative sense (i.e., a graphical sketch would suffice) the relationship between the speed of transmission vs channel bandwidth vs modulation methods—in the presence of noise.

18. Which type of analog modulation method exhibits superior performance in the presence of noise?

19. What is a "tie line?" Under what conditions would a tie line be more advantageous than any other kind of line?

20. What is a multidrop operation? What application would be designed according to the criteria that the multidrop line organization would be the most important consideration?

21. What are the three "landmark" FCC decisions and what was the impact of each of these on data communications technology?

22. Explain each of the following five issues that were among those raised by the FCC's investigation of common-carrier tariffing procedures and the proposed consumer communications Reform Act (CCRA):
    a. Cross-subsidization
    b. Long-run incremental cost method (value of service pricing)
    c. Rate of return
    d. Local exchange areas
    e. Message-toll service (flat-rate pricing)

27. What is FCC Tariff #260?

28. What are the different names by which private-leased voice channel services are known?

29. Discuss in a qualitative sense, the interrelationships of message block sizes to communication-channel error rates. How does this enter the system design picture?

30. Continue the discussion of the previous question to include considerations of half-duplex vs full-duplex operations.

31. What is VRC? What is LRC? Discuss the advantages and disadvantages of each taken individually and in combination. Under what circumstances would the use of only VRC be satisfactory?

32. What is CRC? Where is it used? What are its advantages and disadvantages?

33. What is the purpose of communication codes? Why have so many?

34. What is the meaning of the "transparency" in data communications?

35. What is the meaning of the term "escape characters" in data communications?

36. Why do people feel that there is a need for standardization of communication codes? What progress has been made in that effort?

37. Define the term "system response time" and indicate the subtleties in interpretation that your definition would entail.

38. Projections for expenditures for all data-communications equipment, except modems, shows an average 20% annual growth over the next decade. Explain why the projections for modem expenditures are shown to be decreasing over the next decade.

39. Compute a comparative per hour charge for each of the following common-carrier services for a 1500-mile two-station point-to-point connection where each station is located 3 miles from a rate center exchange office. Draw up a table *and* show your calculations. (Use 176 hours per month.)
    a. DDD day-time
    b. WATS FBD
    c. WATS MTS
    d. DDS
    e. SPCC—voice-grade line
    f. MCI—voice-grade line
    g. Western Union Satellite (use Dallas–San Francisco) voice channel.

Glossary

ACK A positive acknowledgement as a code character or message representation.

ACK/NAK Acknowledge/do-not-acknowledge receipt of message used in request for retransmission systems (see **ARQ**)

Acknowledge character Used in communications protocol to acknowledge that no errors were detected in a received message.

Acoustic coupler A portable modem device that operates with telephone handsets to send frequency-shift-keyed modulated tone signals.

Acoustic delay line A device that transmits and delays sound pulses by recirculating them in a liquid or solid medium.

Adaptive equalization System circuitry capable of automatically changing the characteristics of envelope delay and frequency attenuation of input signals by sampling those signals.

Alternating current (ac) Current that is continually changing in magnitude and reversing in polarity. A periodic current whose average value over a period is zero.

Amplifier A device which enables an input signal to control power from a source independent of the signal and thus be capable of delivering output which is generally greater than the input signal.

Amplitude Maximum displacement from the zero position of an alternating current or any other periodic phenomena. Amplitude-frequency response characteristics. Of a device or system, the variation of its transmission gain or loss with frequency.

Amplitude modulation (AM) Modulation where the amplitude of the carrier varies.

Analog The representation of numerical quantities by nominally continuous physical variables such as voltage, resistance, temperature, etc.

Antenna Any structure or device used to detect or radiate electromagnetic waves.

ARQ Automatic request for repetition. A system whereby the receiver sends a negative acknowledgement indicating that the previous message be retransmitted.

ASCII American Standard Code for Information Interchange. A seven-bit code proposed by the American National Standards Institute (ANSI).

Asynchronous transmission Transmitting characters that have start and stop symbols appended to them. Also called start–stop transmission.

Attenuation The decrease in amplitude of a wave which accompanies propagation or passage through equipment lines or space, as in radio. Usually measured in decibels (dB).

Attenuation-frequency distortion Form of wave distortion in which the relative magnitudes of the different frequency components are changed.

Audio frequency Frequency which can be detected by the human ear. The range of audio frequencies extends approximately from 15 to 20,000 Hz.

Automatic calling unit (ACU) A telephone-company-supplied device that permits a machine to automatically dial cells over the telephone network.

Background noise Total system noise independent of whether or not a signal is present. Known as thermal noise, Gaussian noise, or white noise.

Band Range of frequency spectrum defined between two limits. A group of radio frequencies assigned to a particular type of radio service.

Bandpass filter Filter which has a single transmission band and in which cutoff frequencies are neither zero or infinity (see **filter**).

Bandwidth Range within limits of a band. The range of frequencies of a channel. Not related to the frequency of transmission nor carrier frequency.

Bank An aggregation of similar devices connected together and used in cooperation.

Baseband The band of frequencies produced by an originating device such as a microphone, video camera, terminal, etc. The band of frequencies occupied by the signal before it modulates a carrier frequency.

Baud A unit signaling speed derived from the reciprocal time of the shortest code element or signal pulse. The baud is the unit of modulation rate.

Baudot code Teleprinter code containing five binary information symbols and two additional symbols, one indicating start and the other stop. See **Asychronous transmission.**

Bel The fundamental unit in a logarithmic scale for expressing the ratio of two amounts of power. See **Decibel.**

Bias distortion In teleprinter circuits, a distortion that causes mark and space pulses to be lengthened or shortened.

Binary Characteristic or property involving a selection, choice, or condition in which there are two possibilities: *on* or *off,* or 0 or 1. Number representation system with a base of two.

Binary-coded decimal system (BCD) System of number representation in which each decimal digit is represented by a group of binary digits. Usually 4 bits for packed decimal, and 6 bits for the full character set.

Bipolar waveform A waveform using opposite polarity for consecutive mark pulses and a neutral signal for space pulses. Used in digital transmission systems.

Bit (1) Abbreviation of binary digit. (2) Unit of information content. It equals one binary decision, or the designation of one of two possible and equally likely values or states of anything used to convey information.

Bit error rate The average number of bits in error per the number of bits transmitted over a communication channel.

Block (1) A group of contiguous characters transmitted as a message unit. (2) Group of computer words considered as a unit by virtue of their being stored in successive locations.

Block error rate The average number of blocks that contain at least one bit in error per the number of blocks transmitted over a communication channel. This varies with the block size for a channel of specified bit error rate.

Broadband A term used by Western Union for their wideband service offerings.

Buffer storage A device for the temporary storage of information during data transfers to compensate for speed differential.

Burst error The nature of certain communications channels that have errors occurring close together, in clusters, and then have long error-free intervals which average out to the bit error rates.

Bus A term used to specify a conductor or a circuit over which data or power is transmitted.

Byte Group of binary digits usually operated upon as a unit. Common usage refers to 8-bit bytes.

Cable Assembly of one or more conductors, usually within an enveloping protective and insulating sheath, in such structural arrangement of the individual conductors as to permit their use separately or in groups.

Capacitance Ability to story electrical energy, measured in farads, microfarads, or picofarads, when potential differences exist between the conductors.

Carrier, common communications A company regulated by appropriate regulatory agencies having a vested interest in providing communications services.

Carrier frequency Frequency of the unmodulated fundamental output of a radio transmitter, usually measured in Hertz (Hz).

Cathode-ray tube Vacuum tube in which the instantaneous position of a sharply focused electron beam, deflected by means of electrostatic and/or electromagnetic fields is indicated by a spot of light produced by the impact of the electrons on a fluorescent screen at one end of the tube.

CCITT Consultative Committee on International Telephony and Telegraphy.

Central office Office in a telephone system that provides service to the general public where orders for, or signals controlling, telephone connections are received and established. Also known as an exchange office or end-office.

Channel (1) Portion of the spectrum assigned for the operation of a specific carrier and the minimum number of sidebands to convey intelligence. (2) Single path for transmitting electrical signals.

Channel group A frequency-division-multiplexed subdivision containing 12 voice channels occupying the frequency band 60–108 kHz.

Character One symbol of a set of elementary marks, such as bits pulses, or events, that may be combined to express information.

Chip A term referring to a microelectronic circuit.

Circuit (1) Electronic path between two or more points, capable of providing a number of channels. (2) Number of conductors connected together for the purpose of carrying an electrical current. (3) Connected assemblage of electrical components such as transistors, resistors, capacitors, etc., having desired electrical characteristics.

Circuit, four-wire A two-way circuit where the electrical waves can be transmitted in both directions at any given time. Sometimes known as a full-duplex circuit.

Coaxial cable An electrical conductor that has a conducting tube with a wire running down its center, the tube and wire kept aligned and separated by the use of insulator spacers. Used for high-frequency transmissions.

Code (1) Any system of communications in which arbitrary groups of symbols represent units of plain text of varying length. (2) System of signaling using dot-dash-space, mark-space, or other methods where each letter or figure is represented by prearranged combinations.

Codec A circuit for the conversion of a voice analog signal to a pulse code modulated signal.

Coherent detection A system where the received signal contains information to establish a reference (frequency or phase) at the receiver.

Common carrier See carrier, common communications.

Commutator (1) Device used in multiplex systems to connect the line to various channels. (2) Device used on electric motors or generators to maintain a unidirectional current.

Compandor Device which combines the functions of a compressor with an expandor. Used to reduce the volume range of signals at the compressor while the expandor restores the original volume rage. Its purposes is to improve the ratio of the signal to the interference on a channel.

Concentrator (1) Buffer switch (analog or digital) that serves to reduce the number of trunks required. (2) Storage memory that serves to gather messages from many lines to output on fewer lines usually at a higher rate. Process may be reversed.

Conditioning Equipment modifications or adjustments necessary to flatten out the transmission-channel responses of frequency-attenuation and envelope delay. Available as a Telco service on private-lease voice channels.

Contention Organization of a multidrop system whereby each terminal competes for a transmission path with other terminals. This is contrasted with polling.

Control character The communication codes, characters defined for the purpose of controlling the message exchange.

Crosstalk (1) Undesired power injected into a communications circuit from other communication circuits. May be intelligible or unintelligible. (2) Sound heard in a receiver associated with a given telephone channel resulting from telephone currents in another telephone channel.

Cycle (1) Complete set of any recurrent or periodic values. (2) One complete positive and negative alternation of current.

Cyclic redundancy check (CRC) Characters appended to a message block for the purpose of error detection. Usually formed by determining the remainder of a synthetic division operation on the bits of the message block by a generating polynomial.

DAA Data access arrangement. A requirement by the telephone company tariffs that a device must be used to protect the dial network whenever a nontelephone-company-manufactured device is attached to the dial network.

Data (1) Items of fact, events, or symbol, or facts that refer to or describe an object, idea, condition, situation, or other factors. (2) Basic elements from which information can be derived.

Data link (1) Communications system whose terminals are suitable for the transmission of data. (2) A communications system in which intelligence is represented by digital data rather than by literal means.

Dataphone (1) A trademark and service mark of the Bell System that describes a tariffed service using the switched-telephone network for data transmission. (2) Also describes Western Electric-manufactured modems.

Datasped A trademark and service mark of the Bell System that describes a tariffed data transmission service for paper tape operations and terminal devices.

DDD Direct distance dialing. The message-toll charge scheme for using the public-switched telephone network.

Decibel Dimensionless unit for expressing the ratio of two values, the number of decibels being 10 times the logarithm to the base 10 of a power ratio, or 20 times the logarithm of a voltage or intensity ratio.

Delay distortion (1) Phase-delay distortion: variation of the phase angle of a transmission with frequency over the transmission band. (2) Envelope delay: a transmitted signal. Usually expressed in milliseconds from an average delay time at a central frequency.

Delta modulation Pulse modulation technique in which a continuous signal is converted into a binary pulse pattern for transmission through low-quality channels.

Differential detection The receiver process of comparing the results of the current signal sample with a previous sample to determine the transmitted signal level.

Digitize To convert an analog measurement of a physical variable into a numerical value of finite precision, thereby expressing the quantity in digital form.

Distortion An undesired change in waveform.

Dropout Reduction in output signal level during the reception of a message sufficient to cause an error.

E&M piece A telephone term for the telephone handset.

Echo Wave which has been reflected or otherwise returned with sufficient magnitude and delay to be perceived. Usually occurring in transmission circuits because of impedence imbalances.

Echo checking Checking system in which the transmitted information is returned to the transmitter and compared with what was transmitted.

Echoplexing See **Echo checking**.

Echo suppressor Voice device for use in a two-way telephone channel to alternate echo currents in one direction caused by telephone currents in the other direction.

Electromagnetic spectrum The frequencies or wavelengths present in a given electromagnetic radiation. A particular spectrum could include a single frequency or a wide range of frequencies.

Electronic Industries Association (EIA) A group comprised of electronic equipment manufacturers representatives that propose industry-wide standards for hardware and interfaces.

Envelope-delay distortion See **Delay distortion**.

Equalitization The process by which added electronic circuitry conditions the received signal in modem equipment.

Error-correcting code (1) Redundancy added to the message for the purpose of error detection and correction. Capacity of the message channel is reduced. (2) Code in which the forbidden pulse combination produced by gain or loss of a bit indicates which bit is wrong.

Exchange office See **Central office**.

Facility The physical plant, including equipment, providing the means for assisting in the performance of a function.

Facsimile Term used for the process by which transmission of reproductions of photographs, drawings, or other fixed graphic material is accomplished. The material is scanned and the information is converted into electrical signals for transmissions to remotely reproduce a likeness of the subject copy. Sometimes called telephoto.

Fading Variation of radio-field intensity caused by changes in the transmission medium.

FDM Frequency-division-multiplexed channel.

FDX Full-duplex channel.

Federal Communications Commission (FCC) The government regulatory agency created by the communications Act of 1934 and charged with regulating all interstate and foreign communications and broadcasting in the United States.

Fieldata code Interim common language code used with AUTODIN.

Filter (1) A circuit which offers little opposition to certain frequencies while blocking the passage of other frequencies. (2) A tuned circuit designed to pass alternating current of a specified frequency.

Flip-flop (1) Device having two stable states and two input terminals (or types of input signals) each of which corresponds to one of the two states. The circuit remains in either state until caused to change to the other state by application of the corresponding signal. (2) A similar bistable device with an input which allows it to act as a single-stage binary counter.

Fortuitous distortion Distortion in a telegraph system which includes effects that cannot be classified as bias or characteristic distortion. The direct opposite of systematic distortion.

Four-wire circuit See **Circuit, four-wire**.

Frequency The number of recurrences of a periodic phenomenon in a unit of time expressed in units of hertz (Hz). The older unit was cycles per second (cps).

Frequency modulation Angle modulation of a sinusoidal carrier in which the instantaneous frequency of the modulated wave differs from the carrier frequency by an amount proportional to the instantaneous value of the modulating wave. Commonly referred to as FM.

Frequency-shift keying (FSK) Form of frequency modulation in which the modulating wave shifts the output frequency between predetermined values, and the output wave has no phase discontinuity. Also called frequency-shift modulation.

Full-duplex operation (FDX) Simultaneous communications in both directions between two points.

Gray code Modified binary code used for analog to digital conversion such as changing an angle to a binary value. Also called cyclic binary code and reflective code.

Ground (1) Point in a circuit used as a common reference or datum point in measuring voltages. (2) Conducting connection, whether intentional or accidental, between an electric circuit or equipment and earth, or to some connecting body which serves in place of earth.

Group. See **Channel group**.

Guard band Narrow frequency band left vacant between adjacent channels to give a margin of safety against mutual interference.

Half-duplex circuit Circuit which permits only one direction of electrical communications between stations.

Handshaking Term used to describe the process of establishing the channel connection between two stations.

Hertz (Hz) The unit of frequency replacing cycles per second.

Homodyne reception System where the receiver uses a locally generated voltage or carrier frequency in the demodulation process.

Hybrid circuit In telephone transmission circuits, a circuit for interconnecting two-wire and four-wire circuits through a differential balance or bridge circuit. Also called two-wire-four-wire terminating set.

Impedance Total opposition offered to the flow of an alternating current.

Impulse noise Noise due to disturbances having abrupt changes of amplitude and of short duration.

Inductance Property of an electric circuit whereby changes in the current flowing in the circuit are such that counter electromotive (emf) force is set up either in the circuit itself (called self-inductance) or in neighboring circuits (called mutual inductance).

Intermodulation Modulation of the components of a complex wave by each other producing waves having frequencies equal to the sums and differences on integral multiples of the component frequencies of the complex wave.

International Telecommunication Union (ITU) Civil international organization established to provide standarized communications procedures and practices, including frequency allocation and radio, telegraph, and telephone regulations on an international basis.

Intersymbol interference In a transmission system, extraneous energy from the signal in one or more keying intervals which tends to interfere with the reception of the signal in another keying interval, or the disturbance which results.

Ionsphere The region of the atmosphere from roughly 40 to 250 miles altitude in which there is appreciable ionization which may cause the reflection to earth of radio waves.

J-carrier system A wideband carrier system providing 12 telephone channels, which uses frequencies up to about 140 kHz by means of effective four-wire transmission on a single open-wire pair.

Jitter Random deviations in phase angle of the received signal due primarily to oscillator instability in long-hand frequency-division-multiplexed systems.

K-carrier system Carrier system providing 12 telephone voice channels with a bandwidth up to 60 kHz either on a 4-wire cable system or on a microwave line-of-sight (LOS) or troposheric scater radio systems.

LASER Light amplification by stimulated emission of radiation, a process of generating coherent light.

L-carrier system Telephone carrier system used on coaxial systems, microwave (LOS), and troposheric scater radio systems. It occupies a frequency band from 68 kHz to over 8 MHz.

Leakage (1) Electrical loss resulting from poor insulation. (2) Undesired flow of electricity over or through insulators that are used to support or separate the conductors of a circuit.

Link A general term to indicate the existence of communications facilities between two points.

Loaded line Wire circuits in which loading coils have been inserted at regular intervals to reduce attenuation and phase lag at the frequencies within the band used.

Loop Commercially, that portion of a connection from a central office to a subscriber in a toll connection.

LRC Longitudinal redundancy check. A character of parity bits for checking all the bits of each character in a block of characters.

LSI An acronym for large-scale integration of electronic circuits.

Mark A telegraphy term for a bit—contrasted with a "space."

Message Any thought or idea expressed briefly in a plain or coded language, prepared in a form suitable for transmission by any means of communication.

Message precedence See protocol.

MICR Magnetic ink character recognition. The machine recognition of characters printed with magnetic ink.

Microwave Term applied to radio waves in the frequency range 1000 MHz and upwards.

Modem A device that performs both modulation and demodulation functions.

Modulation Process (or the result of the process) by which the characteristic, such as amplitude, frequency, or phase, of one wave is varied by another wave.

Multipath effect Condition in which radio waves arrive at a receiver at slightly differing times because they travel over paths of appreciably different lengths.

Multiplex Simultaneous transmission of two or more signals by a common-carrier wave by means such as time division or frequency division.

***N*-ary code** Code using *N* distinguishable types of code elements.

Network (1) Organization of stations capable of intercommunications but not necessarily on the same channel. (2) Two or more interrelated circuits. (3) Connected system of nodes and branches geographically or functionally bounded.

NDT An acronym for the net data throughput, i.e., the actual rate of information on a communications channel.

Node Junction point in a network.

Nominal bandwidth Assigned frequency limits of a channel, e.g., the nominal bandwidth of a voice channel is 4 kHz.

Nyquist interval Maximum separation in time which can be given to regularly spaced instantaneous samples of a wave of a given bandwidth for complete determination of the waveform of the signal.

Nyquist rate The maximum rate of a channel at which independent signal values can be transmitted over the specified channel without exceeding a specified amount of mutual interference. This is equal to twice the highest bandwidth frequency.

Oscillator Electronic device which generates alternating current power at a frequency determined by the values of certain constants.

Pad Nonadjustable passive network which reduces the power level of a signal without introducing appreciable distortion.

Parity bit A bit used to make the total number of ''one'' bits either odd or even. This is primarily used in error detection on characters.

Phase Position of a wave relative to the beginning of an electrical or mechanical wave, usually expressed in angular measurement.

Phase jitter See **Jitter**.

Phase modulation Method of modulation where the amplitude of the modulated wave remains constant while varying in phase with the amplitude of the modulating signal. A phase-modulated wave is electrically identical to a modified frequency-modulated wave.

Phase quadrature See **Quadrature**.

Phase-shift keying Form of phase modulation in which the modulating function shifts the instantaneous phase of the modulated wave between predetermined discrete values.

Pilot tone Single frequency transmitted over a narrow channel to operate an alarm or automatic control or to provide a reference signal for the demodulator.

Private branch exchange (PBX) Telephone exchange serving a single organization and having connections to a public telephone exchange.

Propagation The delay of an electronic signal sent over a communications channel. It is estimated at about 1.6×10^8 meters per second over wire systems and 3×10^8 meters per second over radio systems.

Protocol The rules or procedures for the control of communications over a channel.

Quadrature modulation Modulation of two carrier components 90 degrees apart in phase by separate modulating functions.

Quantization Process in which the continuous range of values of an input signal is divided into subranges and to each subrange a discrete value of the output is uniquely assigned. Whenever a signal falls within a given subrange, the output has the corresponding discrete value.

Radio Use of electromagnetic waves to transmit or receive electric impulses or signals without a connecting wire.

RS-232 An Electronic Industries Association interface standard between a modem and a terminal device.

Sensor Element or device that detects a change in a selective physical quantity and converts that change into an electrical signal for use as an input to a measuring, recording, or control system.

Shift register Computer circuit for conversion of a sequence of input signals into a parallel binary number or vice versa.

Signal Event, phenomenon, or electrical quantity that conveys information from one point to another.

Skin effect Tendency of alternating currents to flow near the surface of the conductor as the frequency is increased thus being restricted to a small part of the total sectional area and producing the effect of increased resistance.

Space A telegraphy term for a "zero" bit; contrasted to a "mark."

Strapping Connecting two or more points in a circuit or device with a short piece of wire or metal.

Stunt box A device to control the nonprinting functions of a teletypewriter terminal.

Subscriber line See **Loop**.

Supergroup In carrier frequency-division-multiplexed systems, 5 groups (60 voice channels) treated as a unit and occupying the band between 312 kHz and 552 kHz.

Systematic distortion Periodic or constant distortion, such as bias or characteristic distortion. The direct opposite of fortuitous distortion.

Tariff A common-carrier published contract which describes the services provided and the rates charged for those services.

Telephone channel A nominal 4 kHz voice channel for audio signals

Teletypewriter exchange service (TWX) A semiautomatic switching service provided by Western Union for interconnecting public teletypewriter subscribers.

TELEX Same as teletypewriter exchange service.

Tera The SI (Systéme International) metric prefix for 10^{12}.

Text That part of a message which conveys the information to be transmitted.

Tie-line Leased communication channel or circuit.

Time-division multiplexing (TDM) Process of transmitting two or more channels of information over a single link by allocating a different time interval for the transmission of each channel.

TTL An acronym for transistor-transistor logic interface circuits.

Transducer A device that converts the physical properties of a signal from one energy form to another.

TRIB An acronym for transfer rate of information bits. See **NDT**.

Tropospheric scatter A microwave transmission method that uses the ionized layer of the earth's atmosphere to reflect a narrow beam signal to a distant antenna.

Trunk A communication channel between two switching equipments.

USART A universal synchronous/asynchronous receiver/transmitter LSI chip that is used in binary serial communication interfaces. This chip performs serialization and deserialization of characters, internal baud-rate generation, loop-back self-testing, EIA modem control, etc.

Volume Expression generally taken to by synonomous with power level.

VLSI An acronym for very large-scale integrated electronic circuits.

VRC Vertical redundancy check. A parity bit on each character of a transmitted block of characters.

Waveform Shape of the wave obtained when instantaneous values of an alternating current quantity are plotted against time in rectangular coordinates.

WATS Wide area telephone service provided by AT&T for inward or outward calling on the public dial network at specified rates.

White noise Random noise having equal energy per cycle over a wide frequency band.

Wideband A term used for transmission over two or more combined voice channels at rates of 19,200 bps and higher.

Word In telegraphy, a word consists of six characters including the blank character.

References and Suggested Reading

References for Chapter 1

1. Rosen, S., Electronic computers: A historical survey, *Computing Surveys* **1** (1), (March 1969), pp. 7–36.
2. Denning, P. J., Third generation computer systems, *Computing Surveys* **3** (4), (Dec. 1971), pp. 175–216.
3. Aron, J. D., Information systems in perspective, *Computing Surveys* **1** (4), (Dec. 1969), pp. 213–236.
4. Goldstine, H. H., *The Computer from Pascal to von Neumann,* Princeton University Press, Princeton, New Jersey (1972).
5. Project MAC, developed at the Massachusetts Institute of Technology in 1963 under the direction of J. Corbato.
6. Kemeny, John G., and Kurtz, Thomas E., developed BASIC at Dartmouth College in 1965; subsequently became known as the Dartmouth–GE BASIC time-sharing system.
7. Frost and Sullivan, Inc., *Data Communications Equipment Market in the USA,* Report No. 331 (1975) as summarized in Exciting developments spur data communications growth, *Communications News,* December (1975), pp. 16–27, and in Data communications growing at 22.5% a year, *Data Communications,* May/June (1975), p. 16.

References for Chapter 2

1. Gray, J. P., Line control procedures, *Proc. IEEE* **60** (Nov. 1972), pp. 1301–1312.
2. Grubb, D. S., Data communications system throughput performance using high-speed terminals on the dial telephone network, *National Bureau of Standards Technical Note 779* (May 1973).
3. Gentry, M. L., Effective line speed of high speed communications lines, *Modern Data* (Nov. 1975) pp. 47–50.

References for Chapter 3

1. Hamsher, D. H., ed., *Communication Systems Engineering Handbook,* McGraw-Hill, New York (1967).
2. *Transmission Systems for Communications*, Bell Telephone Labs, Raleigh, North Carolina, (1971), pp. 20–23.
3. Bennet, W. R., and Davey, J. R., *Data Transmission*, McGraw-Hill, New York (1965), pp. 14–16, 83, 84.
4. Flood, J. E., *Telecommunication Networks*, P. Peregrinus Ltd., Stevenage, England (1975), pp. 30–32.

References for Chapter 4

1. Martin, J., *Telecommunications and the Computer,* Prentice-Hall, Englewood Cliffs, New Jersey (1969), pp. 194–202.
2. Bennett, W. R., and Davey, J. R., *Data Transmission,* McGraw-Hill, New York (1965), Chapters 4 and 5.
3. Carlson, A. B., *Communication Systems,* McGraw-Hill, New York (1975), pp. 29–32.
4. Brown, J., and Glazier, E. V. D., *Telecommunications,* Chapman and Hall and Science Paperbacks (1974), pp. 22–36.
5. Shannon, C. E., The mathematical theory of communication, *Bell System Technical Journal,* **50** (July–October 1948).
6. Lucky, R. W., Common-carrier data communication, in *Computer-Communication Networks,* eds. N. Abramson and F. S. Kuo, Prentice-Hall, Englewood Cliffs, New Jersey (1973), pp. 167–173.
7. Brown, J., and Glazier, E. V. D., *Telecommunications,* Chapman and Hall and Science Paperbacks (1974), pp. 210–214.

References for Chapter 5

1. Gregg, W. D., *Analog and Digital Modulation,* John Wiley and Sons, Santa Barbara, California (1977).
2. Bennett, W. R., and Davey, J. R., *Data Transmission,* McGraw-Hill, New York (1965).
3. Carlson, A. B., *Communication Systems,* McGraw-Hill, New York (1968).
4. Panter, P. F., *Communications Systems Design,* McGraw-Hill, New York (1972), pp. 1–19.
5. Krechmer, K., Integrating medium-speed modems into communications networks, *Computer Design* (Feb. 1978), pp. 43–46.
6. Bell System Technical Reference Manual, Pub. No. 41209, Data Set 208A Interface Specification, New York.
7. Davey, J. R., Modems, *Proceedings of the IEEE,* **60**(11) (Nov. 1972), pp. 1284–1292.
8. Stuart, R., Advancement in dataset design, *Telecommunications* **11** (June 1977), pp. 42–46.
9. Bell System Technical Reference Manual, Pub. No. 41213, Data Set 209A Interface Specification, New York.

References for Chapter 6

1. Bennett, W. R., and Davey, J. R., *Data Transmission,* Mcgraw-Hill, New York (1965), p. 245.
2. Hamsher, D. H., ed., *Communication System Engineering Handbook,* McGraw-Hill, New York (1967), pp. 10-1 to 10-40.

3. Freeman, R. L., *Telecommunication Transmission Handbook,* John Wiley and Sons, New York (1975), pp. 82–130.
4. Doll, D. R., *Data Communications,* John Wiley and Sons, New York (1978), pp. 311-322.
5. Chu, W. W., Design considerations of statistical multiplexors, *Proceedings of the First ACM Symposium on Problems in the Optimization of Data Communication Systems,* American Computer Machinery, Pine Mountain, Georgia (Oct. 1969), pp. 35–60.
6. Evans, R. L., Cost savings with multiplexers and concentrators, *Telecommunications* **11**(5) (May 1976), pp. 25–28, and (6) (June 1976), pp. 39–43.
7. Smith, R. S., Multiplexing cuts cost of communications lines, *Electronics Desk Book* **1**(1) (1972), pp. 67–74.
8. Held, G., Multiplexing data with flexible modems, *Data Communications* **4**(6) (Nov/Dec 1975), pp. 33–36
9. Held, G., Inverse multiplexing with multipost modems, *Data Communications* **5**(1) (Jan/Feb 1976), pp. 45–50.
10. Yeh, L. P., Telecommunications transmission media, *Telecommunications* **10**(4) (April 1976), pp. 51–56; (5) (May 1976), pp. 34–36; and (6) (June 1976), pp. 44–46.
11. *Transmission Systems for Communications,* Bell Telephone Laboratories, Raleigh, North Carolina (1971), p. 21.
12. Anonymous, Industrial microwave market, *Communication News*, Oct. (1976), pp. 56–57.
13. *L*-5 coaxial carrier transmission system, *Bell System Technical Journal* **53** (Dec. 1974), pp. 1897-2267.
14. DeWitt, R. G., Digital microwave radio, *Telecommunications* **9**(4) (April 1975), pp. 25-31.
15. Boxall, F., Digital transmission via microwave radio, *Telecommunications* **6**(4) (April 1972), pp. 17–22.
16. Freeman, R. L., *Telecommunication Transmission Handbook,* John Wiley and Sons, New York (1975), pp. 177–263.
17. Roche, A. H., Transoceanic cable system planning and design, *Telecommunications* **4**(1) (Jan. 1970), pp. 15–20.
18. TAT-6, *Communication News* Nov. (1975), p. 35; and Oct. (1975), p. 20.
19. Dawidziuk, B. M., Have satellites sunk the submarine cable?, *Telecommunications* **9**(3) (Mar. 1975), pp. 25–41.
20. Kirkland, F. E., and McDonald, K. M., Overseas communication by submarine cable, *Telecommunications* **13**(3), May (1979), pp. 45–59.
21. Bedwell, C., Communications aid the flow of North Sea oil, *Telecommunications* **9**(5) (May 1975), pp. 46–52.
22. Edelson, B. H., Global satellite communications, *Scientific American*, No. 2 (Feb. 1977), pp. 58–73.
23. Kao, K. C., and Collier, M. E., Fibre-optic systems in future telecommunication networks, *Telecommunications* **11**(4) (April 1977), pp. 25–32.
24. Miller, S. E., Optical communications research progress, *Science* **170** (13 Nov. 1970), pp. 685–695.

References for Chapter 7

1. Thompson, G., Communication administrations in Europe. Home of Monopoly, *Communications News* **12**(11) (November 1975), pp. 28–29.
2. CCITT (Comite Consultif International Telephone Telegraph), *Series Rec. G* and *Series Rec. Q.45,* Green Books, Geneva (1972).
3. *Transmission Systems for Communications,* Bell Telephone Laboratories, Raleigh, North Carolina (1971).

4. Fuhrmann, J. J., A glance at the electronic switching world, *Telecommunications* **10**(2) (February 1976), pp. 41–46.
5. Pitroda, S. G., A review of telecommunications switching concepts, *Telecommunications* **10**(2) (February 1976), pp. 29–36.
6. Hamsher, D. H., ed., *Communication System Engineering Handbook,* McGraw-Hill, New York (1967), pp. 6–33, 6–36.
7. Data communications using the switched telecommunications network, Bell System Technical Reference Pub. 41005, New York (May 1971).

References for Chapter 8

1. Bennett, W. R., and Davey, J. R., *Data Transmission*, McGraw-Hill, New York (1965), pp. 100–118.
2. Lucky, R. W., Common-carrier data communication, in *Computer-Communication Networks,* N. A. Abramson and F. F. Kuo, eds., Prentice-Hall, New Jersey (1973), pp. 167–168.
3. Salz, J., Communications efficiency of certain digital modulation Systems, *IEEE Trans. Commun. Technol. COM-18* (April 1970).
4. Bennett, W. R., and Davey, J. R., *Data Transmission*, McGraw-Hill, New York (1965), pp. 225–229.
5. Lucky, R. W., Common-carrier data communication, in *Computer-Communication Networks,* N. A. Abramson and F. F. Kuo, eds., Prentice-Hall, New Jersey (1973), pp. 167–171.
6. Kelly, J., The relationship of phase jitter to the measurement of other voice channel parameters, *Telecommunications,* Oct. (1972), pp. 46–50.
7. Kelly, J., Phase jitter and its measurement, *Telecommunications,* July (1970), pp. 28–31.
8. Lucky, R. W., in *Computer-Communication Networks,* N. A. Abramson and F. F. Kuo, eds., Prentice-Hall, New Jersey (1973), pp. 155, 166.
9. Phase Jitter, Technical Note No. 1, Farinon Electric Co., New York (1972)
10. Freeman, R. L., *Telecommunication Transmission Handbook*, John Wiley and Sons (1975), pp. 131–152.
11. Freeman, R. L., *Telecommunication Transmission Handbook,* John Wiley and Sons (1975), pp. 131–152.
12. Data communications using the switched telecommunications network, *Bell System Technical Reference Pub. 41005,* New York (May 1971).
13. Data communications using voice band private-line channels, *Bell System Technical Reference Pub. 41004,* New York (Oct. 1975).
14. Attenuation and envelope delay characteristics from the 1969–70 switched telecommunications network connection survey, *Bell System Technical Reference Pub. 41006,* New York (June 1973).
15. Alexander, A. A., Gryb, R. M., and Nast, D. W., Capabilities of the telephone network for data transmission, *Bell System Technical Journal* **39** (May 1960), pp. 431–476.
16. Duffy, F. P., and Thatcher, T. W., Analog transmission performance on the switched telecommunications network, *Bell System Technical Journal* **50** (April 1971), pp. 1311–1347. Also in 1969–70 switched telecommunications network connection survey, *Bell System Technical Reference Pub. 41007* (April 1971).
17. Balkovic, M. D., *et al.*, High-speed voiceband data transmission performance on the switched telecommunications network, *Bell System Technical Journal* **50** (April 1971), pp. 1349–1384. Also in 1969–70 switched telecommunications network connection survey, *Bell System Technical Reference Pub. 41007* (April 1971), and in Green, P. E., and Lucky, R. W., *Computer Communications,* IEEE Press, New York (1974), pp. 79–114.

18. FCC Tariff 260, Rates, practices and procedures governing use of interstate leased lines, filed by American Telephone and Telegraph Co. with the Federal Communications Commission, New York.
19. Transmission parameters affecting voiceband data transmission measuring techniques, *Bell System Technical Reference Pub. 41009,* New York (May 1975).

References for Chapter 9

1. Mathison, S. L., and Walker, P. M., *Computers and Telecommunications Issues in Public Policy,* Prentice-Hall, Englewood Cliffs, New Jersey. (1970).
2. Regulatory policy and future data transmission services, in *Computer-Communication Networks,* N. Abramson and F. Kuo, eds., Prentice-Hall, Englewood Cliffs, New Jersey (1974), Chapter 10.
3. Walker, P. M., Regulatory developments in data communications—The past five years, *AFIPS Proc. Spring Joint Computer Conference, Vol. 40,* Spartan Books, New York (1972), pp. 593–609.
4. Mathison, S. L., and Walker, P. M., Regulatory and economic isues in computer communications, *Proc. IEEE* **60**(11) (Nov. 1972), pp. 1254–1272.
5. Dunn, D. A., The FCC computer inquiry, *Datamation,* Oct. (1969), pp. 71–77.
6. FCC Docket #16979, Final Decision and Order 28 FCC 2d 267 (1971).
7. Peniston, G., An overview of the specialized common-carrier industry, *Telecommunications,* Sept. (1975), pp. 53–57.

References for Chapter 10

1. McNamara, J. E., *Technical Aspects of Data Communication,* Digital Equipment Corp., Maynard, Massachusetts (1977), Chapters 5 and 9.
2. EIA Standard RS-232-C, Interface between data terminal equipment and data communication equipment employing binary serial data interchange, Engineering Department, Electronic Industries Association, Washington, D.C. (August 1969).
3. Application Notes for EIA-Standards RS-232-C, Engineering Department, Electronic Industries Association, Washington, D.C. (May 1971).
4. Holts, H. C., and Cotton, I. W., Interfaces: new standards catch up with technology, *Data Communications,* Volume 6.
5. Vilips, V. V., *Data Modem Selection and Evaluation Guide,* Artech House, Dedham, Massachusetts (1972).
6. Doll, D. R., *Data Communications,* John Wiley and Sons, New York (1978), pp. 244–252.
7. Davey, J. R., Modems, *Proc. IEEE Volume* **60**(11) (November 1972), pp. 1284–1292.
8. Bryant, P., Giesin, F. W., and Hayes, R. M., Experiments in line quality monitoring, *IBM Systems Journal* **15**(2) (1978), pp. 124–142.
9. Foschini, G. J., Gitlin, R. D., and Weinstein, S. B., On the selection of a two-dimensional signal constellation in the presence of phase jitter and gaussian noise, *Bell System Technical Journal* **52**(6) (July-August 1973), pp. 927–965.
10. Puchkoff, S. J., A modem eye-pattern looks at telephone lines, *Telecommunications* **6**(8) (August 1972).

References for Chapter 11

1. Kamman, A. B., How to pick CRT terminals, *Data Processing Magazine* **13**(4), April (1971), pp. 41–45.

2. Martin, J., *Systems Analysis for Data Transmission,* Prentice-Hall, Englewood Cliffs, New Jersey (1973), pp. 170–179.
3. *Data Pro Research Reports,* Data Pro Research Corporation, Newark, New Jersey (annually updated).

Suggested Reading for Chapter 12

Doll, D. R., topology and transmission rate considerations in the design of centralized computer-communication networks, *IEEE Trans. on Comm. Tech.* (June 1971) pp. 339–344.

Doll, D. R., Data communications systems: basics of network design, *Data Communication,* **1**(1), (1972), pp. 13–22.

Gourley, D. E., Data communications: initial planning, *Datamation* (October 1972).

Kershenbaum, A., Tools for planning and designing data communications networks, *Proceedings National Computer Conference* (1974), Association for Computer Machinery, New York pp. 583–591.

McGregor, P., Effective use of data communications hardware, *Proceedings of the National Computer Conference*, (1974), Association for Computer Machinery, New York pp. 565–575.

Nestle, E., Design workshop: configuring an actual data system, *Data Communications,* **1**(1), (1972), p. 97–100.

Pan, G. S., Communications information systems, *Telecommunications* (June 1970).

References for Chapter 13

1. Bennett, W. R., and Davey, J. R., *Data Transmission*, McGraw-Hill, New York (1965), pp. 1–21.
2. Still, A., *Communication Through the Ages,* Murray Hill Books Inc., New York (1946).
3. Bennett, W. R., and Davey, J. R., *Data Transmission,* McGraw-Hill, New York (1965), p. 292.
4. Peterson, W. W., *Error Correcting Codes,* M.I.T. Press and John Wiley and Sons, New York (1961).
5. Lin, S., *An Introduction to Error Correcting Codes,* Prentice-Hall, Englewood Cliffs, New Jersey (1970).
6. Hamming, R. W., Error detecting and error correcting codes, *Bell System Technical Journal* **29** (April 1950), pp. 147–160.
7. Gaushell, D. J., Error control in digital transmission, *Control Engineering,* June (1972), pp. 58–64.
8. Chen, C. L., and Rutledge, R. A., Error correcting codes for satellite communication channels, *IBM Journal of Research Development,* March (1976), pp. 168–175.
9. Espeland, L. R., and Nesenbergs, M., Exhaustive search for the best cyclic (20,8) code, *ESSA Technical Report ERL 174-ITS 111* (April 1970).

References for Chapter 14

1. Berglund Assoc., Variations in line control procedures, *Modern Data,* April (1974), pp. 74–77.
2. Gray, J. P., Line control procedures, *Proc. IEEE* **60**(11) (Nov. 1972), pp. 1301–1312.
3. Eisenbis, J. L., Conventions for digital data communication link design, *IBM Systems Journal* **6**(4) (1967), pp. 267–302.
4. Donman, R. A., and Kersey, J. R., Synchronous data link control: a perspective, *IBM Systems Journal* **13**(2) (1974), pp. 140–162.
5. D.E.C., Specification for: DDCMP digital data communications message protocol, Digital Equipment Corp., Maynard, Massachusetts (10 Dec. 1974), Edition 3.

6. I.B.M., General information—binary synchronous communications, Systems Reference Library Manual No. GA27-3004, IBM Corp. (Oct. 1970).
7. I.B.M., Synchronous data link control—general information No. GA27-3093, IBM Corp., Data Processing Division, White Plains, New York.
8. Kersey, J. R., Synchronous data link control, *Data Communications* **3** (May/June 1974), pp. 49–60.
9. Lynch, W. C., Reliable full-duplex file transmission over half-duplex telephone lines, *Commun. ACM* **11**(6) (June 1968), pp. 407–410; and **12**(5) (May 1969), pp. 260–265.
10. Martin, J., *Teleprocessing Network Organization,* Prentice-Hall, Englewood Cliffs, New Jersey (1970), pp. 96–117.
11. Stein, P. G., Communications protocols: the search for SYN, *Datamation*, April (1973), pp. 55–57.
12. Stutzman, B. W., Data communication control procedures, *Computing Surveys* **4**(4) (Dec. 1972), pp. 197–220.
13. U.S.A.S.I., Code extension procedures for information interchange, *Commun. ACM* **11**(12) (Dec. 1968), pp. 849–852.
14. U.S.A.S.I., Data communication control procedures for the USA Standard Code for Information Interchange, X3.4 Document, *Commun. ACM* **12**(3) (Mar. 1969), pp. 166–178.
15. U.S.A.S.I., Heading format for data transmission (a USAAI tutorial), *Commun. ACM* **11**(6) (June 1968), pp. 441–448.
16. Wecker, S., DEC's protocol DDCMP, *Data Communications* **3**, (Sept/Oct. 1974), pp. 36–46.

References for Chapter 15

1. Herres, P. B., Why digital?, *Business Communications Review,* Nov.–Dec. (1978), pp. 3–9.
2. A digital wave begins to sweep industries; new products emerge, *Wall Street Journal*, Wednesday, May 30 (1979), pp. 1, 22.
3. FCC authorization to satellite venture overturned by court, *Wall Street Journal,* Thursday, August 31 (1978), p. 16.
4. Anderson, H. IBM versus bell in telecommunications, *Datamation,* May (1977), pp. 91–95.
5. Behind AT&T's change at the top, *Business Week,* Nov. 6 (1978), pp. 115–139.

Index